Conten

This atlas is divided into the four Provinces of Ireland. [...] [...]oductory page followed by a section of road maps and ends with an [...]abetical list of places of interest within that Province.

All of the telephone numbers on the introduction and places of interest pages are local numbers.

To phone Northern Ireland from the Republic of Ireland, replace the 028 with 048 e.g. 028 9023 1221 becomes 048 9023 1221.

To phone the Republic of Ireland from Northern Ireland (or anywhere else in the United Kingdom) replace the first '0' of the area code with 00 353 followed by the remainder of the number e.g. 071 61201 becomes 00 353 71 61201

Published by Collins
An imprint of HarperCollins*Publishers*
77-85 Fulham Palace Road, Hammersmith, London W6 8JB

HarperCollins website: www.fireandwater.com

Copyright © HarperCollins*Publishers* Ltd 2002

Mapping © Bartholomew Ltd 2002

Collins® is a registered trademark of HarperCollins*Publishers* Limited

Mapping generated from Bartholomew digital databases

Bartholomew website: www.bartholomewmaps.com

Printed in Great Britain   ISBN 0 00 712884 3   OC11058
CDU   Imp 001   e-mail: roadcheck@harpercollins.co.uk

Route planning

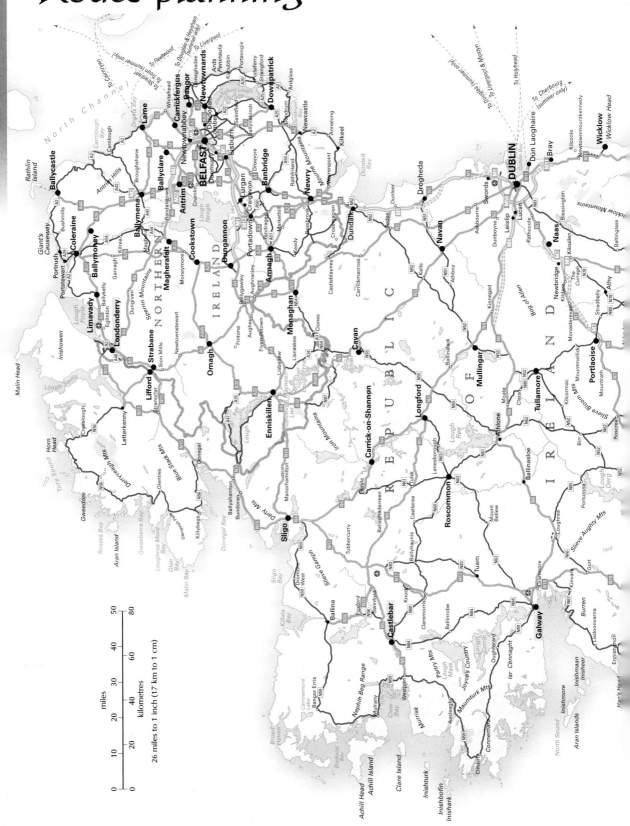

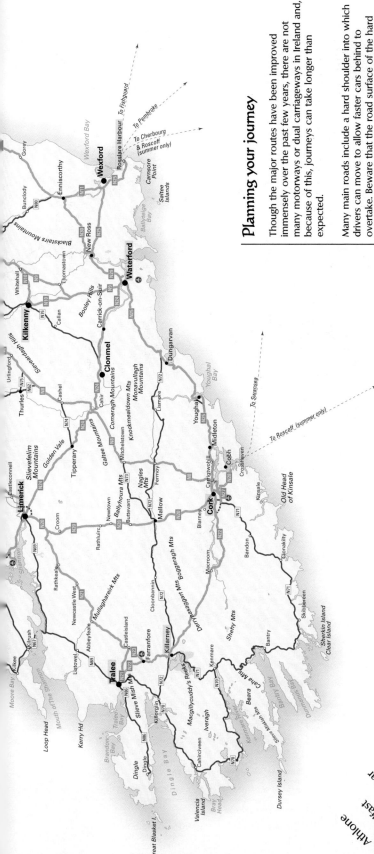

Planning your journey

Though the major routes have been improved immensely over the past few years, there are not many motorways or dual carriageways in Ireland and, because of this, journeys can take longer than expected.

Many main roads include a hard shoulder into which drivers can move to allow faster cars behind to overtake. Beware that the road surface of the hard shoulder is frequently in a poorer state of repair than the main carriageway.

The road surfaces of rural roads are variable in quality and caution is advised. On poor, single track roads it can be prudent to observe where possible turning points are passed, as roads can suddenly deteriorate to the point of being impassable making a long reverse necessary.

However, it does not take long to familiarise oneself with the idiosyncrasies of Irish motoring and the rewards make it worthwhile as, off the major routes, the roads are quiet and the local road users courteous, often giving a cheery wave as they pass.

Road distances

The distance between two selected towns is shown in miles and will be found at the intersection of the respective vertical and horizontal rows, e.g. distance between Belfast and Dublin is 104 miles. In general, distances are based on the shortest routes by classified roads.

	Athlone	Belfast	Castlebar	Cork	Donegal	Dublin	Dundalk	Galway	Kilkenny	Killarney	Limerick	Larne	Londonderry	Roscrea	Rosslare Harbour	Sligo	Tralee
Belfast	141																
Castlebar	81	182															
Cork	134	264	177														
Donegal	114	112	94	250													
Dublin	78	104	151	160	138												
Dundalk	90	52	157	202	98	53											
Galway	58	190	50	130	127	136	148										
Kilkenny	78	177	155	92	192	73	123	97									
Killarney	144	271	183	54	253	192	219	120	123								
Limerick	163	22	204	287	118	126	192	74	199	293							
Larne	75	201	114	65	184	123	150	65	212	70	224						
Londonderry	130	73	138	266	43	147	97	169	208	69	274	216					
Roscrea	40	167	118	95	153	77	116	68	114	31	188	46	181				
Rosslare Harbour	130	205	218	129	243	101	153	101	171	62	227	131	247	100			
Sligo	73	128	54	209	41	135	104	86	213	152	150	84	113	203			
Tralee	117	266	178	74	255	188	215	98	289	20	269	65	181	110	178		
Waterford	108	207	185	78	222	151	137	120	229	30	229	80	68	51	182	130	

Key to Provinces

Ulster	6 – 27
Connaught	28 – 43
Leinster	44 – 63
Munster	64 – 87

The atlas is divided into the four Provinces of Ireland as shown above.

Each Province has an introductory page followed by a section of road maps, ending with an alphabetical list of places of tourist interest within that area. All places of interest are also referenced in the main index at the back of the atlas.

Addresses and telephone numbers of the Tourist Boards which cover part of a Province are listed on the introductory page for that Province.

Contact details for tourist information offices are listed at the side of the mapping page on which the town appears.

Key to map symbols

Road map symbols

M2	Motorway		Motorway / Road under construction		National boundary
limited access 3 / 11 full access	Motorway with junction number	13	Road distance (in miles)		County boundary
dual A3 / N6	Primary / National primary route		Railway and tunnel		National park / Forest park
dual A55 / N52	'A' road /National secondary route		Car ferry		Beach
B170 / R420	'B' road / Regional road		Lake / Lough and river		International airport / Regional airport
	Other road		Canal	▲ 607	Height in metres

SCALE

0	5	10	15 Miles
0	5	10	15	20	25 Kilometres

1:380,160   6 miles to 1 inch / 3.8 km to 1 cm

0	165	490	984	1312	1640	2297	2953	feet
water 0	50	150	300	400	500	700	900	metres

City centre maps

	Main road / Throughroute	P	Car park
	Pedestrian street	WC	Public toilets
	Shopping street	Pol •	Police Service of Northern Ireland / Garda Síochana
	Notable building	+	Religious building
	Railway station	→	One way street

Tourist features

i / i	Tourist Information Centre (all year / seasonal)		Country park / Forest park / National park		Racecourse
	Ancient monument		Garden	†	Religious building
	Art gallery / Museum		Golf course		Viewpoint
	Battlefield		Historic house		Zoo / Wildlife park
	Bird sanctuary / Nature reserve		Historic house with garden	★	Other place of interest
	Castle		Motor racing circuit		

Ulster

Ulster (population 1,923,251) is the most northerly province of Ireland. It comprises the whole of Northern Ireland – Antrim, Armagh, Londonderry, Down, Fermanagh and Tyrone, and also Cavan, Donegal and Monaghan from the South. The earliest written sources about the history of Ulster date back to the 7th century.

The Troubles have had an effect on the number of tourists but with this period in Irish history hopefully drawing to a close with the signing of the Good Friday Agreement in April 1998, the number of visitors has been increasing in recent years.

The scenic mountains, lakes and spectacular coastline, together with the famous Irish hospitality and 'craic' – the Irish for 'a good time' – means that Ulster still has a huge amount to offer.

Live Traditional Music

Northern Ireland Tourist Board
St. Anne's Court, 59 North Street,
Belfast BT1 1NB
☎ 028 9023 1221   www.discovernorthernireland.com

North West Regional Tourism
Aras Reddan, Temple Street, Sligo
☎ 071 61201   www.ireland-northwest.travel.ie

Map pages in this region

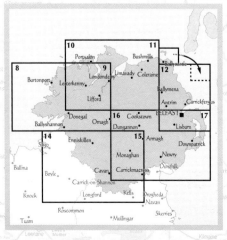

Stormont

History

The Easter Rising of 1916 started the chain of events that ended in 1921 with the creation of the 26 counties of the Irish Free State and the six counties of Northern Ireland. Violent clashes between police and Civil Rights demonstrators in 1969 saw the introduction of British forces to restore order.

In 1972 the Northern Ireland Parliament at Stormont was suspended having sat for 50 years. This was in the wake of 'Bloody Sunday' when thirteen civilians were shot dead by British paratroopers during an anti-internment rally in Londonderry. In 1994 an historic ceasefire by both IRA and Loyalists has restored hope, despite setbacks along the way, that a permanent and lasting peace will be created in Northern Ireland.

Golf

There are over 100 golf courses in Ulster including superb links courses along the coasts of Donegal, Londonderry, Antrim and Down. There are also championship courses at Royal County Down and Royal Portrush in County Antrim, the only Irish club to have hosted the Open Championship, won by Max Faulkner in 1951.

Golf

Wall Mural

Industrial Belfast

In Belfast the traditional industries of ship building, linen and tobacco, which grew up during the Industrial Revolution, have declined in recent years. Harland & Wolff, builders of the Titanic, was the largest shipbuilder in the world in the late 19th century and, at that time, Belfast Ropeworks employed 4000 people but is now closed.

Angling in the Southern Counties

Angling for all tastes is catered for particularly in the southern counties of Cavan, Monaghan and Fermanagh. From the wide open spaces of Loughs Erne, Gowna, Oughter, Sheelin, Ramor, Sillan, Muckno and Egish to the more secluded smaller lakes and stretches of river which are abundant throughout the region. The area frequently hosts International events and Arvagh, Belturbet and Cootehill host annual angling festivals.

Fishing

County Donegal

The peninsula west of Donegal town contains many places of interest. Amongst them Killybegs, the busiest fishing port in Ireland, Slieve League, at 601m (1972ft) are the highest sea cliffs in Europe and the megalithic remains around Glencolumbkille. This area is also part of the largest Gaeltacht (Irish speaking) area in Ireland.

The inland mountain ranges of the Derryveagh and Blue Stack Mountains run through the centre of Donegal and at 752m (2467ft) Errigal is the highest and most distinctive mountain in either range. The Glenveagh National Park contains a wider variety of landscape and also contains the largest herd of red deer in Ireland.

Ardara is the focal point for weaving in Donegal including the famous Donegal Tweed. Demonstrations of the craft can be seen in some of the stores.

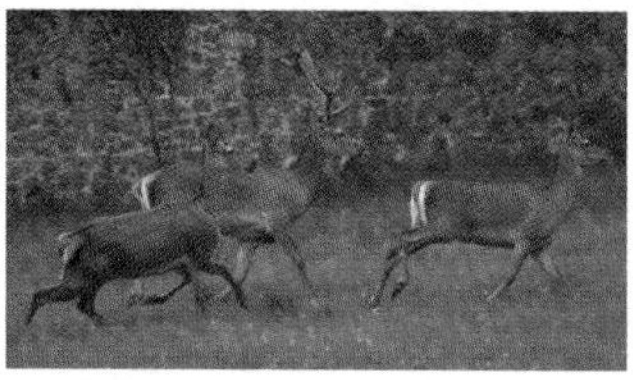

Red Deer

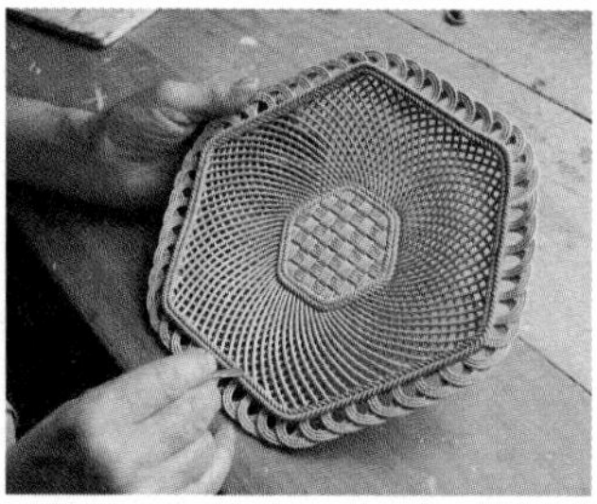

Belleek Pottery

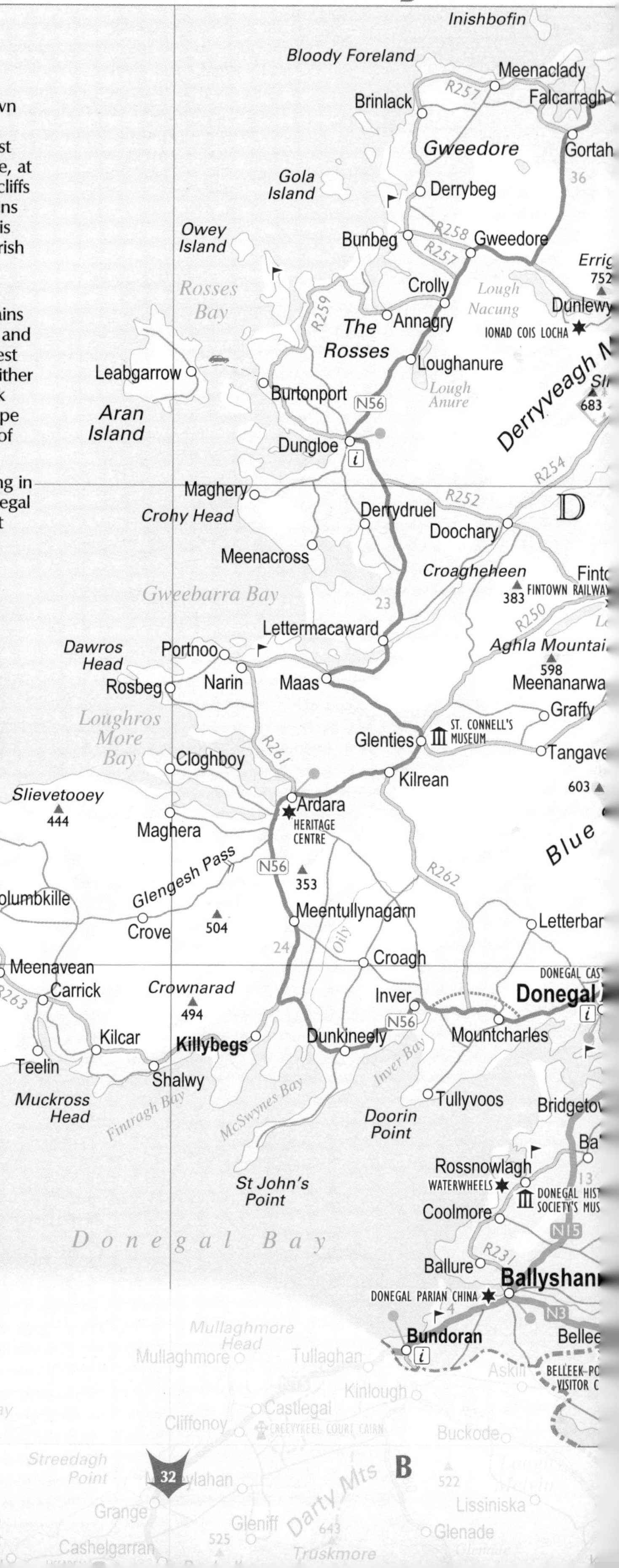

Map labels

Inishbofin

Bloody Foreland

Brinlack · Meenaclady · Falcarragh · R257

Gweedore · Gortah · 36

Gola Island · Derrybeg

Owey Island · Bunbeg · R258 · Gweedore · R257 · Errig 752

Rosses Bay · Crolly · Lough Nacung · Dunlewy

The Rosses · Annagry · IONAD COIS LOCHA

R259 · Loughanure · Sli 683

Leabgarrow · Burtonport · Lough Anure · N56

Aran Island · Dungloe · ℹ

Maghery · Derryveagh M

Crohy Head · Derrydruel · R252 · D

Doochary · R254

Meenacross · Croagheheen · Finto

Gweebarra Bay · 383 · FINTOWN RAILWAY

Dawros Head · Portnoo · 23 · R250 · Le

Rosbeg · Narin · Maas · Aghla Mountai · 598

Loughros More Bay · Meenanarwa · Graffy

Glenties · ST. CONNELL'S MUSEUM · Tangave

Cloghboy · R261 · Kilrean · 603

Slievetooey 444 · Port · Ardara · HERITAGE CENTRE · Blue

Maghera · N56 · 353

Glen Bay · Glencolumbkille · Glengesh Pass · 504 · Meentullynagarn · Letterbar

Rossan Point · GLENCOLUMBKILLE FOLK VILLAGE MUSEUM · Crove · R262

Malin More · Croagh · DONEGAL CAS

Malin Bay · OIDEAS GAEL · Inver · N56 · Donegal · ℹ

Slieve League 601 · Meenavean · Carrick · Crownarad 494 · Dunkineely · Mountcharles

Rathlin O'Birne Island · Malin Beg · R263 · Kilcar · Killybegs

Teelin · Shalwy · Inver Bay · Tullyvoos · Bridgeto

Muckross Head · Fintragh Bay · McSwynes Bay · Doorin Point · Ba

St John's Point · Rossnowlagh · WATERWHEELS · DONEGAL HIST SOCIETY'S MUS · 13

Coolmore · R231 · N15

Donegal Bay · Ballure · Ballyshan

DONEGAL PARIAN CHINA

Mullaghmore Head · Bundoran · ℹ · Bellee · N3

Mullaghmore · Tullaghan · BELLEEK-PO VISITOR C

Inishmurray · Kinlough · Askin

Cliffoney · Castlegal · CREEVYKEEL COURT CAIRN · Buckode

Streedagh Point · 32 · ylahan · Darty Mts · 522

Grange · Glenade

Roskragh Point · Gleniff 643 · Truskmore · Lissiniska

Cashelgarran

miles
0 · 5 · 10

0 · 5 · 10 · 15
kilometres

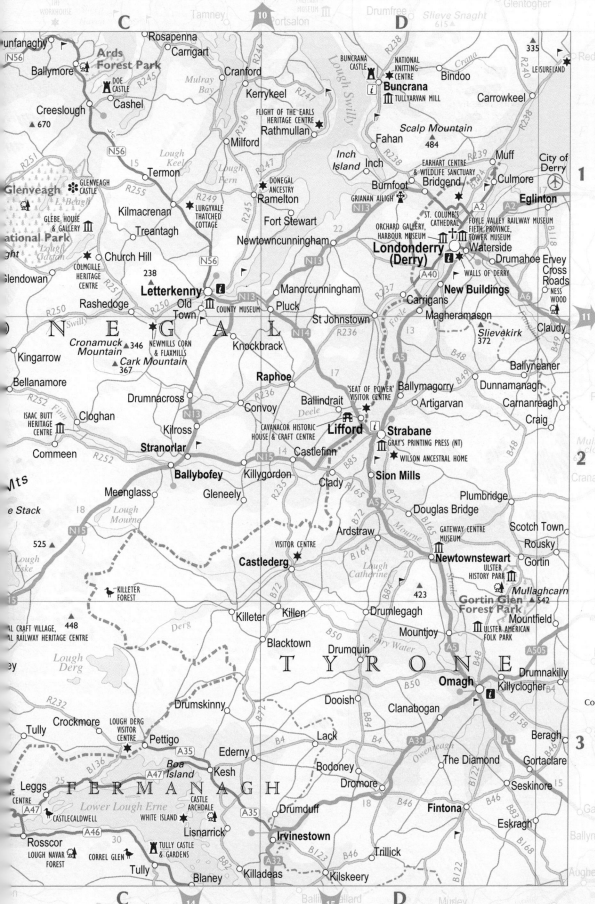

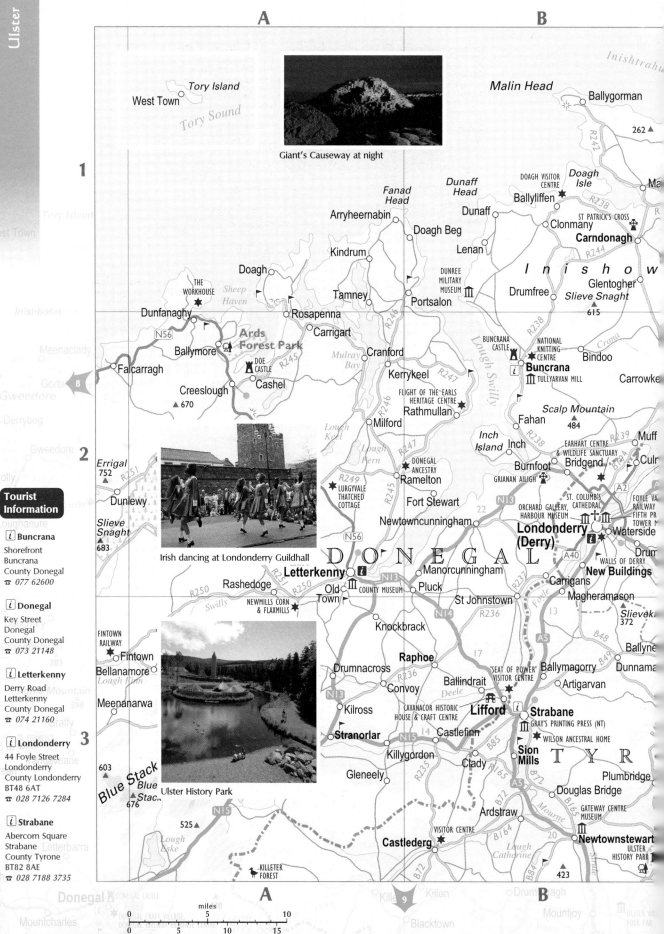

A   B

1

Tory Island

West Town

Tory Sound

Giant's Causeway at night

Malin Head

Ballygorman

262 ▲

DOAGH VISITOR CENTRE   *Doagh Isle*

Dunaff Head   Ballyliffen   R238   Ma

ST PATRICK'S CROSS

Fanad Head   Dunaff   Clonmany

Arryheernabin   Lenan   **Carndonagh**

Doagh Beg   R244

Kindrum   *I n i s h o w*

DUNREE MILITARY MUSEUM   Drumfree   Glentogher

Doagh   Tamney   Portsalon   *Slieve Snaght*

THE WORKHOUSE   *Sheep Haven*   615

Dunfanaghy   Rosapenna   BUNCRANA CASTLE   NATIONAL KNITTING CENTRE   Bindoo

N56   Carrigart   *Lough Swilly*   **Buncrana**

Ards Forest Park   Cranford   TULLYARVAN MILL   Carrowke

Ballymore   *Mulray Bay*   Kerrykeel   R247

DOE CASTLE   FLIGHT OF THE EARLS HERITAGE CENTRE   Fahan   *Scalp Mountain*

Falcarragh   Cashel   Rathmullan   484

Creeslough   Milford   Inch Island   Muff

▲ 670   *Lough Keel*   Inch   R238

EARHART CENTRE & WILDLIFE SANCTUARY   Culr

2   *Errigal 752*   *Lough Fern*   DONEGAL ANCESTRY   Burnfoot   Bridgend

R251   LURGYVALE THATCHED COTTAGE   Ramelton   GRIANAN AILIGH   FOYLE VA RAILWAY

Dunlewy   R249   Fort Stewart   N13   ST. COLUMB'S CATHEDRAL   FIFTH PR TOWER M

Slieve Snaght 683   Newtowncunningham   ORCHARD GALLERY   **Londonderry (Derry)**   Waterside

N56   HARBOUR MUSEUM

Irish dancing at Londonderry Guildhall   22   WALLS OF DERRY   Drum

D O N E G A L   A40

Letterkenny   Manorcunningham   **New Buildings**

Rashedoge   Old Town   Pluck   Carrigans

R250   COUNTY MUSEUM   St Johnstown   13   Magheramason

Swilly   NEWMILLS CORN & FLAXMILLS   N14   R236   *Slievek 372*

FINTOWN RAILWAY   Knockbrack   A5   B48   Ballyne

Fintown   **Raphoe**   17   Dunnama

Bellanamore   *Lough Finn*   Drumnacross   'SEAT OF POWER' VISITOR CENTRE   Ballymagorry   Artigarvan

Meenanarwa   Convoy   R236   Ballindrait   *Deele*

3   603 ▲   Kilross   CAVANACOR HISTORIC HOUSE & CRAFT CENTRE   **Lifford**   **Strabane**

Blue Stack   **Stranorlar**   N15   Castlefinn   GRAY'S PRINTING PRESS (NT)

Blue Stack 676   N13   Killygordon   Clady   **Sion Mills**   WILSON ANCESTRAL HOME

Ulster History Park   Gleneely   R235   **T Y R**

525 ▲   N15   Ardstraw   Plumbridge

Lough Eske   KILLETER FOREST   **Castlederg**   VISITOR CENTRE   *Mourne*   Douglas Bridge

GATEWAY CENTRE MUSEUM

Lough Catherine   20   **Newtownstewart**

B164   423 ▲   ULSTER HISTORY PARK

Tourist Information

[i] **Buncrana**
Shorefront
Buncrana
County Donegal
☎ 077 62600

[i] **Donegal**
Key Street
Donegal
County Donegal
☎ 073 21148

[i] **Letterkenny**
Derry Road
Letterkenny
County Donegal
☎ 074 21160

[i] **Londonderry**
44 Foyle Street
Londonderry
County Londonderry
BT48 6AT
☎ 028 7126 7284

[i] **Strabane**
Abercorn Square
Strabane
County Tyrone
BT82 8AE
☎ 028 7188 3735

A   B

miles
0   5   10
0   5   10   15
kilometres

9

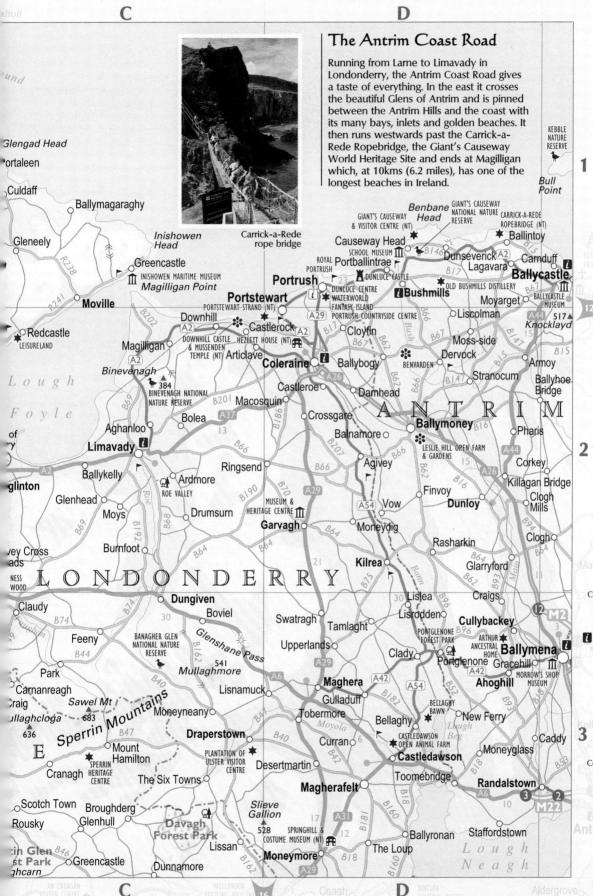

The Antrim Coast Road

Running from Larne to Limavady in Londonderry, the Antrim Coast Road gives a taste of everything. In the east it crosses the beautiful Glens of Antrim and is pinned between the Antrim Hills and the coast with its many bays, inlets and golden beaches. It then runs westwards past the Carrick-a-Rede Ropebridge, the Giant's Causeway World Heritage Site and ends at Magilligan which, at 10kms (6.2 miles), has one of the longest beaches in Ireland.

Carrick-a-Rede rope bridge

Map labels

C · D

Glenglad Head
Portaleen
Culdaff
Gleneely
R238
Ballymagaraghy
Inishowen Head
Greencastle
Inishowen Maritime Museum
Magilligan Point
R241
Moville
R238
Redcastle
LEISURELAND
Downhill
Magilligan
A2
Binevenagh
Binevenagh National Nature Reserve
384
Downhill Castle & Mussenden Temple (NT)
Hezlett House (NT)
Castlerock
Articlave
A2
Coleraine
Portstewart
Portstewart Strand (NT)
Royal Portrush
Portrush
Dunluce Castle
Dunluce Centre Waterworld Fantasy Island Portrush Countryside Centre
A29
Portballintrae
School Museum
Giant's Causeway & Visitor Centre (NT)
Causeway Head
Benbane Head
Giant's Causeway National Nature Reserve
Carrick-a-Rede Ropebridge (NT)
Ballintoy
B146
Dunseverick
A2
Carnduff
Lagavara
Ballycastle
B15
Bushmills
Old Bushmills Distillery
B67
Moyarget
Ballycastle Museum
Liscolman
A44
Knocklayd 517
B15
Kebble Nature Reserve
Bull Point
Fair Head
Ballyvoy
Cloyfin
Ballybogy
B67
Moss-side
Dervock
B147
Stranocum
Armoy
Ballyhoe Bridge
Castleroe
Damhead
ANTRIM
Benvarden
B66
Pharis
Corkey
Magilligan
Aghanloo
Bolea
A37
Macosquin
B201
B186
Crossgare
Balnamore
Ballymoney
B62
B16
A44
Corkey
Killagan Bridge
Clogh Mills
Limavady
Ballykelly
Ardmore
Roe Valley
Ringsend
B66
Agivey
B62
Finvoy
Dunloy
Clogh
Glenhead
Moys
B69
Drumsurn
Museum & Heritage Centre
B70
A29
Vow
A54
Moneydig
Rasharkin
B64
Burnfoot
Garvagh
B64
B64
Kilrea
B75
Glarryford
Craigs
LONDONDERRY
Claudy
B74
Dungiven
Boviel
Swatragh
Tamlaght
Lislea
Lisrodden
Cullybackey
M2
Feeny
B44
Banagher Glen National Nature Reserve
Glenshane Pass
B162
Mullaghmore 541
Upperlands
Clady
Portglenone Forest Park
Arthur Ancestral Home
Ballymena
Park
Carnanreagh
Sawel Mt 683
Moneyneany
Lisnamuck
B41
Maghera
A42
A54
Gulladuff
Portglenone
Gracehill
Morrow's Shop Museum
Ahoghill
Craig ullaghcloga 636
Sperrin Mountains
B47
Draperstown
B40
Tobermore
Curran
Bellaghy Bawn
Bellaghy
New Ferry
Caddy
Mount Hamilton
Sperrin Heritage Centre
Plantation of Ulster Visitor Centre
Desertmartin
Castledawson Open Animal Farm
Castledawson
Moneyglass
Cranagh
The Six Towns
Magherafelt
Toomebridge
Randalstown
A6
Scotch Town
Broughderg
Glenhull
Davagh Forest Park
Slieve Gallion 528
Springhill & Costume Museum (NT)
Ballyronan
The Loup
Staffordstown
M22
in Glen st Park ghcarn
Greencastle
Lissan
Dunnamore
Moneymore
A29
Lough Neagh
B162

C · D
Cookstown

Tourist Information

Tourist Information

Ballycastle
Sheskburn House
7 Mary Street
Ballycastle
County Antrim
BT54 6QH
☎ 028 2076 2024

Ballymena
76 Church Street
Ballymena
County Antrim
☎ 028 2563 8494

Coleraine
Railway Road
Coleraine
County Londonderry
BT52 1PE
☎ 028 7034 4723

Giant's Causeway
44 Causeway Road
Bushmills
County Antrim
BT57 8SU
☎ 028 2073 1855

Limavady
Council Offices
7 Connell Street
Omagh
County Londonderry
BT49 0HA
☎ 028 7776 0307

Portrush
Dunluce Centre
Sandhill Drive
Portrush
County Antrim
BT56 8BF
☎ 028 7082 3333

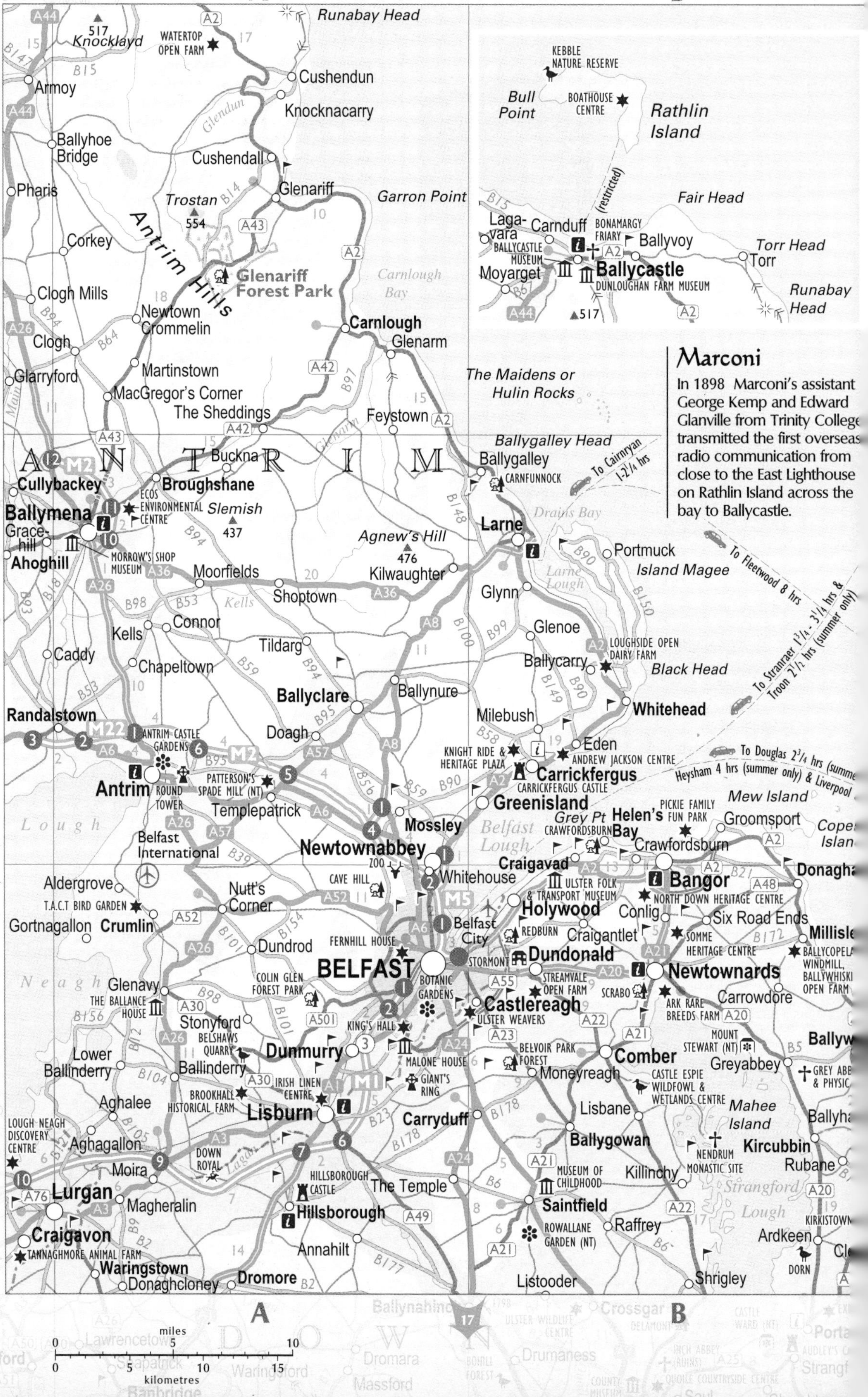

Marconi

In 1898 Marconi's assistant George Kemp and Edward Glanville from Trinity College transmitted the first overseas radio communication from close to the East Lighthouse on Rathlin Island across the bay to Ballycastle.

Tourist Information

Antrim
16 High Street
Antrim
County Antrim
BT41 4AN
☎ 028 9442 8331

Ballymena
76 Church Street
Ballymena
County Antrim
☎ 028 2563 8494

Bangor
34 Quay Street
Bangor
County Down
BT20 5ED
☎ 028 9127 0069

Carrickfergus
Heritage Plaza
Antrim Street
Carrickfergus
County Antrim
BT38 7DG
☎ 028 9336 6455

Hillsborough
The Courthouse
The Square
Hillsborough
County Down
BT26 6AG
☎ 028 9268 9717

Larne
Narrow Gauge Road
Larne
County Antrim
BT40 1XB
☎ 028 2826 0088

Lisburn
Irish Linen Centre
Market Square
Lisburn
County Antrim
BT28 1AG
☎ 028 9266 0038

Newtownards
31 Regent Street
Newtownards
County Down
☎ 028 9182 6846

Belfast (Population: 287,000)

Situated on the River Lagan at the entrance to Belfast Lough, Belfast expanded during the industrial revolution when linen, rope making and ship building became the major industries of the area – the Titanic was built here and is home to the world's largest dry dock.

There has been a period of major regeneration in recent years especially in the city's riverfront area where the Waterfront Hall, a major concert venue, and more recently an entertainment complex, the Odyssey have been constructed. The 'Golden Mile', the area west of the City Hall, is a vibrant area of pubs, clubs and restaurants which has come to life even more since the peace process began.

The murals of West Belfast which adorn the gable ends of many houses, express the political viewpoints of the Protestant Shankill Road and the Catholic Falls Road and have become just as much a part of the tourist industry as the more traditional sites of the city.

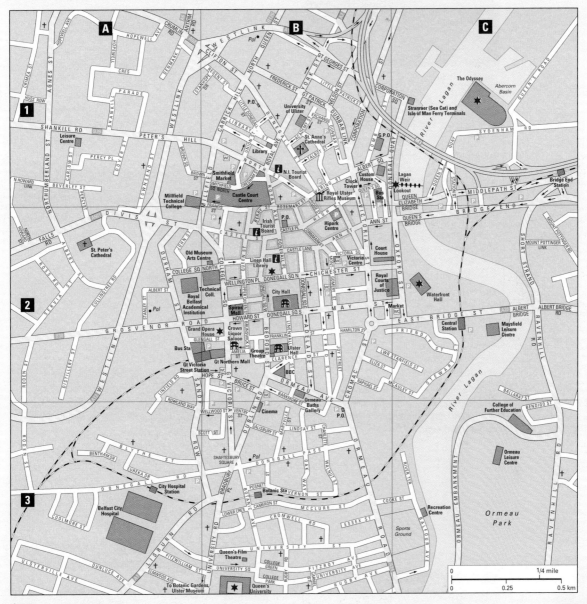

Index to street names

Tourist Information

Belfast Welcome Centre
47 Donegall Place
☎ 028 9024 6609

N.I. Tourist Board
59 North St
☎ 028 9023 1221

Bord Failte
(Irish Tourist Board)
Castle St
☎ 028 9032 7888

A 9 B

Enniskillen Castle

Enniskillen

Eniskillen is the county town of Fermanagh and stands on an island in the River Erne between the Upper and Lower Loughs. It is unfortunate that Enniskillen is probably most famous for the outrage on Remembrance Day in 1987 when 11 people were killed by a terrorist bomb blast, as the town has so much more to offer.

The Buttermarket was built in the 1830s for the export of, amongst other produce, butter which was the main produce exported from Fermanagh in the 19th century. It now houses the Enniskillen Craft and Design Centre.

A climb of 108 steps to the top of Cole's Monument in Forthill Park is rewarded with a magnificent view of the town centre.

Devenish Island

Lough Erne

The Southern Counties

The counties of Cavan, Monaghan and Fermanagh are characterised by rolling drumlin countryside and the abundance of inland waterways and lakes making it a haven for boating and angling. In fact Fermanagh is known as 'Lakeland' because of the sprawling Upper and Lower Lough Erne. Cavan is known as 'The Lake County' and includes the source of the Shannon which rises in the Cuilcagh Mountains in the west of the county.

That is not to say that water activities – angling, cruising, canoeing, windsurfing – are the only attraction. There are megalithic tombs, craft centres such as the famous Belleek pottery, Cavan and Fermanagh Crystal and the contrasting scenery of the forests of Lisnaskea, Mullaghfad, Belmore, Killikeen, Rossmore.

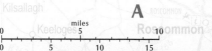

A 34 B

miles
0   5   10
0   5   10   15
kilometres

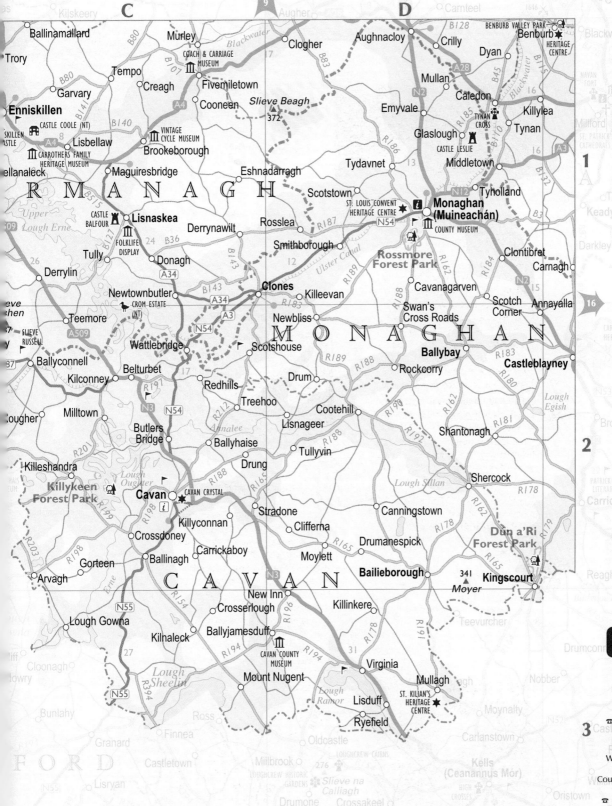

9

16

Irvinestown
Eskragh
Ballymackilroy
Ballygawley
GRANT ANCESTRAL HOME
Eglish
Moy

Trillick
Kilskeery
Murley
Blackwater
Clogher
Aughnacloy
Crilly
BENBURB VALLEY PARK
Benburb
HERITAGE CENTRE
Blackwater

Ballinamallard
COACH & CARRIAGE MUSEUM
B83
Dyan
B45
Charle

Trory
C
Tempo
B107
Fivemiletown
B128
Mullan
Caledon
NAVAN FORT
B110

Garvary
B80
Creagh
Cooneen
Slieve Beagh 372
Emyvale
A28
N2
TYNAN CROSS
Killylea
A3

Enniskillen
Brookeborough
Glaslough
CASTLE LESLIE
Middletown
Tynan

SKILLEN ASTLE
CASTLE COOLE (NT)
VINTAGE CYCLE MUSEUM
Lisbellaw
Tydavnet
R185
B132

ellanaleck
CARROTHERS FAMILY HERITAGE MUSEUM
Maguiresbridge
Eshnadarragh
R186
Tyholland
1

R M A N A G H
Scotstown
R187
Monaghan (Muineachán)
B3

Upper
CASTLE BALFOUR
Lisnaskea
Derrynawilt
Rosslea
ST LOUIS CONVENT HERITAGE CENTRE
N12
COUNTY MUSEUM
Clontibret
Darkley

Lough Erne
Tully
FOLKLIFE DISPLAY
B36
Smithborough
Ulster Canal
Rossmore Forest Park
R162
R184
Carnagh

Derrylin
Donagh
A34
B143
Ulster Canal
R189
Cavanagarven
Scotch Corner
N2
Annayalla
15

Newtownbutler
CROM ESTATE (NT)
Clones
Killeevan
Swan's Cross Roads

eve
Teemore
A509
A34
A3
R193
Newbliss
M O N A G H A N
R183
Castleblayney

SLIEVE RUSSELL
Wattlebridge
N54
Scotshouse
R189
R188
Ballybay
R180

Ballyconnell
Belturbet
Scotshouse
Drum
Rockcorry
Lough Egish

Kilconney
R191
Redhills
R212
Treehoo
Cootehill
R162
R181
Creggan
Cross

Milltown
N3
N54
Annalee
Lisnageer
R190
Shantonagh
Cullaville
Broomfield

R201
Butlers Bridge
Ballyhaise
Tullyvin
R188
Lough Sillan
Inniskeen

Killeshandra
Lough Oughter
Drung
R165
Shercock
R178
Carrickmacross

Killykeen Forest Park
R199
R198
Cavan
CAVAN CRYSTAL
R188
Canningstown
R162
Dún a'Ri Forest Park

Cavan
Killyconnan
Stradone
Clifferna
R178
Drumanespick
R179

Crossdoney
Ballinagh
Carrickaboy
Moylett
R165
2

Arvagh
Gorteen
C A V A N
Bailieborough
341 Moyer
Kingscourt
Reaghstown

R203
Erne
N3
New Inn
Killinkere
R191
Teevurcher

Lough Gowna
Crosserlough
R196
R178
Drumcon

Kilnaleck
Ballyjamesduff
CAVAN COUNTY MUSEUM
R194
Virginia
Nobber

N55
R394
Mount Nugent
Lough Ramor
Mullagh
ST. KILIAN'S HERITAGE CENTRE
3

Lough Sheelin
Lisduff
Moynalty

Ryefield
Carlanstown
Castleblayney

F O R D
Granard
Castletown
Millbrook
Oldcastle
LOUGHCREW CAIRNS
276
Kells (Ceanannus Mór)
Oristown

Lisryan
LOUGHCREW HISTORIC GARDENS
Slieve na Calliagh
HIGH CROSSES
Kilberry

Edgeworthstown
Coole
TULLYNALLY CASTLE
Drumone
Crossakeel
Cross Keys
Kilskeer
Matry
DONAGHM

Rathowen
Castlepollard
FORE ABBEY
Castlepollard
Fordstown
M E A

Tourist Information

i **Cavan**
Farnham Street
Cavan
County Cavan
☎ 049 433 1942

i **Enniskillen**
Wellington Road
Enniskillen
County Fermanagh
BT74 7EF
☎ 028 6632 3110

i **Monaghan**
Market House
Monaghan
County Monaghan
☎ 047 81122

Ulster

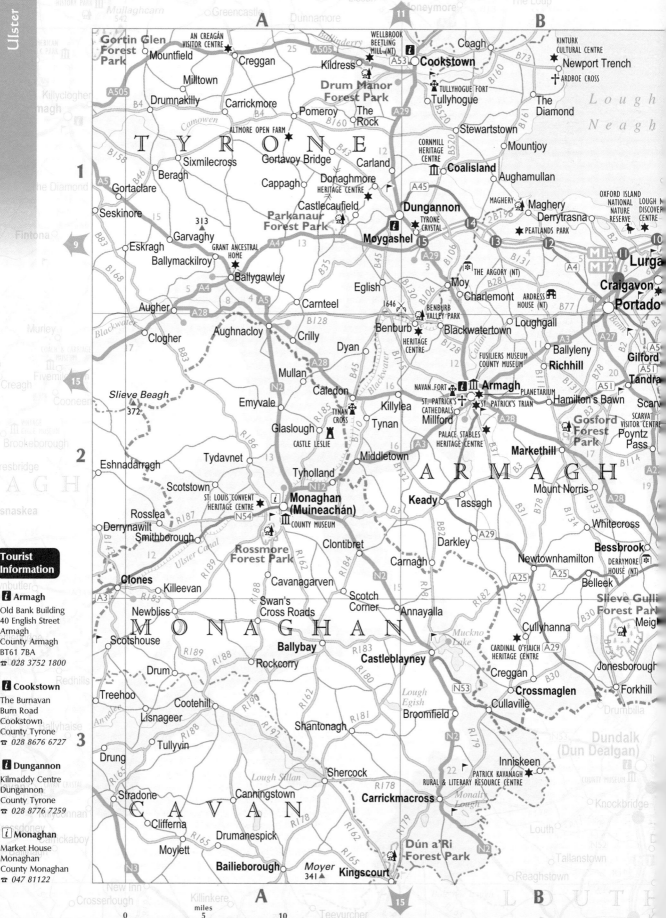

Tourist Information

i Armagh
Old Bank Building
40 English Street
Armagh
County Armagh
BT61 7BA
☎ 028 3752 1800

i Cookstown
The Burnavan
Burn Road
Cookstown
County Tyrone
☎ 028 8676 6727

i Dungannon
Kilmaddy Centre
Dungannon
County Tyrone
☎ 028 8776 7259

i Monaghan
Market House
Monaghan
County Monaghan
☎ 047 81122

A
B

TYRONE
ARMAGH
MONAGHAN
CAVAN

Gortin Glen Forest Park
Mountfield
An Creagán Visitor Centre
Creggan
Kildress
Wellbrook Beetling Mill (NT)
Coagh
Kinturk Cultural Centre
Cookstown
Newport Trench
Ardboe Cross
Drum Manor Forest Park
Tullyhogue Fort
Tullyhogue
The Diamond
Lough Neagh
Milltown
Drumnakilly
Carrickmore
Pomeroy
The Rock
Stewartstown
Mountjoy
Altmore Open Farm
Sixmilecross
Gortavoy Bridge
Carland
Cornmill Heritage Centre
Coalisland
Aughamullan
Beragh
Cappagh
Donaghmore Heritage Centre
Maghery
Maghery
Derrytrasna
Oxford Island National Nature Reserve
Lough Discovery Centre
Gortaclare
Castlecaufield
Dungannon
Tyrone Crystal
Peatlands Park
Seskinore
Grant Ancestral Home
Parkanaur Forest Park
Moygashel
Garvaghy
Eskragh
Ballymackilroy
Ballygawley
Eglish
Moy
Charlemont
Ardress House (NT)
Lurgan
Craigavon
Portadown
Augher
Carnteel
The Argory (NT)
Richhill
Gilford
Clogher
Aughnacloy
Crilly
Benburb Valley Park
Benburb Heritage Centre
Blackwatertown
Loughgall
Ballyleny
Tandragee
Dyan
Fusiliers Museum County Museum
Hamilton's Bawn
Scarva
Mullan
Caledon
Killylea
Navan Fort
Armagh
Planetarium
Gosford Forest Park
Scarva Visitor Centre
Emyvale
Tynan Cross
Tynan
St. Patrick's Cathedrals
St. Patrick's Trian
Poyntz Pass
Slieve Beagh
Glaslough
Castle Leslie
Middletown
Millford
Palace Stables Heritage Centre
Markethill
Eshnadarragh
Tydavnet
Mount Norris
Scotstown
Tyholland
St. Louis Convent Heritage Centre
Monaghan (Muineachán)
Keady
Tassagh
Whitecross
Rosslea
County Museum
Darkley
Newtownhamilton
Bessbrook
Derrynawilt
Smithborough
Clontibret
Carnagh
Derrymore House (NT)
Belleek
Ulster Canal
Rossmore Forest Park
Slieve Gullion Forest Park
Clones
Killeevan
Cavanagarven
Scotch Corner
Annayalla
Cullyhanna
Meigh
Newbliss
Swan's Cross Roads
Cardinal O'Fiaich Heritage Centre
Scotshouse
Ballybay
Castleblayney
Creggan
Crossmaglen
Jonesborough
Drum
Rockcorry
Cullaville
Forkhill
Treehoo
Cootehill
Broomfield
Lough Egish
Lisnageer
Dundalk (Dun Dealgan)
Drung
Tullyvin
Shantonagh
Inniskeen
Patrick Kavanagh Rural & Literary Resource Centre
Shercock
Stradone
Canningstown
Carrickmacross
Clifferna
Drumanespick
Dún a' Ri Forest Park
Moylett
Moyer
Kingscourt
Bailieborough

Silent Valley

The Antrim Coast

The Mourne Mountains sweep down to the Irish Sea south of Newcastle. Slieve Donard, the highest peak in the range, rises straight out of the sea to a height of 852m (2795ft) and on a clear day the Isle of Man can be seen from the summit. The Silent Valley Reservoirs west of Slieve Donard are surrounded by a massive dry stone wall over 35kms (22 miles) in length.

For those travelling between Dublin and Belfast with a little more time on their hands, a scenic alternative route from Newry is along the A2 coast road alongside Carlingford Lough, through Newcastle and then onto the A24 to Belfast.

Linen Centre, Lisburn

✱ Altmore Open Farm `16 A1`
32 Altmore Road, Pomeroy, Co. Tyrone. Essentially a sheep farm but with rare breeds of domestic fowl and opportunities for pony trekking and fly fishing. Also a traditionally furnished thatched cottage museum and working water wheels.
☎ 028 8775 8977

✱ An Creagán Visitor Centre `16 A1`
Creggan, Omagh, Co. Tyrone. To be found in the foothills of the Sperrin Mountains, the centre interpretes the archaeology, natural environment and culture of the area. Besides Irish language, archaeology and history courses and lectures, the centre includes traditional arts, crafts, music, song, dance and storytelling in its regular programme of events. Walking and cycling is also available from the centre.
☎ 028 8076 1112   www.an-creagan.com

✱ Andrew Jackson Centre `12 B2`
Boneybefore, Carrickfergus, Co. Antrim. Housed in a thatched Ulster-Scots farmhouse of 1750, the centre commemorates Andrew Jackson, 7th President of the US from 1829 – 1837 whose parents emigrated from Carrickfergus in 1765. The centre's homestead has been restored and furnished in traditional style. Besides exhibits relating to the life of Andrew Jackson, there are displays of Ulster patchwork quilts and farm implements. An exhibition dedicated to the First Battalion US Rangers raised in Carrickfergus in 1942 stands in the grounds.
☎ 028 9336 6455

❉ Antrim Castle Gardens `12 A2`
Randalstown Road, Antrim, Co. Antrim. Restored 17th century water gardens in Anglo-Dutch style including parterre with plants of the period, ornamental canals, round pond and riverside and woodland walks. An ancient motte stands in the grounds as well as the ruins of the castle which was destroyed by fire in 1922. The carriage house and stables of the former castle houses the Clotworthy Arts Centre where there are displays illustrating the development of the gardens.
☎ 028 9442 8000

♟ Antrim Round Tower `12 A2`
Steeple Road, Antrim, Co. Antrim. The remains of a Celtic monastic settlement, the tower is around 1000 years old and over 28m (83ft) tall. Although possibly used as a bell tower, it would have served a defensive purpose for the monks.
☎ 028 9442 8331

✱ Ardara Heritage Centre `8 B2`
Ardara, Co. Donegal. Donegal tweed is world famous and the centre presents the history of tweed production in the Ardara region by means of old photographs, displays and models. Weavers demonstrate how a loom works and the exhibition explains the tweed making process from the shearing of the sheep through to the manufacture of the woven cloth.
☎ 075 41262

✝ Ardboe Cross `16 B1`
Newport Trench, Coagh, Co. Tyrone. Believed to be the first high cross of Ulster and dating from the 10th century, Ardboe Cross stands around 6m (19ft) high and is richly carved with biblical scenes. During the 18th century this National Monument became a place of pilgrimage.
☎ 028 8676 6727

⌂ Ardress House `16 B1`
64 Ardress Road, Annaghmore, Portadown, Co. Armagh. Originally a 17th century farmhouse, Ardress became more of a small mansion after 18th century additions. Owned by the National Trust, the house has an Adam-style drawing room with fine plasterwork, a collection of paintings and 18th century furniture. Old farm tools are on display in the farmyard which is stocked with some rare breed farm animals. Examples of early Irish roses are found in the gardens and apple orchards are a particular feature of the estate.
☎ 028 3885 1236   www.nationaltrust.org.uk

🌲 Ards Forest Park `9 C1`
Ballymore, Co. Donegal. Situated on the Rosguill peninsula on Sheep Haven Bay, Ards Forest Park comprises sand-dunes and seashore, salt marsh, freshwater lakes and broadleaved and coniferous woodland and consequently has a great diversity of plant, bird and wildlife. Walks and trails through the forest have viewing points which offer spectacular views of the surrounding countryside. Several megalithic tombs and four ring forts are amongst the features of archaeological interest in the park.
☎ 074 21160

❄ Argory, The `16 B1`
Derrycaw Road, Moy, Dungannon, Co. Armagh. Set in wooded countryside and overlooking the Blackwater River, the house dates from 1824. Originally built for Walter McGeough, it remained in the same family until it was given to the National Trust in 1979 and is full of generations of family treasures. It is furnished as it would have been in 1900 and is still without electricity; the acetylene plant which made the gas to light the house can be seen in the courtyard. The 130ha (321 acre) estate is particularly notable for spring flowering bulbs.
☎ 028 8778 4753   www.nationaltrust.org.uk

✱ Ark Rare Breeds Open Farm `12 B3`
296 Bangor Road, Newtownards, Co. Down. Situated in 16ha (40 acres) of countryside with picnic areas, this rare breeds farm has over 80 domestic species of cattle, sheep, goats, pigs and poultry. The young lambs and goats can be bottle fed. Other attractions include pony rides, llamas and red deer.
☎ 028 9182 0445

🏛 Armagh County Museum `16 B2`
The Mall East, Armagh, Co. Armagh. Reveals the varied history of both the city and the county of Armagh with archaeology, natural history, military, railway and costume collections; also an art gallery, library and annual programmme of temporary exhibitions.
☎ 028 3752 3070

✱ Armagh Planetarium `16 B2`
College Hill, Armagh, Co. Armagh. Ireland's only planetarium with multimedia shows, interactive computers and a wide variety of astronomical exhibits displayed in the Hall of Astronomy and in the Eartharium. The 10ha (24 acre) landscaped Astropark features a scale model of the universe. Nearby is the Armagh Observatory, an astronomical research centre.
☎ 028 3752 3689   www.armagh-planetarium.co.uk

✱ Arthur Ancestral Home `11 D3`
Dreen Road, Cullybacky, Co. Antrim. Restored ancestral home of Chester Alan Arthur, 21st US President 1881 – 1885, his father having emigrated from Dreen in 1816. An 18th century farmhouse with open flax straw thatched roof and an interior with open hearth, clay floor and open dresser. Displays illustrate Arthur's life; also traditional baking and craft demonstrations.
☎ 028 2588 0781/ 2563 8494

♜ Audley's Castle `17 D2`
Strangford, Downpatrick, Co. Down. On a rocky prominence overlooking Strangford Lough, Audley's Castle is a tower house with an enclosing 15th century bawn (courtyard). Latrines and window seats are still visible.
☎ 028 4461 2233

🏛 Ballance House, The `12 A3`
118a Lisburn Road, Glenavy, Co. Antrim. John Ballance, Prime Minister of New Zealand 1891-1893, was born here in 1839; audiovisual presentations and a library highlight the many links between New Zealand and Ireland as a result of emigration and also illustrate pioneer life and Maorie culture. The parlour is furnished as it would have been in 1850.
☎ 028 9264 8492

🏛 Ballycastle Museum `12 B1`
59 Castle Street, Ballycastle, Co. Antrim. Located in Ballycastle's 18th century courthouse, the museum collection has items relating to the social history and folklore of the area.
☎ 028 2076 2942

✱ Ballycopeland Windmill `12 B3`
Windmill Road, Millisle, Co. Down. Situated to the west of Millisle, this 18th century windmill was used until 1915 for milling oats and making animal feed and is still in working order. In the former miller's house there is an electrically operated model of the mill, audiovisual displays and the chance for visitors to have a go at milling.
☎ 028 9054 3037

✱ Ballywhiskin Open Farm `12 B3`
216 Ballywalter Road, Millisle, Newtownards, Co. Down. Animals and birds including sheep, rabbits, ducks and peafowl can be seen in a natural environment.
☎ 028 9186 2262

🐦 Banagher Glen National Nature Reserve `11 C3`
Moneyneaney, Draperstown, Co. Londonderry. Mature oak and ash trees predominate in this steep sided glen with an abundance of wild flowers in spring; buzzards and sparrowhawks are amongst the birds which can be seen. A 5km (3 mile) track leads to Altnaheglish Reservoir.
☎ 028 7772 2074   www.ehsni.gov.uk

⚔ Battle of Ballynahinch `17 D2`
Ballynahinch, Co. Down. The last major battle in Ulster of the 1798 uprising by the United Irishmen. Irish forces led by Henry Munro were defeated on June 13th at Windmill Hill on the edge of the town by government troops under General Nugent.
☎ 028 4461 2233

⚔ Battle of Benburb `16 B2`
Benburb, Co. Tyrone. One of the biggest Irish victories over the Plantation settlers when Owen Roe O'Neill defeated the Scottish forces of General Monro on 5th June 1646 in the Drumflugh and Derrycreevy Hills to the west of Benburb.
☎ 028 3752 1800

✝ Belfast Cathedral `13 B1`
Donegall Street, Belfast, Co. Antrim. Built on the site of the former parish church, the Hiberno-Romanesque Cathedral Church of St Anne was consecrated in 1904 but not finally completed until 1981. Architect W. H. Lynn created an awe inspiring baptistry in 1928 with over 15,000 pieces of coloured glass depicting the Creation. There is fine stained glass, notably in the Great West Window, and mosaics by Gertrude Stein. Lord Carson, leader of the opposition to Home Rule who died in 1935, is buried here in the south aisle.
☎ 028 9032 8332

✱ Belfast City Hall `13 B2`
Donegall Square, Belfast, Co. Antrim. A striking classical Renaissance style building of Portland stone, built to commemorate Queen Victoria giving city status to Belfast in 1888 and completed in 1906. The great copper dome which crowns the City Hall rises to 53m (173ft), providing a landmark throughout the city. The impressive grand staircase is made of Italian marble.
☎ 028 9027 0456   www.belfastcity.gov.uk

⚘ Belfast Zoo `12 A2`
Antrim Road, Belfast, Co. Antrim. Set in landscaped parkland on the slopes of Cave Hill, over 160 species are housed in family groups or colonies in enclosures designed to replicate their natural environment. Gorillas and chimpanzees, big cats, free-flight aviaries, underwater viewing of sea-lions and penguins and a children's farm are among the attractions. The zoo increasingly focuses on wildlife facing extinction and has specialised collections with breeding programmes for endangered species.
☎ 028 9077 6277   www.belfastzoo.co.uk

✱ **Bellaghy Bawn** `11 D3`
Castle Street, Bellaghy, Co. Londonderry. In 1622 Bellaghy became one of the first planned settlements in Ulster at the time of the Plantation of Ulster and parts of the original fortified enclosure remains together with a restored 18th century house. An interpretative centre presents the history of the Bawn and of south Londonderry. There is also an exhibition about contemporary Irish poetry and in particular that of Nobel Prize winning poet Seamus Heaney who was born in Bellaghy.
☎ 028 7938 6812

✱ **Belleek Pottery & Visitors Centre** `8 B3`
Belleek, Co. Fermanagh. The pottery was established in 1857 by John Caldwell Bloomfield who had inherited nearby Castle Caldwell. A tour of the pottery demonstrates the continuing production of the award winning highly decorated lustrous parian ware and the museum exhibits many pieces from all periods of the pottery's working life.
☎ 028 6865 9300/8501 www.belleek.ie

🐦 **Belshaw's Quarry Nature Reserve** `12 A3`
Lisburn, Co. Antrim. A haven for native wildlife in a quarry abandoned in 1950. Dragonflies and butterflies are plentiful. Bulrushes fringe the pond and the drier parts of the quarry support common spotted orchids. Of geological interest, the quarry walls illustrate how the landscape of this area has changed from being a desert, a sea bed, engulfed with molten lava and then covered in ice.
☎ 028 3832 2398 www.ehsni.gov.uk

🐿 **Belvoir Park Forest** `12 B3`
Belvoir Drive, Belfast, Co. Down. On the banks of the River Lagan, Belvoir Forest was formerly an estate and contains mixed woodland. Forest walks, a nature reserve, a small arboretum and a Norman motte are among the attractions of the park. The RSPB is based here and the park is ideal for bird watching.
☎ 028 9049 1264

✱ **Benburb Heritage Centre** `16 B2`
89 Milltown Road, Benburb, Dungannon, Co. Tyrone. 19th century linen weaving factory beside the old Ulster canal with displays of linen and other industrial machinery from 1850-1950, including two steam engines. Nearby is the site of the 1646 Battle of Benburb; a scale model of the battle can be seen in the centre.
☎ 028 3754 9752

🐿 **Benburb Valley Park** `16 B2`
Main Street, Benburb, Co. Tyrone. Riverside walks along the wooded Blackwater river valley and limestone gorge, past the ruins of 17th century Benburb Castle and derelict parts of the former Ulster canal.
☎ 028 3754 8241

❊ **Benvarden** `11 D2`
Dervock, Ballymoney, Co. Antrim. One of the oldest estates in Northern Ireland dating back to the 1630s. Most of the landscaping was carried out by the Montgomery family in the early 19th century with grounds stretching down to the River Bush. The walled garden originated in 1788 and there are herbaceous borders, shrubs, roses and a kitchen garden. Other features include a Victorian woodland pond and an 18th century cobbled stable yard with cart and coach houses and a small collection of garden and farm tools.
☎ 028 2074 1331

🐦 **Binevenagh National Nature Reserve** `11 C2`
Limavady, Co. Londonderry. Binevenagh mountain towers above the flat coastal plain and from the basalt outcrops there are panoramic views over Magilligan Strand, Lough Foyle and the hills of Inishowen. The area supports a rich variety of plant life while buzzards, fulmars and kittiwakes can be seen overhead.
☎ 028 7772 2074 www.ehsni.gov.uk

✱ **Boathouse Centre** `12 B1`
Rathlin Island Harbour, Co. Antrim. Exhibition relating to the history, culture and ecology of the island, with a growing collection of photographs, documents and artefacts. The Rathlin Community Quilt, created by the women of Rathlin, depicts many of the special features and events of the island.
☎ 028 2076 3951/2024

🐦 **Bohill Forest Nature Reserve** `17 D2`
Drumaness, Co. Down. A small reserve of deciduous woodland comprising oak, holly, birch, rowan and hazel. Bohill was first established to protect the Holly Blue butterfly and a colony still exists here. Native woodland birds are joined by summer migrants such as the blackcap and chiffchaff and red deer may also be seen.
☎ 028 4461 2233 www.ehsni.gov.uk

✝ **Bonamargy Friary** `12 B1`
Ballycastle, Co. Antrim. Substantial ruin of a Franciscan friary founded by Rory McQuillan in about 1500 and occupied until the mid 17th century. The vault contains the coffins of several McDonnell chiefs.
☎ 028 2076 2024

❊ **Botanic Gardens** `12 A3`
Stranmillis Road, Belfast, Co. Antrim. One of Belfast's most popular parks with notable rose garden and herbaceous borders established in 1920. The Palm House was built in 1840 by Richard Turner of Dublin and is one of the earliest examples of a curved glass and wrought iron glasshouse. The Victorian tropical ravine, completed in 1889, has a raised balcony which overlooks the plants growing in a sunken glen including bromeliads, orchids, bananas, cinnamon and papyrus.
☎ 028 90324902

✱ **Brontë Homeland Interpretive Centre** `17 C2`
Church Hill Road, Rathfriland, Newry, Co. Down. Drumballyroney Church and School where Patrick Brontë first preached and taught has been converted into a centre to illustrate the life of the literary family in this area; Patrick being the father of the novelist sisters, Emily, Anne and Charlotte. Starting at the centre is a signposted 16km (10 mile) Brontë Homeland drive through the Bann valley which takes in Patrick's birthplace at Emdale.
☎ 028 4063 1152

✱ **Brookhall Historical Farm** `12 A3`
2 Horse Park, Ballinderry Road, Lisburn, Co. Antrim. Rare breeds animals, a farm museum and a wildlife pond are among the attractions at this family-run farm. A holy well, reputed to have healing properties, is found within the grounds and the enclosed landscaped gardens were once an ancient burial ground.
☎ 028 9262 1712

🏰 **Buncrana Castle** `10 B2`
Buncrana, Co. Donegal. The ruins of Buncrana Castle date back to the 16th century but the castle was largely re-built in 1718; Wolfe Tone is reputed to have been imprisoned here following his capture in 1798 after the Anglo-French naval encounter in Lough Swilly.
☎ 077 62600

✱ **Burren Heritage Centre** `17 C3`
15 Bridge Road, Warrenpoint, Newry, Co. Down. Housed in a restored 1839 National School, the centre presents the archaeology and social history of the locality from Neolithic times to the 19th century.
☎ 028 4177 3378

✱ **Cardinal O'Fiaich Heritage Centre** `16 B3`
Slatequarry Road, Cullyhanna, Co. Armagh. An exhibition depicting the life of Cardinal O'Fiaich 'Father Tom' (1923 – 1990), who was born near Cullyhanna. O'Fiaich, a professor of modern history, was appointed Archbishop of Armagh in 1977 and Cardinal and Primate of all Ireland in 1979. The items displayed include photographs, video interviews as well as personal memorabilia.
☎ 028 3086 8757

🐿 **Carnfunnock Country Park** `12 B2`
Coast Road, Larne, Co. Antrim. Woodland and gardens which feature a maze in the shape of Northern Ireland and a collection of sundials; also miniature railway, golf and a driving range. Situated on Drains Bay, the park encompasses beaches and coastline with panoramic views of the Antrim coast.
☎ 028 2827 0541

✱ **Carrick-a-Rede Ropebridge** `11 D1`
Ballintoy, Co. Antrim. A 20m (66ft) bridge of planks with wire handrails which swings 24m (80ft) above the sea and rocks, separating Larrybane Cliffs from a small rocky island. Now in the care of the National Trust, this bridge has been erected here every spring for at least 200 years by the salmon fishermen of the island.
☎ 028 2073 1159/1582 www.nationaltrust.org.uk

🏰 **Carrickfergus Castle** `12 B2`
Marine Highway, Carrickfergus, Co. Antrim. Dating back to the end of the 12th century when it was built by John de Courcy, the castle is well preserved with three remaining medieval courtyards within the walls, a massive keep with barrel-vaulted chambers and a Great Hall. Standing on a rock overlooking the harbour, the castle dominates the town's skyline. Among the historical events associated with the castle are the landing of William of Orange in 1690 and the first action by an American ship in European waters in 1778. It was garrisoned until 1928.
☎ 028 9335 1273

🏛 **Carrothers Family Heritage Museum** `15 C1`
Carrybridge Road, Lisbellaw, Co. Fermanagh. An unique and quirky collection comprising thousands of items acquired by the Carrothers family; fossils, bird's eggs, bottles, newspapers and letters from the front in World War I.
☎ 028 6638 7278

🐿 **Castle Archdale Country Park** `9 C3`
Irvinestown, Co. Fermanagh. Featuring an exhibition which explains how the loughs of the area were formed and illustrates how Lough Erne has influenced the people who live around its shore. The archaeological heritage of the area is presented along with the rich diversity of landscape.
☎ 028 6862 1588

🏰 **Castle Balfour** `15 C1`
Main Street, Lisnaskea, Co. Fermanagh. The substantial ruin of a three storey tower house overlooking the town of Lisnaskea which has undergone recent restoration. Built in about 1618 by Sir James Balfour, a Scottish planter, the castle was occupied continuously until the 19th century.
☎ 028 6632 3110

🏯 **Castle Coole** `15 C1`
Enniskillen, Co. Fermanagh. Restored by the National Trust, this elegant mansion was designed in neo-classical style at the end of the 18th century. The interior has ornate plaster work by Joseph Rose, marble chimney pieces carved by Westmancott and rooms filled with original Regency furnishings and furniture. A visit includes the servant's tunnel, ice house and the Belmore private coach in the original coach house. Castle Coole is set in beautiful landscaped parkland with mature oak woodland and a lake, which is home to a breeding colony of Greylag Geese.
☎ 028 6632 2690 www.nationaltrust.org.uk

🐦 **Castle Espie Wildfowl and Wetlands Trust** `12 B3`
78 Ballydrain Road, Comber, Newtownards, Co. Down. Castle Espie on the shores of Strangford Lough has the largest collection of geese, ducks and swans in Ireland. In autumn and winter the birds are increased in great numbers by migrants such as Brent geese and godwits. Hides allow visitors to watch birds undisturbed and there are woodland walks and wildfowl gardens with ponds and lakes.
☎ 028 9187 4146

🏰 **Castle Leslie** `15 D1`
Glaslough, Co. Monaghan. Set in wooded parkland overlooking a lake, Castle Leslie has been home to the Leslie family since 1665, although the present house was built in 1870. The interior has Italian Renaissance features while the exterior is in Scottish Baronial style. Castle Leslie is now run by the family as a hotel and conference venue.
☎ 047 88109 www.castle-leslie.ie

❋ Castle Ward
`17 D2`

Strangford, Downpatrick, Co. Down. Situated in over 200ha (490 acres) of walled parkland on the shores of Strangford Lough, Castle Ward is a half Gothic, half Palladian masterpiece built in 1765 for the first Viscount Bangor and his wife, who both favoured different styles. There is a Victorian laundry, a working cornmill driven by water and old sawmill on the estate. Close to the house is Old Castle Ward, a small Plantation tower house built in 1610, and there are walks through the woodland and alongside Strangford Lough. A National Trust property.
☎ 028 4488 1204   www.nationaltrust.org.uk

🦆 Castlecaldwell
`9 C3`

Beleek, Co. Fermanagh. The ruined 17th century Caldwell family castle is situated on a wooded peninsula on the shores of Lower Lough Erne and the three sheltered bays here are now a RSPB reserve. There are inspiring views across the lough from the estate, where wildfowl hides give visitors the opportunity to view the flocks of waterfowl. Way-marked walks and nature trails lead from an exhibition centre through beech and conifer forest to the shoreline.
☎ 028 6863 1253

❋ Castledawson Open Animal Farm
`11 D3`

46 Leitrim Road, Castledawson, Co. Londonderry. Home to a wide variety of rare domestic animal and fowl breeds including dexter cattle and jacob sheep; also pets and shetland ponies.
☎ 028 7946 8207

❋ Castlederg Visitor Centre
`10 B3`

26 Lower Strabane Road, Castlederg, Co. Tyrone. A celebration of Castlederg and its people through the presentation of several stories on an innovative video wall. Connections with the town are found to include Davy Crocket and the creator of Irish Coffee, Joe Sheridan.
☎ 028 8167 0795

❋ Castlewellan Forest Park
`17 C2`

Main Street, Castlewellan, Co. Down. Mixed woodland predominates at Castlewellan which is the location of the national arboretum, first established in 1740. The park also has gardens with Queen-Anne style courtyards, a glasshouse with tropical birds, a 4km (3 mile) sculpture trail around the lake and the hedged Peace Maze, the largest maze in the world opened in 2001. Castlewellan offers opportunities for outdoor activities such as fishing, canoeing and pony trekking.
☎ 028 4377 8664

🏛 Causeway School Museum
`11 D1`

52 Causeway Road, Bushmills, Co. Antrim. Re-creation of a 1920s classroom in a former National School designed by Clough Williams Ellis where visitors try out copperplate handwriting and playground games from a past era. Located next to the Giant's Causeway Centre.
☎ 028 2073 1777

🏛 Cavan County Museum
`15 D3`

Virginia Road, Ballyjamesduff, Co. Cavan. Housed in a splendid 19th century building set within extensive grounds, the museum presents the history and heritage of Cavan from earliest times. Among the rare artefacts is the Killycluggin stone dating back 4000 years, the 1000 year old Lough Errol Log Boat, medieval Sheela-na-gigs (carved female figures set into church and castle walls) and the 18th century Cavan Mace. For sports enthusiasts there is a recently opened Gaelic Athletic Association gallery reflecting the history of the GAA in Cavan.
☎ 049 8544070

❋ Cavan Crystal
`15 C2`

Dublin Road, Cavan, Co. Cavan. Visitors are given an insight into the production of the crystal which is mouth-blown and hand-cut, and the audiovisual theatre also presents a brief history of Cavan and the surrounding area. The work of innovative craft and design artists from all over Europe is displayed in the showroom as well as the locally handcrafted crystal.
☎ 049 4331800   www.cavancrystaldesign.com

🏤 Cavancor Historic House and Craft Centre
`10 B3`

Ballindrait, Lifford, Co. Donegal. James II is reputed to have dined at Cavancor in April 1690. Later the house was to become the ancestral home of James Knox Polk, who was 11th U.S. President between 1845 and 1849. Built in the early 17th century, Cavancor is furnished in Jacobean and Georgian style and contains a museum, art gallery and pottery.
☎ 074 41143

🏕 Cave Hill Country Park
`12 A3`

Antrim Road, Belfast, Co. Antrim. The park comprises heath and moorland, meadows and woodland and is rich in wild plants and birdlife. Walks to McArt's Fort opens up panoramic views. Other archaeological sites include Neolithic caves and the remains of a stone cairn and crannog. The Heritage Centre explains the archaeology, natural history and folklore of the area.
☎ 028 9077 6925

♟ Clough Castle
`17 D2`

Clough Village, Downpatrick, Co. Down. Clough is an Anglo Norman motte-and-bailey earthwork castle with an added stone tower. Excellent views can be enjoyed from the top of the mound.
☎ 028 4461 2233

🏛 Coach & Carriage Museum
`15 C1`

17 Murley Road, Blessingbourne, Fivemiletown, Co. Tyrone. Coaches on display include an impressive 1825 London-to-Oxford stagecoach while the diverse carriage collection exhibits range in age from 1790 to 1910. Horse drawn farm machinery and costumes are also on show.
☎ 028 8952 1221

🦆 Colin Glen Forest Park
`12 A3`

163 Stewartstown Road, Dunmurry, Belfast, Co. Antrim. 80ha (198 acres) of beautiful broadleaved woodland, grassland, waterfalls and ponds in West Belfast, reclaimed from a landfill site and disused brickworks. The Forest Park Centre provides information about the history of the park, which was originally a game estate and the wide variety of flora and fauna to be found.
☎ 028 9061 4115   www.colinglentrust.org

❋ Colmcille Heritage Centre
`9 C1`

Gartan, Church Hill, Letterkenny, Co. Donegal. An exhibition about the life and work of St Colmcille (St. Columba) who is said to have been born in the area around 521AD; artefacts associated with the saint are on display and visitors can see how early Christian manuscripts were illuminated.
☎ 074 37306

❋ Corn Mill
`17 C3`

Marine Park, Annalong, Co. Down. Overlooking Annalong harbour, the water-powered mill which was built around 1830 has demonstrations of flour and oatmeal production. The mill has a restored grain drying kiln and three pairs of millstones. Visitors have the opportunity to grind their own corn.
☎ 028 4376 8736

🏛 Cornmill Heritage Centre
`16 B1`

Dungannon Road, Coalisland, Co. Tyrone. Local history and the industrial development of Coalisland is brought to life through photographs, paintings, recordings of people's memories and by means of audiovisual presentations.
☎ 028 8774 8532

🌿 Correl Glen
`9 C3`

Tully, Co. Fermanagh. The Sillees River runs through Correl Glen and a nature trail follows the river up through shady native woodland to a panoramic viewpoint on heathland above. Meadow pipits and curlews nest on the reserve from April to July. Correl Glen is just part of the extensive Largalinny National Nature Reserve which contains some rare plants and most of the Irish native species of butterfly.
☎ 028 6632 3110

🏕 Crawfordsburn Country Park
`12 B2`

Bridge Road, Helen's Bay, Co. Down. 16km (10 miles) east of Belfast on Helen's Bay and alongside the North Down Coastal Path, Crawfordsburn Country Park has two fine sandy beaches, stretches of rocky coastline, meadows and a wooded glen with a waterfall at its head. Walks and nature trails cross the park and there is a countryside centre with interactive natural history exhibits. Grey Point Fort, a defensive gun site built to protect Belfast Lough, is situated within the park and has a small military museum.
☎ 028 9185 3621

🌿 Crom Estate
`15 C1`

Newtownbutler, Co. Fermanagh. Comprising 770ha (1901 acres) of oak woodland and parkland on the SE shores of Upper Lough Erne, Crom is an important nature conservation area in the care of the National Trust. Abundant wildlife includes fallow deer and pine martens whilst spotted flycatchers and curlews are amongst the birds to be seen; there is the facility of an overnight woodland hide. The area supports many rare plants and the estate is notable for flowering shrubs in Culliaghs Wood in spring. The landscape is enhanced by several old buildings including the ruin of Crom Old Castle. The visitor centre has a wildlife exhibition.
☎ 028 6773 8118/8174   www.nationaltrust.org.uk

🏤 Crown Liquor Saloon
`13 B2`

46 Great Victoria Street, Belfast, Co. Antrim. Dating from Victorian times and one of the most famous public houses in Belfast. A National Trust property.
☎ 028 9024 9476   www.nationaltrust.org.uk

🦆 Davagh Forest Park
`11 C3`

Cookstown, Co. Tyrone. Wilderness area of mixed conifer forest covering 1200ha (2964 acres) on the north facing slope of Beleevamore Mountain; abundant wildlife including a herd of sika deer. Nature trails and a scenic forest drive.
☎ 028 8676 6727

🦆 Delamont Country Park
`17 D2`

Mullagh, Killyleagh, Downpatrick, Co. Down. Comprising gardens, woodland and parkland adjoining Strangford Lough, Delamont also has the longest miniature railway in Ireland, an adventure playground and opportunities for boat trips. Standing within the park is the tallest megalith in Ireland, the Strangford Stone.
☎ 028 4482 8333

❋ Derrymore House
`16 B2`

Bessbrook, Newry, Co. Armagh. This elegant thatched house, dating back to the 18th century, is set in picturesque parkland laid out in the style of Capability Brown. Once home to Isaac Corry, who represented Newry in the Irish House of Commons for 30 years from 1776 and was General in Chief of the Irish Volunteers. A National Trust property.
☎ 028 3083 0353   www.nationaltrust.org.uk

✝ Devenish Island
`14 B1`

Lower Lough Erne, Enniskillen, Co. Fermanagh. Devenish is remarkable for its well preserved 12th century round tower which belonged to a monastic settlement originally founded by St Molaise in the 6th century. This island in Lower Lough Erne also has the remains of an Augustinian abbey and an intricately carved medieval cross still standing in the graveyard.
☎ 028 6862 1588

❋ Doagh Visitor Centre
`10 B1`

Doagh Island, Ballyliffen, Inishowen, Co. Donegal. An outdoor museum which recreates the life and traditions of the people of Inishowen from the 1840s and the time of the Great Famine through to the 1970s. Scenes from past times are re-enacted including a Presbyterian meeting and an eviction and there are several reconstructed buildings ranging from a turf house to a landlord's mansion.
☎ 077 78078

Doe Castle
9 C1

Creeslough, Co. Donegal. A ruined medieval fortress well protected on three sides by the sea and on the other by a moat hewn from rock. The castle did not fall to the English until 1650 when it was attacked from the sea. Once guarded by a drawbridge and portcullis, the moat is now spanned by a bridge. Considerable alterations to the castle were made in the 19th century by General Vaughan Harte.
☎ 074 21160

Donaghmore Heritage Centre
16 A1

Pomeroy, Donaghmore, Co. Tyrone. Housed in a converted late 19th century National School, the centre offers the facility to research family history with the aid of a large computerised database. There are also collections of photographs, documents, land registration ledgers, maps, name scrolls and coats of arms along with arts and crafts memorabilia and artefacts from local industries.
☎ 028 8776 1306

Donegal Ancestry
9 C1

The Quay, Ramelton, Co. Donegal. Ramelton's story from the time it was a Gaelic stronghold through to its prosperity in the Georgian era is portrayed in an exhibition housed in a restored quayside warehouse, while the adjacent warehouse is a genealogical centre providing a service for people who wish to research their family history. Since the 1600s there has been widespread emigration from Donegal which was accelerated in the mid 19th century as a result of the Great Famine and compounded by evictions and clearances.
☎ 074 51266

Donegal Castle
8 B3

Donegal, Co. Donegal. Overlooking the River Eske, the restored late 15th century castle is just off the main square of this market town. Originally the seat of the O'Donnells, the castle was built by Red Hugh II O'Donnell in 1505, whilst additions, including the magnificent fireplace in the banqueting hall, were made in the 17th century by Sir Basil Brooke, who was responsible for the fine Jacobean fortified house that forms part of the castle. The castle furnishings include French tapestries and Persian rugs.
☎ 073 22405

Donegal County Museum
9 C1

High Road, Letterkenny, Co. Donegal. The museum has a wide range of exhibits which illustrate all aspects of life in Donegal from prehistoric times to the 20th century and is housed in buildings which were once part of the Letterkenny Workhouse which functioned between 1846 and 1922.
☎ 074 24613

Donegal Craft Village
8 B3

Ballyshannon Road, Donegal, Co. Donegal. Resident professional craftspeople can be seen at work in their workshops which are clustered round a central courtyard. Pottery, sculpture, metalwork, batik and jewelry are among the crafts on view.
☎ 073 22225

Donegal Historical Society's Museum
8 B3

Rossknowlagh, Co. Donegal. Housed in a room in a Franciscan friary, the museum documents Irish history from the Stone Age to World War II with a collection which includes prehistoric artefacts, items from the Spanish Armada including an anchor, coins and medals and Belleek pottery. There is also a genealogical section.
☎ 072 51342   www.donegalhistory.com

Donegal Parian China
8 B3

Ballyshannon, Co. Donegal. A pottery producing delicate handcrafted parian china including figurines and ceramic woven baskets and plates; the visitor centre has an extensive showroom and video of the production process. The company was only founded in 1986 but carries on a 150 year old tradition of parian china manufacture in this part of Ireland.
☎ 072 51826   www.donegalchina.ie

Donegal Railway Heritage Centre
8 B3

The Old Station House, Donegal, Co. Donegal. Located in the old Donegal Town Station, the centre displays restored carriages, models and memorabilia from the time when Donegal was served by an extensive narrow gauge rail network.
☎ 073 22655

Dorn Nature Reserve
12 B3

Ardkeen, Co. Down. An extensive area of sheltered bays, saltmarsh and mud-flats on the east side of Strangford Lough supporting a remarkable diversity of marine life including sponges, sea squirts, anemones and star fish. The channel which connects several bays to the lough has rock sills which hold back the water as the tide falls, creating saltwater rapids. Common seals and large numbers of wintering wildfowl can be seen on the foreshore. At the north end of the reserve a spit of shingle and bedrock extends over 1km (0.6 mile) into the lough.
☎ 028 4272 9882   www.ehsni.gov.uk

Down Cathedral
17 D2

English Street, Downpatrick, Co. Down. A fine Gothic cathedral of the Church of Ireland with beautiful stained glass windows; originally built in 1183 as part of a Benedictine monastery, substantially destroyed in the 14th century, restored and remodelled in the late 18th century and the interior comprehensively renovated in 1987. The organ, one of the finest in Ireland, has a magnificent oak case. In the grounds lies a grave reputed to be that of St Patrick.
☎ 028 4461 4922   www.cathedral.down.anglican.org

Down County Museum
17 D2

The Mall, Downpatrick, Co. Down. Housed in an 18th century gaol with restored cells, the museum's changing exhibitions and activities bring to life the history of County Down. There is a room dedicated to St Patrick and carved stones from Saul, the traditional site of St Patrick's first church.
☎ 028 4461 5218

Down Royal Racecourse
12 A3

Maze, Lisburn, Co. Down. National Hunt and Flat racing course with 12 race meetings a year including the Ulster Oaks and the Ulster Derby in June, and the Northern Ireland Festival of Racing held in November. Down Royal was first established by royal charter in 1685.
☎ 028 9262 1256   www.downroyal.co

Downhill Castle & Mussenden Temple
11 C2

Bishop's Gate, 42 Mussenden Road, Castlerock, Co. Londonderry. Now a ruin, this massive palace was built in 1780 by the eccentric Frederick Hervey, Earl of Bristol and Bishop of Derry. The temple folly, inspired by the Tivoli Temple of Vesta, is perched on the clifftop and from the landscaped Downhill estate and ornamental gardens there are stunning views over the north coast. A National Trust property.
☎ 028 7084 8728   www.nationaltrust.org.uk

Downpatrick Racecourse
17 D2

Ballydugan Road, Downpatrick, Co. Down. National Hunt and Flat racing course with eight race days a year. 1685 saw the first race meeting in Downpatrick and racing has taken place on the present course for over 200 years.
☎ 028 4461 2054

Downpatrick Railway Museum
17 D2

Market Street, Downpatrick, Co. Down. Steam and diesel locomotives, carriages and working engines on display; also a model railway in the station house. Train rides take place along 2km (1mile) of a restored section of the BCDR Belfast-Newcastle main line; this is eventually to be extended to over 11km (9 miles).
☎ 028 4461 5779   www.downrail.icom43.net

Drum Manor Forest Park
16 A1

Drum Road, Cookstown, Co. Tyrone. A 92ha (227 acre) forest with 11km (7 miles) of walking trails and an interpretative centre. Drum Manor no longer exists but the tower and outside walls remain. Two ornamental ponds have various species of waterfowl, a butterfly garden, an arboretum and demonstration forest plots planted with both evergreen and deciduous trees.
☎ 028 8676 2774

Dún a'Ri Forest Park
15 D2

Cabra, Cootehill, Co. Cavan. Located in the River Cabra glen, the forest comprises 229ha (565 acres), more than half of which is managed commercially to produce Norway spruce and oak. The park has a wide variety of plants and animals including squirrels, stoats, Irish hares, pigmy shrews, mink and otters. Forest walks pass many places associated with the legends and history of the valley; a holy well, the ruins of Fleming's Castle, a flax mill, lake and an old ice house.
☎ 049 4331942

Dundrum Castle
17 D2

Dundrum, Newcastle, Co. Down. Built by John de Courcy in about 1177 and later occupied by the Magennises, Dundrum is one of the finest Norman castles in Northern Ireland. A massive circular stone tower is enclosed by stone walls and further protected by a ditch hewn from rock. The castle affords panoramic views of the Mourne Mountains and across Dundrum Bay.
☎ 028 9054 3037

Dunloughan Farm Museum
12 B1

92 Torr Road, Ballycastle, Co. Antrim. An old Farmhouse and a range of farm exhibits, including farm machinery are on display.
☎ 028 2076 2739

Dunluce Castle
11 D1

Portrush, Co. Antrim. An extensive dramatic cliff top ruin on a rocky headland, the site of which has been fortified for over 1500 years. The mainly 16th and 17th century remains of the castle incorporate two Norman towers dating from 1305. Successively occupied by Ulster clans, the McQuillens, O'Neills and McDonnells, until the 17th century when, during a storm, the kitchens fell into the sea and all the servants were killed.
☎ 028 2073 1938

Dunluce Centre
11 D1

10 Sandhill Drive, Portrush, Co. Antrim. Indoor family entertainment centre which includes a multimedia display of the folklore of the surrounding area, Turbo Tours where action on a giant screen is synchronised with moving seats, interactive nature exhibits and a soft play area. The viewing tower offers panoramic views of Portrush and the north coast.
☎ 028 7082 4444

Dunree Military Museum
10 B1

Fort Dunree, Buncrana, Inishowen, Co. Donegal. The museum is set within the old military fort at Dunree Head which had a strategic role in defending the entrance to Lough Swilly. With an audiovisual theatre, an extensive collection of military artefacts and large artillery pieces in their original location, the museum explains the role of coastal artillery and the military history of the area. The Old Fort Hospital has a wildlife exhibition illustrating the flora and fauna of the surrounding area.
☎ 077 61817

Earhart Centre & Wildlife Sanctuary
10 B2

Ballyarnet Country Park, Londonderry, Co. Londonderry. Commemorates Amelia Earhart, the first woman to fly solo across the Atlantic, who landed unexpectedly in the field here on 21st May 1932.
☎ 028 7135 4040

ECOS Environmental Centre
12 A2

Kernohans Lane, Broughshane Road, Ballymena, Co. Antrim. Standing in a 60ha (150 acre) park, interactive displays focus on the environment and alternative energy production from renewable sources. On site willow coppicing, wind turbines and solar energy account for 60% of the centre's energy requirements.
☎ 028 2566 4400

Enniskillen Castle & Heritage Centre `15 C1`

Castle Barracks, Wellington Place, Enniskillen, Co. Fermanagh. Overlooking the River Erne, Enniskillen Castle dates back to the 15th century and was once the stronghold of the Gaelic Maguire chieftains. The medieval keep remains intact and is surrounded by 18th and 19th century barracks buildings, while the 17th century turrets of the Water-gate give the castle its distinctive appearance. The keep houses the Royal Inniskilling Fusiliers museum which explains the history of the regiment from its formation in 1689. The Heritage Centre, located in a modern purpose built building within the castle, houses the Fermanagh County Museum and Fermanagh's archaeological heritage is portrayed in the curved barracks building.
☎ 028 6632 5000

✱ Erne Gateway Centre `9 C3`

Corry, Belleek, Co. Fermanagh. Featuring an exhibition which explains how the loughs of the area were formed and illustrates how Lough Erne has influenced the people who live around its shore. The archaeological heritage of the area is presented along with the rich diversity of landscape and wildlife.
☎ 028 6865 8866

✱ Exploris `17 D2`

The Ropewalk, Castle Street, Portaferry, Co. Down. Aquarium attraction with some of the largest tanks in Britain, simulating the experience of underwater exploration of Strangford Lough and the Irish Sea. Attractions include a touch tank, marine discovery lab and a recently opened seal sanctuary where sick or orphaned seals are rehabilitated to return to the wild.
☎ 028 4272 8062   www.exploris.org.uk

✱ Fantasy Island `11 D1`

2-8 Kerr Street, Portrush, Co. Antrim. Indoor adventure play area for young children with ball ponds and climbing frames.
☎ 028 7082 3595

Fernhill House: The People's Museum `12 A3`

Glencairn Road, Belfast, Co. Antrim. The history of the Shankill district of Belfast is told in the words of local people focussing on the Home Rule Crisis and the World Wars. Of additional interest is the re-creation of a 1930s terraced 'kitchen house', typical of the district at that time.
☎ 028 9071 5599

Fifth Province `10 B2`

Calgach Centre, Butcher Street, Londonderry, Co. Londonderry. Museum with multimedia exhibits which dramatically illustrate the history of the Celts; local history and the impact of emigrants on the U.S.A. are also featured.
☎ 028 7137 3177

✱ Fintown Railway `8 B2`

Fintown, Co. Donegal. The only operational narrow gauge railway in Donegal which was re-opened in 1995; visitors can take a 6km/4m return journey along the shore of Lough Finn.
☎ 075 46280

✱ Flight of the Earls Heritage Centre `10 B2`

Rathmullan, Co. Donegal. In 1607 the O'Neill and O'Donnell chieftains fled the country for Spain in what became known as The Flight of the Earls. The heritage centre traces the history of these times and their consequences with lively and interesting displays including works of art and costume.
☎ 074 58229

Florence Court `14 B1`

Florencecourt, Enniskillen, Co. Fermanagh. Once the home of the Earls of Enniskillen, 18th century Florence Court built in the Palladian style is one of the finest historic houses in Ulster. It was named after Florence, the wife of the first Earl of Enniskillen. Beautiful rococo ceilings and panels decorate the interior which has original furniture, paintings and artefacts. Within the estate is a 1780s walled garden, ice house, summer house and water-powered sawmill. A National Trust property.
☎ 028 6634 8249   www.nationaltrust.org.uk

Florence Court Forest Park `14 B1`

Florencecourt, Enniskillen, Co. Fermanagh. Adjoining Florence Court House, the forest park covers over 1200ha (2964 acres) encompassing a wide variety of habitats including open blanket bog, coniferous forest and the old estate woodland featuring many oak trees planted around 200 years ago.
☎ 028 6634 8497

Folk Village Museum `8 A2`

Glencolumbkille, Co. Donegal. The museum is built in the form of a village where each cottage is a replica dwelling used by local people in one of the 18th, 19th or 20th centuries with period furnishings and artefacts. A 19th century National School is also featured and has a collection of old photographs, books and items of local history on display. The folk village was established by Father James MacDyer in the 1950s to help ease unemployment and maintain the traditional culture of the area.
☎ 073 30017

Folklife Display `15 C1`

Lisnaskea Library, Drumhaw, Lisnaskea, Co. Fermanagh. An exhibition in Lisnaskea Library depicting rural life in Fermanagh, made up from the bric-a-brac collection of a retired local publican.
☎ 028 6772 1222

Foyle Valley Railway Museum `10 B2`

Foyle Road, Londonderry, Co. Londonderry. Situated on the site of the Great Northern Railway terminus, the centre has a fascinating collection of railway memorabilia, artefacts and rolling stock. 4km (3 miles) of narrow gauge tracks which carried the Donegal Railway and the Londonderry & Lough Swilly Railway are now operated as a tourist railway with diesel railcars from 1932 and runs alongside the River Foyle.
☎ 028 7126 5234   www.foylevalleyrailway.co.uk

Garvagh Museum & Heritage Centre `11 D2`

Main Street, Garvagh, Co. Londonderry. 19th and early 20th century rural and domestic life and industry is portrayed here with exhibits including a jaunting car and eel fisherman's boat. Stone Age artefacts from the Bann valley are also on display at the museum, located in the walled garden of the former Garvagh House
☎ 028 2955 7924

Gateway Centre Museum `10 B3`

21 Moyle Road, Newtownstewart, Co. Tyrone. Exhibition of Victoriana, toys, packaging, photographic equipment and militaria.
☎ 028 8166 2414

✱ Giant's Causeway `11 D1`

Causeway Road, Bushmills, Co. Antrim. Thousands of layered basalt columns, mostly hexagonal, stretching for almost 1km (0.6 mile) into the ocean and resulting from the cooling of molten lava about 60 million years ago. Legend tells it was built by the giant Finn MacCool to enable him to cross to Scotland. The visitor centre has an audiovisual theatre and exhibition area which outlines the geological history of the Causeway and also illustrates the flora and fauna of the area and local history. An UNESCO World Heritage Site in the care of the National Trust.
☎ 028 2073 1159/1582   www.giantscausewayofficialguide.com

☙ Giant's Causeway National Nature Reserve `11 D1`

Bushmills, Co. Antrim. The reserve encompasses the basalt pavement and steps of the Giant's Causeway, dramatic cliffs, sheltered bays and the site where a Spanish galleon, the Girona, sunk in 1588; paths provide easy access. Birds include eider ducks and oystercatchers, rare choughs, buzzards and peregrine falcons. Wild flowers carpet the cliffs in early summer.
☎ 028 2073 1855   www.ehsni.gov.uk

✞ Giant's Ring `17 C1`

Ballylesson, Edenderry, Co. Down. One of Ireland's most important Neolithic sites consisting of a high circular earthbank 183m (600ft) in diameter which encloses a megalithic tomb. Situated beside the River Lagan, the enclosure was used as a horse racing circuit in the 18th century.
☎ 028 9266 0038

Glebe House & Gallery `9 C1`

Church Hill, Letterkenny, Co. Donegal. Glebe House is a Regency house built in 1828 with an interior decorated with William Morris wallpaper and textiles and Japanese and Islamic art. Set in woodland gardens, the house is home to the Derek Hill Collection of over 300 works by leading 20th century artists including Picasso and Kokoshka. Many Irish and English artists are also represented in the collection.
☎ 074 37071   www.heritageireland.ie

Glenariff Forest Park `12 A1`

Glenariff Road, Parkmore, Co. Antrim. Paths and trails lead through the narrow wooded gorge cut by the Glenarrif River to mountain viewpoints. Three spectacular waterfalls cascade down the river and the damp conditions support a variety of mosses and ferns; the woodland comprises oak, hazel, ash and willow. A visitor centre provides information about the park.
☎ 028 2175 8232

Glenveagh Castle `9 C1`

Church Hill, Letterkenny, Co. Donegal. Set within the Glenveagh National Park, the Scottish style castle with its rectangular keep was built between 1870 and 1873 and is surrounded by celebrated gardens. An important collection of trees and shrubs is found at Glenveagh and there are a variety of garden styles skillfully set against the beautiful and rugged Donegal landscape. A formal Italian terrace has antique sculpture and terracotta pots while a fruit, vegetable and flower garden is surrounded by clipped hedges and overlooked by a neo-gothic conservatory.
☎ 074 37090

Glenveagh National Park `9 C1`

Church Hill, Letterkenny, Co. Donegal. Home to a large herd of red deer, the park comprises 16,500ha (40,755 acres) of mountains, lakes, glens and woods. Glenveagh Castle and gardens are found within the park and a visitor centre at the castle has exhibitions and an audiovisual show about the area.
☎ 074 37090   www.heritageireland.ie

Gortin Glen Forest Park `9 D2`

163 Glenpark Road, Omagh, Co. Tyrone. The park has an 8km (5 mile) scenic drive through the forest, walking and bike trails. All afford breathtaking views. Also within the park is a sika deer enclosure, wildfowl enclosure and visitor centre.
☎ 028 8164 8217

Gosford Forest Park `16 B2`

Gosford Road, Markethill, Co. Armagh. The park is made up of the forested former estate of Gosford Castle, a mock-Norman castle built by Sir Arthur Acheson in 1839. Features include an arboretum with 200 year old broadleaved trees and a deer park. Traditional breeds of poultry in open paddocks, ornamental pigeons, nature trails and a walled garden are amongst other attractions.
☎ 028 3755 1277

✱ Grand Opera House `13 B2`

2-4 Great Victoria Street, Belfast, Co. Antrim. Designed by architect Frank Matcham and opened by J F Warden in 1895, the theatre has always seen a rich variety of entertainment from opera to pantomime and serious drama to comedy. Its declining opulence was restored in 1980; transformed into a premier modern theatre whilst retaining the lavish Victorian interior.
☎ 028 9024 1919   www.goh.co.uk

✱ Grant Ancestral Home　　16 A1
45 Dergenagh Road, Dungannon, Co. Tyrone. Ancestral home of Ulysses Simpson Grant who became 18th President of the United States (1869 – 1877). The typical 19th century thatched cottage has original mud walls reinforced with reeds; the farmyard has a turf store, byre and display of agricultural implements. Exhibitions and audiovisual shows tell the story of the Simpson family and their early years in Ireland, of Irish emigration to America and of the American Civil War. A pond and wildlife garden has been created in the grounds of the homestead.
☎ 028 8555 7133

▥ Gray's Printing Press　　10 B3
49 Main Street, Strabane, Co. Tyrone. With a unique Georgian façade, the building houses an 18th century printing press (National Trust) thought to have been used by John Dunlap who was later to print the American Declaration of Independence. An impressive selection of 19th century hand printing machines are also displayed and there are compositor demonstrations from time to time. In the same building is Strabane's local history museum.
☎ 028 7188 4094　　　　　　　　　　www.nationaltrust.org.uk

♜ Greencastle　　17 C3
Cranfield Point, Kilkeel, Co. Down. In medieval times this royal castle on the north shore of the narrow mouth to Carlingford Lough guarded the entrance to the lough and had an eventful history. Greencastle was besieged by Edward Bruce in 1316 and later became a garrison for Elizabeth I. The castle today is substantial, consisting of a curtain wall with a tower at each corner enclosing a large rectangular keep.
☎ 028 4176 2525

✝ Grey Abbey & Physic Garden　　12 B3
Greyabbey, Newtownards, Co. Down. Set within beautiful parkland, Grey Abbey is the substantial remains of a Cistercian abbey founded by Affreca, the wife of John de Courcy, in 1193. Monks made use of many herbs in their medicines and a herb garden has been recreated here as it may have existed in medieval times.
☎ 028 4278 8585

✣ Grianan Ailigh　　10 B2
Burt, Inishowen, Co. Donegal. A huge round stone fort or cashel dating back to 1700BC which stands at the centre of a series of three earthen banks from either late Bronze or early Iron Age. An important stronghold of the kingdom of Ailigh, it retained a mythological importance long after its strategic value had passed away. Restored in the 1870s, the cashel has walls measuring 4m (13ft) thick and 5m (16ft) high with terraces along their interior to allow access to the top of the wall. Situated on a hilltop 242m (800ft) above sea level, there are wonderful views across the Foyle and Swilly.
☎ 077 68080　　　　　　　　　　　　www.griananailigh.ie

✱ Grianan Ailigh Visitor Centre　　10 B2
Burt, Inishowen, Co. Donegal. Housed within a restored church, the centre provides information about the history of the ancient round stone fort of Grianan Ailigh; there is also an interpretative display of the ecosystem of the nearby woodland and wetland habitat, home to Hooper swans, wild geese and many woodland birds and animals.
☎ 077 68000

▥ Harbour Museum　　10 B2
Harbour Square, Londonderry, Co. Londonderry. Maritime museum which includes a replica of the curragh in which St Columba sailed to Iona in 563AD.
☎ 028 7137 7331

▦ Hezlett House　　11 D2
107 Sea Road, Castlerock, Co. Londonderry. Thatched house dating from 1600s, one of few remaining of this age in Ireland, with simple Victorian furnishings. The cruck-truss roof construction may be viewed from the attic and there is a display of farm implements. A National Trust property.
☎ 028 7084 8567　　　　　　　　　　www.nationaltrust.org.uk

♜ Hillsborough Castle　　12 A3
Main Street, Hillsborough, Co. Down. The official residence of the Secretary for State for Northern Ireland and formerly the home of the Governor of Northern Ireland. Built in the 1770s by Wills Hill, first Marquess of Downshire, the mansion is set in impressive grounds with a rose garden and lakeside walks. The state drawing room, dining rooms and the Candlestick Hall are open to visitors. Hillsborough displays silver from H.M.S Nelson and has many items of Georgian furniture.
☎ 028 9268 2244

✝ Inch Abbey　　17 D2
Downpatrick, Co. Down. Situated on an island in the River Quoile and reached by a raised causeway, Inch Abbey is the ruin of a Cistercian monastery founded by John de Courcy in the 1180s. Some earthworks survive from a church which pre-dated the abbey.
☎ 028 4461 2233

▥ Inishowen Maritime Museum & Planetarium　　11 C1
Greencastle, Co. Donegal. Located in the old coastguard station beside the harbour, the museum illustrates the traditions of the community which has one of the busiest fishing fleets in Ireland. The planetarium traces the history of navigation and visitors have the opportunity to view the stars as they would have looked before the birth of Christ and as they are today.
☎ 077 81363

✱ Ionad Cois Locha　　8 B1
Dunlewey Centre, Gweedore, Co. Donegal. Situated beside Dunlewey Lake in a restored farmhouse, this centre presents an insight into life in this Irish speaking area in the 19th century. There are demonstrations of traditional crafts such as spinning, weaving and carding and a programme of cultural events and concerts. Boat trips, a farm museum and a large variety of animals are also amongst the attractions.
☎ 075 31699

✱ Irish Linen Centre　　12 A3
Market Square, Lisburn, Co. Antrim. Linen weaving workshop with working hand looms recreates one of Ulster's greatest industries; also an exhibition on how linen has been produced through the ages and a textile collection. Established in the town's 17th century Market House along with the Lisburn Museum which has a changing programme of local history and art exhibitions.
☎ 028 9266 3377

▥ Isaac Butt Heritage Centre　　9 C2
Cloghan, Ballybofey, Co. Donegal. Isaac Butt (1813 – 1879), born in Cloghan, was a civil rights activist and regarded as founder of the Home Rule party. Exhibitions about his life and times are housed in the restored old school.
☎ 074 31858

♜ Jordan's Castle　　17 D2
Ardglass, Downpatrick, Co. Down. One of several tower house castles built around the port of Ardglass in the 15th century. The four storey ruin is well preserved and houses a local exhibition centre.
☎ 028 4461 2233

🐦 Kebble Nature Reserve　　12 B1
Rathlin Island, Co. Antrim. Situated at the west of Rathlin Island where the cliffs rise more than 100m (328ft) above the rocky seashore, Kebble is renowned for breeding birds. Guillemots, razorbills, kittiwakes, fulmars, peregrine falcons, buzzards and ravens breed on the cliff ledges whilst puffins rear their chicks in burrows in cliff grassland. Breeding waterfowl are found on the lake and marshy areas of the heathland which stretches inland from the cliffs.
☎ 028 2076 2024　　　　　　　　　　www.ehsni.gov.uk

🌳 Kilbroney Forest Park　　17 C3
Shore Road, Rostrevor, Newry, Co. Down. The park covering almost 40ha (99 acres) has a 3km (2 mile) forest drive to views over Carlingford Lough, walks along the Kilbroney River and an arboretum. Part of Kilbroney, known as Rosetrevor Oakwood, is designated a National Nature Reserve.
☎ 028 4173 8134

🐦 Killeter Forest　　9 C2
Killeter, Castlederg, Co. Tyrone. An extensive area of conifer forest with hill loughs and expanses of blanket bogland in the upper Derg valley. Grouse, skylarks and curlew are native birds while Greenland white fronted geese are seen flying overhead in winter; the bogs support a rich variety of specialised plants including sphagnum mosses and bog cotton.
☎ 028 8224 7831　　　　　　　　　　www.ehsni.gov.uk

🌳 Killykeen Forest Park　　15 C2
Cavan, Co. Cavan. The park comprises 240ha (593 acres)of mixed woodland rich in wildlife at the south end of Lough Oughter, the lough forming part of a labyrinth of waterways known as the Erne River system. Lough Oughter and Killykeen are renowned for coarse angling and the forest park also has walking and cycle trails and facilities for watersports.
☎ 049 4332541

✱ King's Hall　　12 A3
Lisburn Road, Balmoral, Belfast, Co. Antrim. Exhibition and conference centre, venue for many international and national events including the Belfast Telegraph Ideal Home Exhibition and the Ulster Motor Show; also venue for concerts and gala shows.
☎ 028 9066 5225　　　　　　　　　　www.kingshall.co.uk

✱ Kinturk Cultural Centre　　16 B1
7 Kinturk Road, Cookstown, Co. Tyrone. The centre tells the story of the fishermen of Lough Neagh and the eel industry with displays of traditional boats and equipment and an audiovisual show. There are boat trips and walks from the centre, situated on the west side of Lough Neagh.
☎ 028 8637 6512

🏁 Kirkistown Race Circuit　　17 D1
Rubane Road, Kircubbin, Newtownards, Co. Down. This 2.5km (1.6 mile) track hosts a variety of motorsport including car, rallycross, motorcycle and kart racing and is the only RAC approved circuit in Northern Ireland. Built on an old wartime airfield, it was opened in 1951 by the 500 Motor Racing Club of Ireland.
☎ 028 4277 1325

✱ Knight Ride & Heritage Plaza　　12 B2
Antrim Street, Carrickfergus, Co. Antrim. A monorail theme ride through a thousand years of the history of Carrickfergus, brought to life by means of sounds, smells and special effects. Comprises a 'high ride' and a 'dark ride' as well as a walk through exhibition.
☎ 028 9336 6455

✱ Lagan Lookout Centre　　13 C1
Donegall Quay, Belfast, Co. Antrim. Multimedia and audiovisual displays explain the history of the £14m weir and the industrial and cultural history of Belfast.
☎ 028 9031 5444　　　　　　　　　　www.laganside.com

✱ Leisureland　　11 C2
Redcastle, Inishowen, Co. Donegal. An indoor heated fun park with attractions including pirate boat rides, remote control boats, safari train, dodgems, small cars, mega trucks, ball pool, shooting gallery and pool tables.
☎ 077 82306

❀ Leslie Hill Open Farm & Gardens　　11 D2
Leslie Hill, Ballymoney, Co. Antrim. 18th century landscaped estate with walled garden and lakes; nature trails and horse-trap rides through the grounds. Working farm and blacksmith's forge along with farm animals, poultry and pets.
☎ 028 2766 6803

✱ Linen Hall Library `13 B2`

Belfast's oldest library and Ireland's last subscription library was founded in 1788 and is the leading centre for Irish and local studies in Northern Ireland. Specialising in Irish culture and politics, the library also has a unique collection of Belfast and Ulster early printed books. The Northern Ireland Political Collection is the definitive archive of the Troubles. The reference service is free and open to the general public.
☎ 028 9032 1707   www.linenhall.com

✱ Lough Derg Visitor Centre `9 C3`

Main Street, Pettigo, Co. Donegal. The visitor centre presents exhibits about St Patrick and the history and myths associated with Lough Derg. St Patrick's Purgatory, an island in the lough, has been a place of pilgrimage since medieval times. St Patrick fasted and prayed there for 40 days and pilgrims endeavour to follow in his footsteps. Lough Derg has also been a place of inspiration to many poets and extracts from their poems are displayed in the centre.
☎ 072 61546

🐾 Lough Navar Forest `15 C1`

Derrygonnelly, Enniskillen, Co. Fermanagh. Red deer and wild goats inhabit Lough Navar Forest, through which there is an 11km (7 mile) scenic drive to a spectacular viewpoint over Lower Lough Erne, Donegal Bay and the Sperrin Mountains and several way-marked walking trails. The forest is managed to enhance the landscape and for the benefit of wildlife by planting more broadleaved trees such as oak, beech and birch amongst the conifers and by clear felling other areas. Several small loughs and rocky crags are also a feature of the forest scenery.
☎ 028 6864 1256

✱ Lough Neagh Discovery Centre `16 B1`

Annaloiste Road, Lurgan, Craigavon, Co. Armagh. Set within the Oxford Island National Nature Reserve, the centre has an award winning interactive exhibition which illustrates the wildlife, management and history of Lough Neagh. A programme of events takes place throughout the year including guided nature walks, pond-dipping and bird watching.
☎ 028 3832 2205

✱ Loughside Open Dairy Farm `12 B2`

Friesian Holstein herd and Jacob sheep together with fallow deer, Highland cattle, ponies and donkeys. The farm also features a pets' corner and bird sanctuary, an adventure playground, trips on a miniature train and refreshments are available.
☎ 028 9335 3312

✱ Lurgyvale Thatched Cottage `9 C1`

Traditional music evenings and craft demonstrations are held in the cottage which is around 150 years old and has the original flagged floor and open hearth. An exhibition of old farm implements is included and there are frequent demonstrations of traditional crafts.
☎ 074 39216

🐾 Maghery Country Park `16 B1`

Maghery, Lurgan, Co. Armagh. A place for birdwatching and woodland nature walks on the shores of Lough Neagh. Fishing is also popular at Maghery canal. Coney Island lies 1km (0.6 mile)offshore and is the only inhabited island in Lough Neagh; boat trips to the island are sometimes available from the park.
☎ 028 3832 2205

🏛 Malone House `12 A3`

Barnett Demesne, Upper Malone Road, Belfast, Co. Antrim. Early 19th century Georgian mansion built for prominent Belfast merchant, William Thomas Legge. Set in beautiful parkland with mature trees and woodland, the house commands views over the Lagan Valley. Home of the Higgin Art gallery and an exhibition about Belfast parks.
☎ 028 9068 1246   www.malonehouse.co.uk

✱ Marble Arch Caves `14 B1`

Marlbank, Florencecourt, Co. Fermanagh. This system of caves with rivers, waterfalls, winding passageways and huge chambers has been formed by the action of three streams on a bed of limestone on Mount Cuilcagh. Underground they converge to form a single river, the Cladagh, which flows via the 9m (30ft) limestone Marble Arch into Lough Macnean. The tour of these spectacular show caves includes a boat ride and the presentation of an array of illuminated and named rock formations including stalactites and stalagmites.
☎ 028 6634 8855

🏛 Monaghan County Museum `15 D1`

1-2 Hill Street, Monaghan, Co. Monaghan. With archaeology, folklife, craft, transport, coin and industrial collections, this award winning museum displays the history of Monaghan since earliest times. The unique 14th century Cross of Clogher is one of the treasures of the museum and there is a fine collection of artefacts from early medieval crannog settlements.
☎ 047 82928

🏰 Monea Castle `14 B1`

Monea, Enniskillen, Co. Fermanagh. Built in 1618 in Scottish Plantation style by the Rev. Malcolm Hamilton and burnt out in 1750. Monea is in a reasonable state of preservation; two imposing barrel shaped towers remain at the front capped with crow-stepped gables.
☎ 028 6632 3110

🏛 Morrow's Shop Museum `12 A2`

13 Bridge Street, Ballymena, Co. Antrim. A former drapers with original shop fittings houses varied collections illustrating the history of Ballymena.
☎ 028 2565 3663

❋ Mount Stewart `12 B3`

Portaferry Road, Newtownards, Co. Down. The 18th century former seat of the Marquess of Londonderry and childhood home of Lord Castlereagh, the 19th century Prime Minister. A severely Classical building, it sits amid 32ha (78 acres) of gardens planted in the 1920s which are renowned for the many rare and unusual plants which flourish in the mild climate. There are colourful parterres and displays of almost every style of gardening. The Temple of the Winds, also in the grounds and overlooking Strangford Lough, is an octagonal banqueting hall built in 1785. A National Trust property.
☎ 028 4278 8387/8487   www.nationaltrust.org.uk

🦅 Murlough National Nature Reserve `17 D2`

Keel Point, Dundrum, Newcastle, Co. Down. Ireland's first nature reserve, Murlough is an area of sand dunes (some of which were formed over 5000 years ago), heath, grassland and woodland surrounded by the estuary of the Carrigs River and the shore of Dundrum Bay. With the diversity of habitats there is a wide range of plants, birds and wildlife including badgers and stoats. The estuary attracts many species of wader, duck and geese, migration times being of particular interest. Common and grey seals are visitors to the beach. A National Trust property.
☎ 028 4375 1467   www.nationaltrust.org.uk

🏛 Museum of Childhood `12 B3`

92 Main Street, Saintfield, Co. Down. A small museum with a large and fascinating collection of toys, books, prams and clothes dating back from the 1960s to Victorian times. Tin toys and a carousel horse are amongst the highlights.
☎ 028 9751 9270

✱ National Knitting Centre `10 B2`

Buncrana, Inishowen, Co. Donegal. A centre of excellence for the hand knitting industry which provides knitting courses and training and is based at the headquarters and factory shop of a knitwear company. An exhibition takes a lighthearted look at the history of knitting and the centre illustrates traditional methods of spinning and dyeing wool.
☎ 077 62355   www.westernconnect.com/companies/crana

♟ Navan Fort `16 B2`

Killylea Road, Armagh, Co. Armagh. Once known as Emain Macha, the earthworks at Navan are of a 7ha (17 acre) hill fort, crowned by a ceremonial tumulus, which together form the remains of the seat of the Ulster kings until 332AD. The visitor centre has exhibitions and audiovisuals to interpret the myths and legends of the area.
☎ 028 3752 5550

✝ Nendrum Monastic Site `12 B3`

Mahee Island, Comber, Co. Down. Three concentric stone wall enclosures are the remains of a pre-Norman monastery associated with St Mochaoi. Also found on the site are the base of a round tower, a sundial and cross slabs from the 12th century. Situated on Mahee Island in Strangford Lough, Nendrum is reached by causeway and has a small museum with displays about monastic life and St Mochaoi.
☎ 028 9182 6846

🐾 Ness Wood Country Park `11 C2`

Londonderry, Co. Londonderry. 19ha (47 acres) of woodland, originally dominated by oak trees but many other species were added from the 17th century. The highlight of Ness is Ulster's highest waterfall, a spectacular 9m (30ft) drop in the River Burntollet, which has also created a series of gorges and rapids.
☎ 028 7772 2074

✱ Newmills Corn & Flax Mills `9 C2`

Churchill Road, Letterkenny, Co. Donegal. A group of buildings, the oldest of which is said to be 400 years old, including both a corn and a flax mill which were powered by the River Swilly. The corn mill, once used for grinding oats and barley, has one of the largest remaining working waterwheels in Ireland, made by the Stevenson Foundry of Strabane in 1867.
☎ 074 25115   www.heritageireland.ie

🏛 Newry Museum & Arts Centre `17 C2`

Bank Parade, Newry, Co. Down. The small museum, located within Newry Arts Centre, has a varied collection relating to the heritage of Newry and the Mourne area, including a robe of the Order of St Patrick and a reconstructed Georgian panelled room from a house in Newry which has since been demolished.
☎ 028 3026 6232

✱ North Down Heritage Centre `12 B2`

Town Hall, The Castle, Bangor, Co. Down. Set in woodland at the rear of Bangor Castle with permanent and temporary exhibitions illustrating the area's history, archaeology and wildlife. Treasures include the Ballycroghan Swords dating from 500BC, a bronze 9th century monastic handbell found near Bangor and a collection of antique objects d'art from the Far East; also railway and toy collections and exhibits showing how Bangor developed as a holiday resort.
☎ 028 9127 1200

✱ Odyssey, The `13 C1`

Queen's Quay, Belfast, Co. Antrim. A multi-functional entertainment centre completed in 2001 which comprises a 10,000 seat arena, W5; an interactive discovery centre run by the Museums and Galleries of Northern Ireland and a cinema and leisure complex.
☎ 028 9045 1055   www.theodyssey.co.uk

✱ Oideas Gael `8 A2`

Ulster Cultural Institute, Glencolumbkille, Co. Donegal. An Irish language and cultural centre which offers courses and cultural activity holidays for adults which include painting, music, dancing, archaeology and hill walking, as well as the Irish language.
☎ 073 30248   www.oideas-gael.com

✦ **Old Bushmills Distillery**   `11 D1`
Distillery Road, Bushmills, Co. Antrim. Established in 1608, this is the world's oldest licensed whiskey distillery and offers tours of the Irish single malt distilling process.
☎ *028 2073 1521*   www.bushmills.com

▥ **Orchard Gallery**   `10 B2`
Orchard Street, Londonderry, Co. Londonderry. Innovative contemporary art gallery with exhibitions of local and international artists.
☎ *028 7126 9675*

☙ **Oxford Island National Nature Reserve**   `16 B1`
Annaloiste Road, Lurgan, Craigavon, Co. Armagh. The 109ha (269 acre) reserve comprises woodlands, ponds and wildflower meadows on the south shores of Lough Neagh. Oxford Island is now a peninsula but was an island prior to the lowering of Lough Neagh in the 1850s. Access for visitors includes 8km (5 miles) of walks and nature trails and the facility of five bird watching hides.
☎ *028 3832 2205*

✦ **Palace Stables Heritage Centre**   `16 B2`
Friary Road, Armagh, Co. Armagh. Characters in period costume recreate many aspects of life during the Georgian period in Armagh in the restored stable and courtyard of the former palace of the archbishop and primate of the Church of Ireland, built in 1770. A guided tour includes the primate's chapel, the ice house, ornamental gardens and a 'garden of the senses'. Near the entrance are the ruins of the Franciscan friary church founded by Archbishop Patrick O'Scanail in 1263; at 50m (163ft) it is the longest friary church in Ireland.
☎ *028 3752 9629*

⛲ **Parkanaur Forest Park**   `16 A1`
Castlecaulfield Road, Castlecaulfield, Co. Tyrone. Home to a herd of white fallow deer and full of colour in spring with daffodils and rhododendrons. There are nature walks through beech and oak woodland and a Victorian garden and wishing well.
☎ *028 8776 7432*

✦ **Patrick Kavanagh Rural and Literary Resource Centre**   `16 B3`
Inniskeen, Co. Monaghan. Housed in the former St Mary's church, the centre commemorates the poet and novelist Patrick Kavanagh who was born in Inniskeen. Paintings and models illustrate his poems 'The Great Hunger' and 'A Christmas Childhood' and the poet's death mask is on display. A unique feature of the centre is the performance tour of 'Kavanagh Country' which takes in many sites associated with the poet and concludes with a one-man show by a local actor. The centre also stages local history exhibitions includes an audiovisual theatre and research library.
☎ *042 9378560*   www.patrickkavanaghcountry.com

✦ **Patterson's Spade Mill**   `12 A2`
Antrim Road, Templepatrick, Co. Antrim. A working water-driven spade-making mill, the last surviving one in Ireland. Demonstrations of how garden and turf spades are made with the original hammers, turbines and a press installed in 1919. A National Trust property.
☎ *028 9443 3619*   www.nationaltrust.org.uk

✦ **Peatlands Park**   `16 B1`
Derryhubert Road, Dungannon, Co. Armagh. Bogs and deciduous woodland make up this park which is crossed by a network of way-marked paths and boardwalks. A visitor centre gives an insight into the increasingly threatened habitat of the peatlands. Commercial turf cutting was carried out here until the 1960s and the narrow gauge railway used in the operation has been reconstructed for use by visitors, who may also experience turf cutting at an outdoor turbary site. The area has a rich variety of flora and fauna and a bog garden enables visitors to see many of the plants and insects in close-up.
☎ *028 3885 1102*

✦ **Pickie Family Fun Park**   `12 B2`
Marine Gardens, Bangor, Co. Down. Entertainment park including a miniature railway, go-karts, adventure playground, paddling pool and swan pedal boats.
☎ *028 9127 4430*

✦ **Plantation of Ulster Visitor Centre**   `11 C3`
50 High Street, Draperstown, Co. Londonderry. An audiovisual show and interactive displays illustrate the story of the Ulster plantation period when the first urban settlements were created outside of Down and Antrim, Draperstown being a typical plantation town. It also traces the life of Hugh O'Neill, Earl of Tyrone, who led a crushing rebellion against the English, and recounts the subsequent events surrounding the exile of the northern earls from Donegal in 1607.
☎ *028 7962 7800*

⛲ **Portglenone Forest Park**   `11 D3`
Portglenone, Ballymena, Co. Antrim. With beech and oak woods and renowned for bluebells in spring, Portglenone has riverside walks and nature trails along the banks of the River Bann.
☎ *028 2955 6000*   www.forestserviceni.gov.uk

✦ **Portrush Countryside Centre**   `11 D1`
8 Bath Road, Portrush, Co. Antrim. Illustrating the geology, seascapes and wildlife of the area, the centre features an indoor rock pool and rock and fossil exhibition; adjacent is a nature reserve where visitors can search for ammonites.
☎ *028 7028 3600*

✦ **Portstewart Strand**   `11 C2`
Portstewart, Co. Londonderry. 3km (2 miles) of beach backed by sand dunes and marram grassland with way-marked nature trail.
☎ *028 7083 6396*   www.nationaltrust.org.uk

✦ **Queen's Visitor Centre**   `13 B1`
Queen's University, University Road, Belfast, Co. Antrim. Established in 1845 as one of three Queen's colleges in Ireland, Queen's became a university in 1908. The visitor centre provides information about the university and presents a varied programme of exhibitions. Located at the heart of the campus in the Lanyon Room, the centre is named after Charles Lanyon who was the architect of the main Queen's building and many other public buildings in Ireland.
☎ *028 9033 5252*   www.qub.ac.uk/vcentre

✦ **Quoile Countryside Centre**   `17 D2`
5 Quay Road, Downpatrick, Co. Down. Situated beside the ruins of 16th century Quoile Castle, the centre has displays on the wildlife of the Quoile Pondage National Nature Reserve. Once a saltwater estuary before a tidal barrage was built in 1957, Quoile Pondage is now freshwater and the wetland reserve is fringed with natural woodland. Paths wend their way along the river and there is an abundance of birds, insects and wildflowers.
☎ *028 4461 5520*

⛲ **Redburn Country Park**   `12 B3`
Old Holywood Road, Holywood, Co. Down. Redburn provides over 30ha (74 acres) of parkland and woodland with displays of bluebells in spring. From the escarpment in the park there are magnificent views over Belfast Lough, the city and the south Antrim Hills.
☎ *028 9181 1491*

⛲ **Roe Valley Country Park**   `11 C2`
Dogleap Road, Limavady, Co. Londonderry. Ulster's first domestic water powered electricity generating station, built in 1896, is to be found in the wooded valley as well as ruined water mills which were once used to produce linen. A visitor centre presents the history of the valley and there is a countryside museum and numerous riverside walks. In spring the woodland floor is carpeted with flowers and wildlife includes otters, foxes, badgers, rare butterflies and sparrowhawks. Opportunities exist for canoeing, rock-climbing and fishing.
☎ *028 7772 2074*

⛲ **Rossmore Forest Park**   `15 D1`
Monaghan, Co. Monaghan. Situated to the SW of Monaghan Town, the forest comprises a mixture of broadleaved and coniferous trees, many of which, including cedars and monkey puzzle trees, are the originals planted in the estate of the 19th century Rossmore Castle, now a ruin. The former walled garden has notable yew hedges and there are two prehistoric tombs. In early summer there is a spectacular display of rhododendrons and azaleas.
☎ *047 81968*

☙ **Rostrevor Oakwood National Nature Reserve**   `17 C3`
Kilbroney Forest Park, Rostrevor, Newry, Co. Down. Within Kilbroney Forest Park, the reserve is a mature oak wood on a steep slope overlooking Carlingford Lough, possibly dating back 1000 years. Rich in woodland birdlife and with a trail through the reserve.
☎ *028 4176 2525*   www.ehsni.gov.uk

❀ **Rowallane Garden**   `12 B3`
Saintfield, Ballynahinch, Co. Down. First established in the 1860s by the Rev. John Moore, this natural-looking garden is planted with many rare trees, shrubs and plants from all round the world. Rowallane is memorable in spring with flowering bulbs, trees and shrubs including rhododendrons and azaleas. In summer, orchids flower in the meadows. Fuchsias and shrub roses flourish in a walled garden where there is also a national collection of penstemon; the rock garden is planted with primulas and heathers. A National Trust property.
☎ *028 9751 0131*   www.nationaltrust.org.uk

⛳ **Royal County Down**   `17 D2`
Newcastle, Co. Down. Magnificent links course founded in 1889 and situated at the foot of the Mourne Mountains. The club has played host to the British Men's and Women's Amateur Championships as well as the Curtis Cup.
☎ *028 4372 2419*   www.royalcountydown.org

▥ **Royal Irish Fusiliers Museum**   `16 B2`
Sovereign's House, The Mall East, Armagh, Co. Armagh. Artefacts on display, including uniforms and medals, illustrate the history of the regiment from its inauguration in 1793 in response to the Napoleonic threat. The regiment was amalgamated with the Inniskilling Fusiliers and Ulster Rifles in 1968. Located in the 18th century former residence of the 'Sovereign' or Mayor of Armagh, the museum also has militaria from the militias of Armagh, Cavan and Monaghan on display.
☎ *028 3752 2911*

⛳ **Royal Portrush Golf Club**   `11 D1`
Dunluce Road, Portrush, Co. Antrim. Founded in 1888, it is the only Irish Club to have hosted the British Open Championship, won by Max Faulkner in 1951, and in 1895 was the first course to host a professional tournament in Ireland.
☎ *028 7082 2311*   www.royalportrushgolfclub.com

▥ **Royal Ulster Rifles Museum**   `13 B1`
War Memorial Building, 5 Waring Street, Belfast, Co. Antrim. Displays relating not only to the Royal Ulster Rifles but also to its predecessors, Regiments of Foot, which was raised in 1793.
☎ *028 9023 2086*   rurmuseum.tripod.com

✝ **St Columb's Cathedral**   `10 B2`
London Street, Londonderry, Co. Londonderry. Standing within the Walls of Derry and built in 'Planters Gothic' style in 1633, the cathedral is dedicated to St Columba who established a Christian settlement here in the 6th century. Stained glass depicts famous people who have been connected with the cathedral, including the governor of the city during the 105 day Jacobite siege of 1688-1689.
☎ *028 7126 7313*   www.stcolumbscathedral.org

🏛 **St Connell's Museum** `8 B2`

Glenties, Co. Donegal. The museum illustrates the history, traditions and heritage of the Glenties area and includes a wildlife exhibition, local writers' corner, Donegal railways collection and a display about the Great Famine of 1845 – 1847.
☎ 075 51277

✴ **St Kilian's Heritage Centre** `15 D3`

Mullagh, Co. Cavan. St. Kilian was born in Mullagh in 640AD and became a missionary at the age of 46 in Wurzburg, Germany, where he was martyred three years later. The heritage centre gives an insight into his life and work, including the cult which developed after his martyrdom and the work of Irish missionaries in Europe in the 6th and 7th centuries. Maps, facsimiles, sculpture and art reproductions are displayed and there is an audiovisual presentation. Also of interest is an exhibition which explains the development of Gaelic script from the Ogham writing of the 4th – 7th centuries and the earliest examples of written Irish in the mid 8th century to the illuminated script of the Book of Kells.
☎ 046 42433

✴ **St Louis Convent Heritage Centre** `15 D1`

St. Louis Convent, Broad Road, Monaghan, Co. Monaghan. Through documents, memorabilia, artefacts, models and commemorative albums, the centre traces the history of the order of the Sisters of St Louis back to their origins in 17th century Turkenstein. An Institute was later established in France in 1842 and the order spread to Ireland in 1859 and then to England, West Africa and the Americas. Particular emphasis is given to the Sisters' work in health care and educational development in Nigeria and Ghana. The heritage centre also displays their traditional crafts.
☎ 047 83529

✴ **St Patrick Centre** `17 D2`

Market Street, Downpatrick, Co. Down. The story of Ireland's patron saint in the 5th century and the introduction of Christianity into Ireland is told using audiovisuals, exhibitions and interactive displays. The impact of Irish missionaries is examined and the arts and crafts produced during this time are on display.
☎ 028 4461 9000   www.saintpatrickcentre.com

✝ **St Patrick's Church of Ireland Cathedral** `16 B2`

Vicar's Hill, Armagh, Co. Armagh. A church has stood on this site for over 1500 years, being destroyed and rebuilt many times. The present cathedral was largely built by Archbishop O'Scanail in medieval times but the present fabric of the building reflects the restoration work which took place between 1834 and 1840 under the direction of Archbishop John George Beresford. Stained glass depicts St Patrick who came to establish his church here in 444AD. There are a number of carved figures, possibly prehistoric, and the remains of high crosses from the 9th or 10th century. Brian Ború, High King of Ireland was killed at the Battle of Clontarf in 1014 and is buried in the cathedral grounds.
☎ 028 3752 3142

✝ **St Patrick's Cross** `10 B1`

Cardonagh, Inishowen, Co. Donegal. Located by the roadside and next to the graveyard of the church at Cardonagh, St Patrick's Cross (also known as the Donagh Cross) is believed to be one of the oldest high cross in Ireland, probably dating back to the 7th century. Cut from red sandstone with low relief carving, the cross is 3.5m (11.6ft) tall and has two short pillar stones on either side.
☎ 074 21160

✝ **St Patrick's Roman Catholic Cathedral** `16 B2`

Cathedral Road, Armagh, Co. Armagh. Construction started on St Patrick's Day in 1840 and was not completed until 24 July 1903 partly due to the disruption caused by the Great Famine. Sited on a hill top, the twin spires are visible from almost anywhere in the city. The interior contains red Armagh marble and was renovated in 1981 with brilliantly coloured frescos, mosaics and stained glass windows.
☎ 028 3752 2638

✴ **St Patrick's Trian Visitor Complex** `16 B2`

40 English Street, Armagh, Co. Armagh. A dramatic and entertaining exhibition centre which touches on history, culture, genealogy and arts and crafts. The legacy of St Patrick and the story of Armagh are brought to life and there is an adaptation of Jonathan Swift's Gulliver's Travels. Writer and clergyman Swift was often a visitor to the area. The visitor complex takes its name from the ancient division of the city of Armagh into three districts or 'trians'
☎ 028 3752 1801

✴ **Scarva Visitor Centre** `16 B2`

Main Street, Scarva, Banbridge, Co. Down. The centre is situated at a basin on the Newry canal where coal used to be unloaded for the linen industry; the canal was built in 1742 and is the oldest summit-level canal in Britain, linking the sea port of Newry with Lough Neagh. The centre describes the building of the canal and the associated development of Scarva as well as illustrating the history of Irish canals.
☎ 028 3883 2163

⛰ **Scrabo Country Park** `12 B3`

Scrabo Road, Newtownards, Co. Down. The landscape around Scrabo is dominated by Scrabo Hill which is crowned by Scrabo Tower, erected in 1857 in memory of the third Marquess of Londonderry. The tower, with magnificent views across Strangford Lough, now houses a museum about it's history and surrounding countryside. Impressive disused sandstone quarries with volcanic features are to be seen in the park and there are woodland walks through beech and mixed woodland and an iron age hill fort.
☎ 028 9181 1491

✴ **Seaforde Butterfly House** `17 D2`

Seaforde Demesne, Seaforde, Downpatrick, Co. Down. Set in Seaforde gardens, the tropical butterfly house has hundreds of free-flying exotic butterflies. The butterfly centre is also home to insects, reptiles, amphibians and parrots.
☎ 028 4481 1225

❇ **Seaforde Gardens** `17 D2`

Seaforde, Downpatrick, Co. Down. A new moghul style observation tower overlooks an 18th century walled garden which features a hornbeam maze and mixed tree and shrub borders. Seaforde has the national collection of eucryphia, an evergreen shrub family from the southern hemisphere. Seaforde Butterfly House stands within the grounds and there is an adjoining tree and shrub nursery.
☎ 028 4481 1225

✴ **Seat of Power Visitor Centre** `10 B3`

The Diamond, Lifford, Co. Donegal. Housed in the restored 18th century courthouse, the centre gives an insight into the history of Lifford and the important role the town played as a seat of power in Donegal. Once an O'Donnell stronghold, Lifford was to become an important administrative centre during the Plantation of Ulster and then the county's legal centre until the courthouse closed in 1938. Cells beneath the courthouse where prisoners awaited trial can be visited and an audiovisual show presents famous trials in which local people were tried and sentenced either to hanging or to deportation to Australia.
☎ 074 41733   www.infowing.ie/seatofpower

✴ **Sheepland Open Farm** `17 D2`

3 Tollumgrange Road, Chapeltown, Ardglass, Co. Down. Ducks, sheep, pigs, hens and goats can be seen on the farm as well as a display of horse ploughs, hayrakes and harrows. Haymaking, sheep shearing and potato digging take place in season.
☎ 028 4484 2268

✴ **Silent Valley** `17 C3`

Head Road, Kilkeel, Co. Down. Silent Valley and Ben Crom reservoirs are set in the beautiful scenery of the Mourne Mountains with landscaped parkland, lakes and ponds in the grounds of the reservoirs. The damming of the Kilkeel river valley was completed in 1933 and today the reservoirs supply a large part of Belfast and most of County Down with water. An information centre explains the development of the Silent Valley and is a starting point for woodland walks.
☎ 028 9074 1166

⛰ **Slieve Gullion Forest Park** `16 B3`

Meigh, Newry, Co. Armagh. Covering over 6000ha (14,820 acres), the park is thickly wooded with the summit of Slieve Gullion rising above to a height of 577m (1894ft). A scenic 13km (8 miles) drive loops through the forest and from the road a trail leads to the mountain summit where there is a passage grave, cairn, volcanic lake and panoramic views of the surrounding mountains known as the Ring of Gullion. There are also woodland trails and a walk through an ornamental garden. The Slieve Gullion Courtyard at the centre of the park provides visitor information for the area as well as an educational facility.
☎ 028 4173 8284

⛳ **Slieve Russell Golf Club** `15 C2`

Ballyconnell, Co. Cavan. Championship parkland course which has hosted the Irish PGA Championship and North West of Ireland Open in recent years.
☎ 049 26444

✴ **Slievenalargy Open Farm** `17 C2`

5 Largy Road, Kilcoo, Newcastle, Co. Down. Situated on a hillside overlooking the sea and the mountains of Mourne, this farm has rare breeds of cattle, sheep and pigs; also a pets corner, pony rides and ornamental pheasants.
☎ 028 4377 8687

✴ **Somme Heritage Centre** `12 B3`

233 Bangor Road, Conlig, Newtownards, Co. Down. Presents a multimedia re-creation of the 1916 Battle of the Somme from a reconstructed trench system. The centre illustrates the contribution made by Irish troops to the First World War and the effects it had on their communities, with the voices of veterans recounting their experiences. Visitors are taken back in time to the recruitment and training of volunteers and in a hands-on activity area can try on uniforms and see trench rations.
☎ 028 9182 3202   www.irishsoldier.org

✴ **Sperrin Heritage Centre** `11 C3`

274 Glenelly Road, Gortin, Co. Tyrone. The Sperrin Mountains, a range of mountains with five summits rising to over 610m (2000ft), is an area of outstanding natural beauty and steeped in history. The Heritage Centre, located in the Glenelly Valley, presents a 'Treasures of the Sperrins Exhibition' which illustrates the geological composition of the area, the wildlife and habitats, and gives an insight into local rural life and customs. Resident ghost Jimmy is the storyteller and visitors can pan for gold in a local stream.
☎ 028 8164 8142

🏠 **Springhill** `11 D3`

20 Springhill Road, Moneymore, Co. Londonderry. 17th century Plantation House, home of the Conyngham family for 300 years and now in the care of the National Trust. Rooms of interest include a library, nursery and gun room and the house is filled with family portraits, furniture, papers and books. Irish costumes dating back to the 17th century are among the colourful collection in the old laundry. The walled gardens and estate paths are open to visitors.
☎ 028 8674 8210   www.nationaltrust.org.uk

🏠 **Stormont** `12 B3`

Upper Newtownards Road, Belfast, Co. Antrim. The Northern Ireland Parliament buildings are not normally open to the public though tours can be arranged for parties in advance. Designed by Sir Anthony Thornley and constructed from Mourne granite and Portland Stone, it was officially opened in 1932 by the Prince of Wales, later to become King Edward VIII .
☎ 028 9024 6609

✴ **Streamvale Open Farm** `12 B3`

38 Ballyhanwood Road, Gilnahirk, Belfast, Co. Down. Family run dairy farm in the Gilnahirk hills on the edge of Belfast with a gallery to enable visitors to view the milking and opportunities to watch calves being born and to feed lambs; also a pets' corner and nature trail.
☎ 028 9048 3244   www.streamvale.com

✻ **T.A.C.T Wildlife Centre** 12 A3
2 Crumlin Road, Crumlin, Co. Antrim. A sanctuary for sick, injured and abandoned birds and small mammals in a 200 year old walled garden. Run by volunteers of the Talnotry Avian Care Trust who return as many to the wild as possible. Those for which this is not possible remain at the centre for the rest of their natural lives. Long term residents include owls, falcons, buzzards, gulls, gannets, foxes, rabbits and hedgehogs.
☎ 028 9442 2900　　www.tactwildlifecentre.org.uk

✻ **Tannaghmore Gardens & Animal Farm** 16 B1
Silverwood, Craigavon, Co. Armagh. Many domestic animal breeds which were traditionally kept on Irish farms at the end of the 19th century, but which are now rare, are to be seen on the farm. These include Irish Moiled, Kerry and Dexter cattle; Galway and Jacob sheep; also Tamworth, Saddleback and Gloucester Old Spot pigs. Formal rose gardens surround the Georgian farmhouse at Tannaghmore and old agricultural artefacts and farming practices are displayed in the barn museum.
☎ 028 3834 3244

✤ **Tollymore Forest Park** 17 C2
Tullybrannigan Road, Newcastle, Co. Down. Covering an area of almost 500ha (1235 acres), Tollymore is situated at the foot of the Mournes with panoramic views of the mountains and sea and with woodland rich in bird and wildlife. The park features an arboretum with a native strawberry tree and notable cork oak from Portugal; also several stone bridges and 19th century follies. Ample opportunities exist for walking and fishing while forestry and wildlife exhibits are displayed in the barn.
☎ 028 4372 2428

🏛 **Tower Museum** 10 B2
Union Hall Place, Londonderry, Co. Londonderry. Illustrates the history of the city from the earliest times with special exhibits on Celtic monasticism, the Plantation of Ulster, the siege of Derry and the Georgian period.
☎ 028 7137 2411

✞ **Tullaghogue Fort** 16 B1
Cookstown, Co. Tyrone. Served as the ceremonial site for the inauguration of the kings of Ulster as O'Neills from 12th – 16th centuries; Hugh O'Neill was the last to be crowned here in 1593. Reached by footpath, the earthwork has fine views over Tyrone.
☎ 028 8676 6727

🏰 **Tully Castle & Gardens** 9 C3
Derrygonnelly, Enniskillen, Co. Fermanagh. Overlooking Lower Lough Erne, Tully castle is the remains of a fortified house and bawn built for the Hume family in around 1613. It was captured and burnt out by the Maguires in 1641 and never re-occupied. In spite of this, the substantial ruin survives almost to its full height of two and a half storeys. In 1988 a formal garden was created with plants that would have been known in the 17th century and incorporating original cobbled paths.
☎ 028 9023 5000

🏛 **Tullyarvan Mill** 10 B2
Buncrana, Inishowen, Co. Donegal. As a cultural and exhibition centre, Tullyarvan Mill is the venue for traditional and folk concerts, visual arts and other cultural events throughout the year. Buncrana's 200 year old textile industry and the wildlife of Inishowen are also illustrated in permanent exhibitions in this restored 19th century corn mill.
☎ 077 61613

✞ **Tynan Cross** 16 A2
Tynan, Co. Armagh. This high cross stands at the roadside in the village of Tynan but has been moved at least twice in its history. Dating back to the 10th century, it was restored in the 19th century and is made up of at least two crosses. The story of Adam and Eve are depicted on the central shaft and the head of the cross is decorated with circular bosses.
☎ 028 3752 1800

✻ **Tyrone Crystal** 16 B1
115 Coalisland Road, Killybrackey, Dungannon, Co. Tyrone. Guided tours give visitors the opportunity to view the processes involved in the manufacture of this world renowned lead crystal.
☎ 028 8772 5335　　www.tyronecrystal.com

🏛 **Ulster American Folk Park** 9 D3
Mellon Road, Castletown, Omagh, Co. Tyrone. An outdoor museum covering 20ha (50 acres) which depicts the story of Irish emigrants to North America in the 18th and 19th centuries. Life in both the Old and New Worlds is illustrated through a wide range of reconstructed period buildings. Visitors are transported via a typical Irish dockside through a full size replica emigrant ship to a typical colonial dockside street. Based at the park is the Centre for Migration Studies which includes a research library and Irish Emigration database.
☎ 028 8224 3292　　www.folkpark.com

🏛 **Ulster Folk & Transport Museum** 12 B3
153 Bangor Road, Cultra, Holywood, Belfast, Co. Down. Buildings from various parts of Ulster have been re-erected here to recreate a village of days gone by with rural crafts, agriculture and industry illustrating how the way of life and traditions of people in Northern Ireland have changed and developed. Also features a typical Ulster town of around 1910 with terraced housing, shops and churches, a bank and school. Indoor galleries have a comprehensive collection of railway, road and aviation exhibits as well as a Titanic exhibition.
☎ 028 9042 8428　　www.nidex.com/uftm

✻ **Ulster Hall** 13 B2
Bedford Street, Belfast, Co. Antrim. Historic venue for concerts and recitals, now owned by Belfast city council but first built in 1862 for the Ulster Hall Company. The classic English theatre organ was installed shortly after the hall was built and is still played today.
☎ 028 9032 3900　　www.ulsterhall.co.uk

🏛 **Ulster History Park** 10 B3
Cullion, Lislap, Omagh, Co. Tyrone. Neolithic houses, a crannog, early monastery, motte and bailey and a plantation house are among the settlements which have been recreated to illustrate how people lived in Ulster from the Stone Age to the Plantation of Ulster in the 17th century. An exhibition and audiovisual presentation aims to give the flavour of Irish life throughout these 10,000 years.
☎ 028 8164 8188

🏛 **Ulster Museum** 13 A3
Botanic Gardens, Stranmillis Road, Belfast, Co. Antrim. Collections of local and worldwide interest are housed in this National Museum including Irish art, history, science, botany, geology and archaeology. The history section features exhibits dating from 10,000 to 1500BC and artifacts from the Spanish Armada.
☎ 028 9038 3000　　www.ulstermuseum.org.uk

✻ **Ulster Weavers** 12 B3
44 Montgomery Road, Belfast, Co. Antrim. Linen weaving factory with displays of damask table linen, linen bedding and tea towels.
☎ 028 9040 4236　　www.ulsterweavers.co.uk

✻ **Ulster Wildlife Centre** 17 D2
3 New Line, Killyleagh Road, Crossgar, Co. Down. Within a walled garden there is a variety of habitats including meadowland, native woodland, raised bogland and a pond, to illustrate the ecology and wildlife of Ulster. A Victorian conservatory has butterflies amongst the flowers and plants which include vines over a century old.
☎ 028 4483 0282

🏛 **Vintage Cycle Museum** 15 C1
64 Main Street, Brookeborough, Co. Fermanagh. A collection of over 100 cycles, pedal cars and toys, many unique or rare. Treasures include a Penny Farthing, an ice-cream tricycle and a folding army bike. Household memorabilia and farm machinery are also to be found in the museum.
☎ 028 8953 1206

✻ **Walls of Derry** 10 B2
Londonderry, Co. Londonderry. Views across the city are afforded from the cobbled walkway on top of the walls which are almost 2km (1 mile) in circumference. In spite of withstanding many sieges, the walls are well preserved and little changed since they were built in 1618.
☎ 028 7126 7284

✻ **Waterfront Hall** 13 C2
Lanyon Place, Belfast, Co. Antrim. A conference and concert centre constructed as part of Belfast's riverfront regeneration.
☎ 028 9033 4400　　www.waterfront.co.uk

✻ **Watertop Open Farm** 12 A1
188 Cushendall Road, Ballycastle, Co. Antrim. Extensive cattle and sheep farm with farm tours and many other family activities including pony trekking, boating, fishing, archery, mountain bike tours and walking. Sheep shearing demonstrations in summer.
☎ 028 2076 2576

✻ **Waterwheels** 8 B3
Rossnowlagh Road, Ballyshannon, Co. Donegal. Two mills with restored waterwheels at the site of the former Cistercian Abbey Assaroe, founded in the late 12th century by monks from Boyle Abbey. A museum in one of the mills presents the legacy the medieval Cistercians gave to Ireland.
☎ 072 51580

✻ **Waterworld** 11 D1
The Harbour, Portrush, Co. Antrim. Pool leisure complex with giant slides and featuring Pirate Cove play area with pirate ship, water cannons and rope bridges; also tenpin bowling.
☎ 028 7082 2001

✻ **Wellbrook Beetling Mill** 16 A1
20 Wellbrook Road, Corkhill, Cookstown, Co. Tyrone. Set in a wooded glen on the banks of the Ballinderry River, Wellbrook is the last working beetling mill in Northern Ireland. Beetling was the last stage in manufacturing linen when the cloth was pounded with heavy wooden hammers to give the distinctive sheen. Wellbrook operated as a mill for nearly 200 years, ceasing commercial production in 1961. There are hands-on demonstrations and an exhibition of how linen was produced. A National Trust property.
☎ 028 8674 8210/8675 1735　　www.nationaltrust.org.uk

✻ **White Island** 9 C3
Lower Lough Erne, Lisnarrick, Co. Fermanagh. Situated on the island in Lower Lough Erne is a ruined 12th century church with a fine Romanesque doorway. Unusual stone figures set into the wall of the church are much older, perhaps dating back to the 6th century. White Island is reached by passenger ferry from Castle Archdale.
☎ 028 6862 1333

✻ **Wilson Ancestral Home** 10 B3
28 Spout Road, Dergalt, Strabane, Co. Tyrone. This cottage with traditional hearth fire has remained virtually unchanged since James Wilson, grandfather of American President Woodrow Wilson, emigrated to America in 1807; authentic period artefacts on display.
☎ 028 7138 2204

✻ **Workhouse, The** 10 A1
Dunfanaghy, Co. Donegal. Presented as a series of tableaux, this 19th century Workhouse building depicts the harsh life endured by many at that time and the effects of the Great Famine of 1845 – 1847 after blight devastated the potato crop.
☎ 074 36540　　www.theirishfamine.com

Connaught

Connaught (population 433,231), also known as Connacht, is the most sparsely populated province in Ireland being 25% of the area of Ireland with only 12% of the country's population.

It comprises counties Galway, Leitrim, Mayo, Roscommon and Sligo and is bounded on the west and north by the Atlantic and in the south and east by the River Shannon.

The Aran Islands, Connemara and North West Mayo are large Gaeltacht areas where Gaelic remains the first language.

Connaught has some of the most spectacular unspoilt scenery in Ireland – from the rugged Atlantic coastline of West Galway, North and West Mayo with its many bays and islands and the spectacular mountains of Connemara to the limestone central plain and the mountains and waterways of the eastern counties of Roscommon and Leitrim.

The climate is mild and can be especially warm in summer though rain is often never far away.

Connemara

Map pages in this region

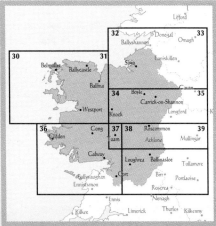

Ireland West Regional Tourism

Aras Failte, Forster Street, Galway
☎ 091 537700
www.westireland.travel.ie

North West Regional Tourism

Aras Reddan, Temple Street, Sligo
☎ 071 61201
www.ireland-northwest.travel.ie

The Aran Islands (Oileán Árann)

The islands of Inishmore, Inishmaan and Inisheer comprise the Aran Islands which lie at the entrance to Galway Bay. The main industries are tourism, sheep raising (providing wool for the world renowned Aran sweaters) and fishing. Many of the fishermen still use the Currach – the traditional Aran boat.

Inishmore (Inis Mór meaning Big Island) is the largest, most populated and most frequently visited of the islands. The sandy beaches of Kilmurvey and Killeany contrast starkly with the sheer cliffs of the south of the island on which the ancient stone fort of Dún Aengus and Dún Eoghanachta sit.

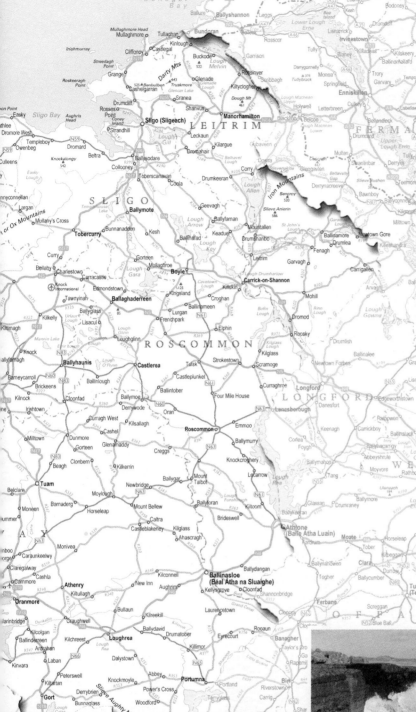

Keel Beach, Achill Island

Gaeltacht

The Gaeltacht are those areas of Ireland where Gaelic (Irish) is the main language and has a total population of around 86,000. They are mainly in the West – counties Donegal, Galway, Kerry and Mayo – though there are also areas in counties Cork, Meath and Waterford.

These areas are important in the future development of the language and link back to the 16th century when most of the population spoke Gaelic. British rule, together with the Great Famine of 1845 to 1849, took its toll on the traditional Irish culture which has seen Gaelic fall from its position in the middle of the 19th century as the dominant language. Currently 40% of the population are now Gaelic speakers, which is the highest percentage since then.

Today it is the responsibility of Údarás na Gaeltachta – the Regional Development Agency in Ireland – to develop the Gaeltacht regions economically, socially and culturally and to ensure that the Irish language not only survives but also thrives in the 21st century.

South East Coast, Inishmore

The way of life on Inishmaan (Inis Meáin meaning Middle Island) is more traditional than almost anywhere else in Ireland and tourism is not of great importance. However, it is this tradition that gives the island it's individuality and the stone fort of Dún Chonchuir is as impressive as any on the islands.

Inisheer (Inis Óirr meaning East Island) is the smallest of the three islands and is closest to the mainland. The sandy beach on the north of the island is as beautiful as any on the west coast of Ireland and the ancient churches, holy wells and the 15th century O'Brien's Castle have archaeological interest.

Dún Aengus, Inishmore

Atlantic Drive, Achill Island

Achill Island

Ireland's largest island, Achill Island is permanently connected to the mainland by a road bridge except when raised for passing boats. At 672m (2205ft) Slieve More is the island's high point, at the foot of which is the village of the same name which was deserted during the Great Famine of 1844–48.

Achill Seafood Festival in July offers delicious gourmet seafood and the Atlantic Drive gives splendid views particularly from the high point of the Minaun Heights.

Westport

The town of Westport (population 3900) was designed by James Wyatt in the 1770s and is distinctive due to its wide tree lined streets and the North and South Malls on either side of the Carrowbeg River.

Clew Bay has numerous sandy beaches and at the entrance to the bay sits Clare Island from where the pirate queen Gráinne Uaile (Grace O'Malley) terrorised English cargo vessels and one of her castles remains on the island's east coast. She died in 1603 and though her final resting place is unknown some think she lies in the small abbey on the island.

Ferries to the island run from Westport and from Roonah Quay.

Gráinne Uaile's Castle, Achill Island

Tourist Information

ⓘ **Achill**

Cashel
Achill Island
County Mayo
☎ 098 45384

Map labels

Erris Head
Stonefield
Broad Haven
Aghadoon
Knocknali
DOONAMO FORT
Corclogh
Belmullet
Barnatra
R314
Binghamstown
Bunnahow
R313
Trawmore Bay
R313
Inishkea North
The Mullet
Aghleam
Gweensa
Inishkea South
Srahnamanragh Bridge
Fallmore
Doohooma
Duvillaun More
Blacksod
Doona
Bay
Ballycro
Slieve More ▲ 672
Valley
Doogort
▲ 668 Croaghaun
Bunacurry
Clagg
Achill Head
Dooagh
Keel
R319
Annagh Island
Achill Island
Achill ⓘ
Dooega
Corrau.
Peninsu
Cloughmore
Corraun
Achillbeg Island
Clare Island
Ballytoohy
Roonah Quay
GRA VISITORS C
Caher Island
Killadoon
Inishturk
Kinnado
Inishbofin
Benbu
Inishark
Cashleen
Rinvyle
Salruck
Killary Harbour
Mv
Ballynakill Bay
OCEANS ALIVE ★ Tully Cross

miles
0   5   10
0   5   10   15
kilometres

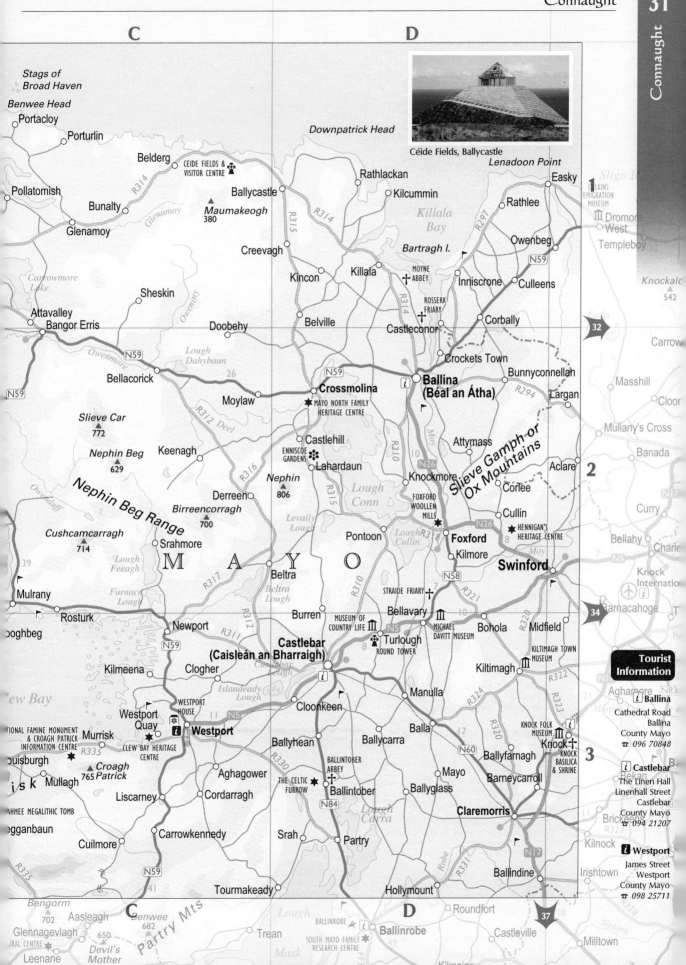

C

D

Stags of
Broad Haven

Benwee Head

Portacloy

Porturlin

Belderg

CÉIDE FIELDS &
VISITOR CENTRE

Pollatomish

Bunalty

Glenamoy

Maumakeogh
380

Downpatrick Head

Céide Fields, Ballycastle

Lenadoon Point

Ballycastle

Rathlackan

Kilcummin

Sligo B

Easky

1

Rathlee

ELKINS
EMIGRATION
MUSEUM

Dromor
West
Templeboy

Creevagh

Kincon

Killala

*Killala
Bay*

Owenbeg

N59

Culleens

Knockalo
542

*Carrowmore
Lake*

Sheskin

Bartragh I.

MOYNE
ABBEY

Inniscrone

32

Attavalley
Bangor Erris

Doobehy

Belville

ROSSERK
FRIARY

Corbally

Carrow

N59

Owenmore

*Lough
Dahybaun*

Castleconor

Crockets Town

Bunnyconnellah

Masshill

N59

Bellacorick

Moylaw

N59

Crossmolina

MAYO NORTH FAMILY
HERITAGE CENTRE

**Ballina
(Béal an Átha)**

Largan

R294

Cloor

Mullany's Cross

Slieve Car
772

R312 Deel

Castlehill

ENNISCOE
GARDENS

Lahardaun

Attymass

Knockmore

Banada

Nephin Beg
629

Keenagh

R316

Nephin
806

10

N26

Slieve Gamph or
Ox Mountains

Aclare

2

Curry

Nephin Beg Range

Derreen

R315

*Lough
Conn*

FOXFORD
WOOLLEN
MILLS

Corlee

Cullin

N17

Cushcamcarragh
714

Birreencorragh
700

Srahmore

*Levally
Lough*

HENNIGAN'S
HERITAGE CENTRE

Bellahy

Owenduff

39

M   A   Y   O

Beltra

*Lough
Feeagh*

R317

Pontoon

*Lough
Cullin*

R318

Foxford

Kilmore

N26

Swinford

Moy

Knock
Internatio

Mulrany

Rosturk

*Furnace
Lough*

Beltra

*Beltra
Lough*

R310

Burren

STRAIDE FRIARY

N58

R321

34

Barnacahoge

oghbeg

Newport

R312

R311

MUSEUM OF
COUNTRY LIFE

N5

Bellavary

MICHAEL
DAVITT MUSEUM

Bohola

Midfield

R320

Kilmeena

N59

Clogher

*Castlebar
Lough*

Turlough
ROUND TOWER

8

KILTIMAGH TOWN
MUSEUM

**Castlebar
(Caisleán an Bharraigh)**

*Islandeady
Lough*

Kiltimagh

R322

Tourist
Information

WESTPORT
HOUSE

Cloonkeen

N5

Manulla

Aghamore

N83

NATIONAL FAMINE MONUMENT
& CROAGH PATRICK
INFORMATION CENTRE

Murrisk

Westport
Quay

CLEW BAY HERITAGE
CENTRE

Westport

Ballyhean

Ballycarra

Balla

17

R324

R323

KNOCK FOLK
MUSEUM

Ballina

Cathedral Road
Ballina
County Mayo
☎ 096 70848

Clew Bay

R335

*Croagh
Patrick*
765

Aghagower

THE CELTIC
FURROW

BALLINTOBER
ABBEY

Ballintober

Mayo

Ballyfarnagh

Knock

KNOCK
BASILICA
& SHRINE

Barneycarroll

3

Castlebar

The Linen Hall
Linenhall Street
Castlebar
County Mayo
☎ 094 21207

risk

Mullagh

Liscarney

Cordarragh

Ballyglass

Claremorris

Kilnock

Brickee

egganbaun

Cuilmore

Carrowkennedy

Srah

Partry

N60

N17

Westport

James Street
Westport
County Mayo
☎ 098 25711

R335

N59

Tourmakeady

Ballindine

Hollymount

Irishtown

Castleville

Milltown

Bengorm
702

Aasleagh

Benwee
682

Partry Mts

Lough

Mask

BALLINROBE

SOUTH MAYO FAMILY
RESEARCH CENTRE

Ballinrobe

Roundfort

37

Glennagevlagh

650

*Devil's
Mother*

Leenane

Trean

Kilmaine

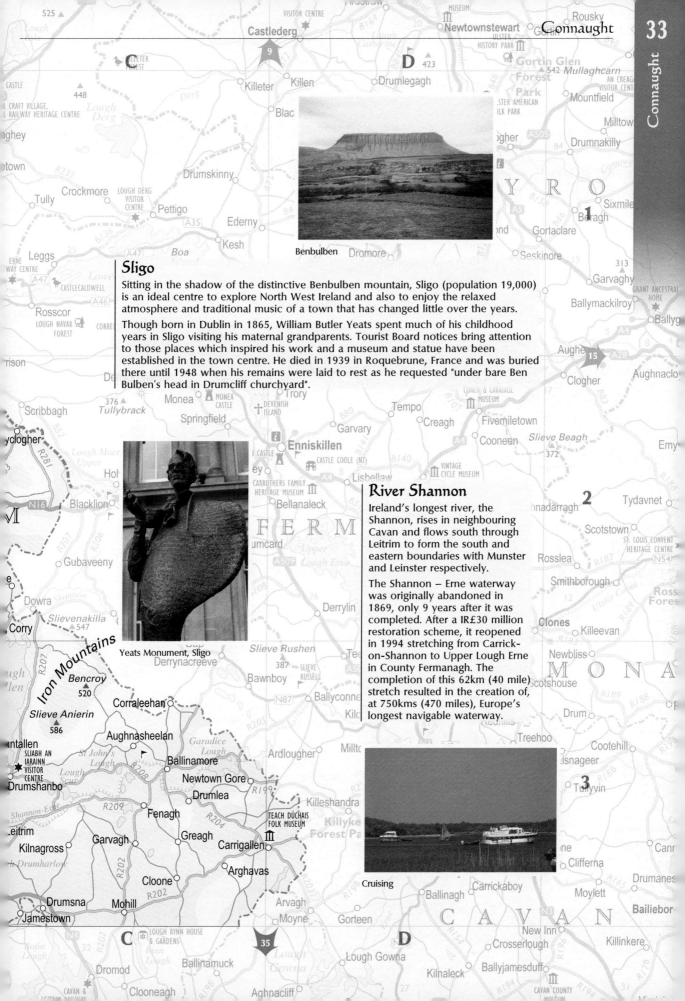

Benbulben

Sligo

Sitting in the shadow of the distinctive Benbulben mountain, Sligo (population 19,000) is an ideal centre to explore North West Ireland and also to enjoy the relaxed atmosphere and traditional music of a town that has changed little over the years.

Though born in Dublin in 1865, William Butler Yeats spent much of his childhood years in Sligo visiting his maternal grandparents. Tourist Board notices bring attention to those places which inspired his work and a museum and statue have been established in the town centre. He died in 1939 in Roquebrune, France and was buried there until 1948 when his remains were laid to rest as he requested "under bare Ben Bulben's head in Drumcliff churchyard".

Yeats Monument, Sligo

River Shannon

Ireland's longest river, the Shannon, rises in neighbouring Cavan and flows south through Leitrim to form the south and eastern boundaries with Munster and Leinster respectively.

The Shannon – Erne waterway was originally abandoned in 1869, only 9 years after it was completed. After a IR£30 million restoration scheme, it reopened in 1994 stretching from Carrick-on-Shannon to Upper Lough Erne in County Fermanagh. The completion of this 62km (40 mile) stretch resulted in the creation of, at 750kms (470 miles), Europe's longest navigable waterway.

Cruising

Connaught

SLIGO

ROSCOMMON

GALWAY

Knockalongy 542

Beltra
Ballysadare
Colooney
Dromahair
FRANXAXA FRIARY
Coll
R289
Byhavel Lough

Corbally
Coolaney
R290
Drumkeeran
R280

Rockets Town
Cullen
Carrowneden
Toberscanavan
Coola
Drumkeeran
R200

Corbally
Carrowmore
N17
R293
Ushin
R284
Geevagh
Altagowla

Masshill
Lavagh
Timehouse Lake
Ballymote
N4
Riverstown
Derry
Lough Arrow
Ballyfarnan

Largan
Cloonacool
Achonry
BALLYMOTE CASTLE
CARROWKEEL MEGALITHIC CEMETERY
Kesh
R295
Ballinafad
Keadue

Slieve Gamph or Ox Mountains
Mullany's Cross
Bunnanadden
Killavil
R293
Lough Key

Banada
24
R296
Crossna

Attymass
Aclare
Tobercurry
Doocastle
Gorteen
FRYBROOK HOUSE, KING HOUSE
BOYLE ABBEY
Lough Key Forest Park

Corlee
N17
R294
Mullaghroe
Boyle
TULLYBOY FARM

Cullin
Curry
Roosky
R293
Kingsland
Carrick-on-Shannon

Foxford
Kilmore
Bellahy
Cloontia
Edmondstown
Lough Gara
125
Killukin

N26
N5
Charlestown
Carracastle
Ballaghaderreen
Croghan

MICHAEL DAVITT MUSEUM
Swinford
Barnacahoge
Knock International
Tawnyinah
Carrownurlar
28 N5
Ballinameen

31 Bohola
Midfield
R375
R325
Ballyglass
85
DR. DOUGLAS HYDE INTERPRETIVE CENTRE
Frenchpark
Lurgan
N61

Manulla
KILTIMAGH TOWN MUSEUM
Kilkelly
R322
Lisacul
Moyne
R361
Ballyroddy
Elphin

Kiltimagh
R323
Aghamore
N83
15
Urlaur Lough
Lough Glinn
Bellanagare
R369

Ballyfarnagh
Mayo
KNOCK FOLK MUSEUM
Knock
Ernit Lough
Cloonagh Lough
Loughglinn
R325
ROSCOMMON
Drumm

Balla
KNOCK BASILICA & SHRINE
Mannin Lake
Brackloon
Gortnasillagh
CRUACHAN AÍ VISITOR CENTRE
Strokestown

Bekan
Ballyhaunis
Lough O'Flynn
CLONALIS
Castlerea
Tulsk
ROSCOMMON HERITAGE & GENEALOGY CENTRE

Barneycarroll
N60
Ballinlough
R361
Castleplunket

Claremorris
Brickeens
N83
BALLINTOBER CASTLE
Ballintober
N61

Kilnock
R327
Garranlahan
Ballymoe
R367
Four Mile Hou

Ballindine
Irishtown
Cloonfad
R360
Derrywode
Ballymacurley
Ballylea

N17
18
R328
Curragh West
Kilsallagh
N60
31
Oran
ROSCOMMON CASTLE

Roundfort
Milltown
Dunmore
R362
Cashel
Keeloges
ROSCOMMON
Roscommon
Emm

GALWAY
Gorteen
Glenamaddy
Creggs
N63
Ballymurry

Knock International Airport
Clonbern
Kilkerrin
R362
Athleague
Scardaun
Knockcroghe

Beagh
R328
Toomard
R366
Ballygar
20
Mount Talbot
R362

CATHEDRAL & CROSS
Tuam
Levally
Newbridge
N63
R363
R357
Lough Funshin

Belclare
LITTLE MILL MUSEUM
Barnaderg
R332
Moylough
Ballyforan

Moneen
R333
R347
Horseleap
Mount Bellew
Ballyvoneen
Brideswe

Cummer
23
N63
Caltra
R363

N17
Ardnasodan
N63
Colmanstown
Castleblakeney
Kilglass
Ahascragh
Bellaneeny

LACKAGH MUS. & HERITAGE PARK
Corranduff
Cloonboo
Caraunkeelwy
Mornea
Gurteen
Trust
Caltraghlea
Newtown

Laghtgeorge
Claregalway
Newcastle
Attymon
Ballinasloe

A 32 B

A 37 38 B

miles
0 5 10
kilometres
0 5 10 15

Strokestown Park House

Strokestown Park House

Roscommon

The county town of Roscommon (population 1400) is a market town of some interest. The old gaol in Main Street, which now houses a variety of shops, had 'Lady Betty' as its executioner. She took the job on as at the appointed hour of her own hanging, there was no one else to carry out the sentence. In return for the revocation of her own death sentence (for the murder of her son) she volunteered to hang those condemned with her and continued to carry out the task willingly until her death early in the 19th century.

The Church of the Scared Heart, built in 1925, has a replica of the Cross of Cong, the original of which is in the National Museum in Dublin.

Old Market House, Roscommon

Church of the Sacred Heart, Roscommon

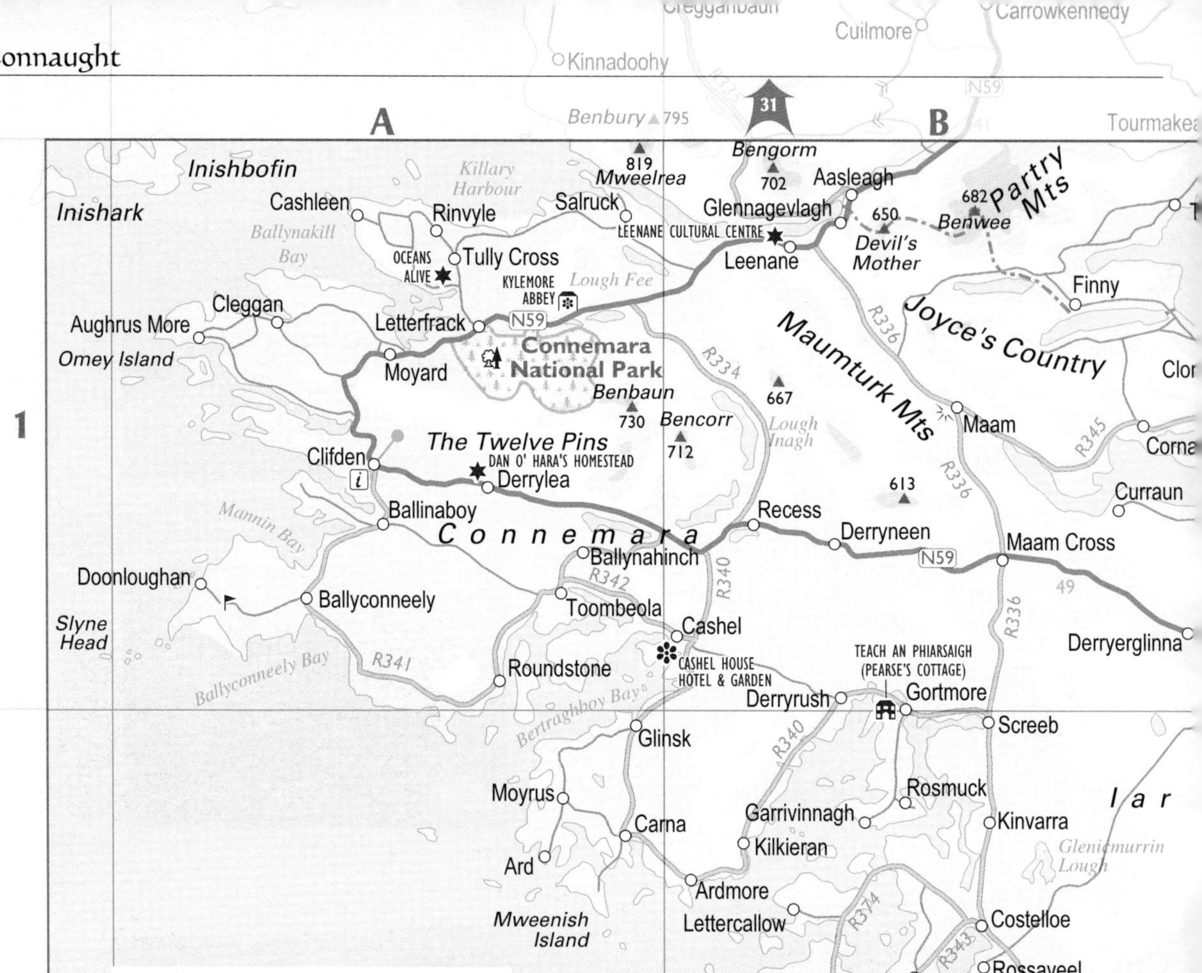

Creggánbaun · Cuilmore · Carrowkennedy · Kinnadoohy · Tourmakea

A · **B**

Benbury ▲795 · **31**

Inishbofin

Inishark

Cashleen

Rinvyle

Salruck

819 Mweelrea

Bengorm

702 Aasleagh

682 Benwee · Partry Mts

650 · N59

Ballynakill Bay

OCEANS ALIVE ★

Tully Cross

LEENANE CULTURAL CENTRE ★

Glennagevlagh

Leenane

Devil's Mother

Finny

Cleggan

KYLEMORE ABBEY ❄

Lough Fee

Aughrus More

Letterfrack

N59

Joyce's Country

Clon

Omey Island

Moyard

Connemara National Park

Benbaun 730

667 ▲

Maumturk Mts

Maam

R345

Corna

1

Bencorr 712

Lough Inagh

R336

Curraun

Clifden ⓘ

The Twelve Pins

DAN O' HARA'S HOMESTEAD ★

Derrylea

C o n n e m a r a

Recess

613 ▲

Derryneen

Maam Cross

Derryerglinna

Ballinaboy

Ballynahinch

R342

R340

N59

49

Mannin Bay

Toombeola

Cashel

Doonloughan

Ballyconneely

CASHEL HOUSE ❋ HOTEL & GARDEN

TEACH AN PHIARSAIGH (PEARSE'S COTTAGE)

Gortmore

Iar

Slyne Head

Roundstone

Derryrush

Screeb

Ballyconneely Bay

R341

Bertraghboy Bay

Glinsk

R340

Rosmuck

Kinvarra

Moyrus

Garrivinnagh

Glencmurrin Lough

Carna

Kilkieran

2

Ard

Mweenish Island

Ardmore

Lettercallow

R374

Costelloe

R343

Rossaveel

Lettermullen

Gorumna Island

Carraroe

Connemara ✈ Inveran

Lough Inagh, Connemara

Golam Head

North Sound

G a l w a

Onaght

Inishmore

DUN AENGUS ✝

ⓘ Kilronan

★ ARAN ISLANDS HERITAGE CENTRE (IONAD ARAINN)

Killeany

Inishmaan

Aran Islands

Inisheer

South Sound

Doolir Point

Connemara

West of Galway towards Clifden the landscape opens out into the majestic, varied landscape of Connemara. The mountain ranges of the Maamturks and Twelve Pins (or Bens) rise out of the largely flat bog which sweeps down to the coastline, dotted with tiny lakes and islands and numerous golden beaches. Even on the warmest summer days the area is seldom busy and the changing colours of the landscape that appear especially at sunrise and sunset is breathtaking.

Connemara is home to *Raidió na Gaeltachta (RnaG)* and *Teilifís na Gaeilge (TG4)*, the national Irish language radio and television stations respectively.

Alcock and Brown

In 1919 Alcock and Brown were the first to fly an aircraft non-stop across the Atlantic. The flight began in Newfoundland and ended 16 hours later when they crash landed into Derrigimlagh Bog south of Ballinaboy near Clifden having mistaken it for a hard landing site. A plaque commemorates the site. The aircraft was a Vickers Vimy bomber intended for use in World War I but the war ended before it could be brought into service.

Tourist Information

ⓘ **Aran Islands**

Kilronan
Inishmore
Aran Islands
County Galway
☎ 099 61263

ⓘ **Clifden**

Market Street
Clifden
County Galway
☎ 095 21163

3

Rinneen

A · **66** · **B**

miles
0 ... 5 ... 10

0 ... 5 ... 10 ... 15
kilometres

Spanish Point

Mal Bay

Mutton

N67

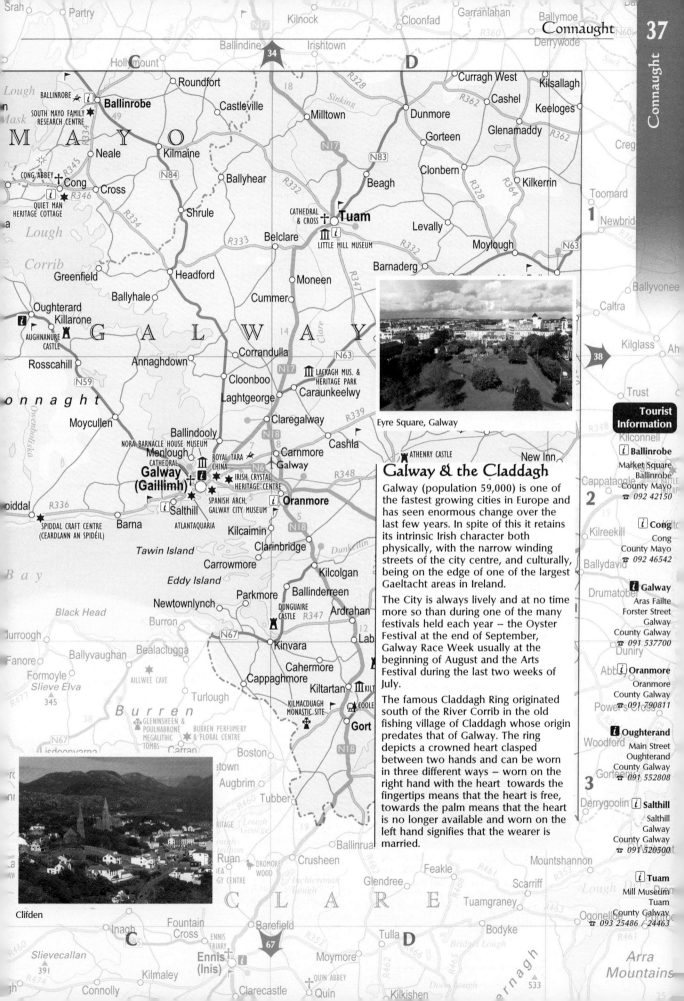

Eyre Square, Galway

Clifden

Galway & the Claddagh

Galway (population 59,000) is one of the fastest growing cities in Europe and has seen enormous change over the last few years. In spite of this it retains its intrinsic Irish character both physically, with the narrow winding streets of the city centre, and culturally, being on the edge of one of the largest Gaeltacht areas in Ireland.

The City is always lively and at no time more so than during one of the many festivals held each year – the Oyster Festival at the end of September, Galway Race Week usually at the beginning of August and the Arts Festival during the last two weeks of July.

The famous Claddagh Ring originated south of the River Corrib in the old fishing village of Claddagh whose origin predates that of Galway. The ring depicts a crowned heart clasped between two hands and can be worn in three different ways – worn on the right hand with the heart towards the fingertips means that the heart is free, towards the palm means that the heart is no longer available and worn on the left hand signifies that the wearer is married.

Tourist Information

ℹ **Ballinrobe**
Market Square
Ballinrobe
County Mayo
☎ 092 42150

ℹ **Cong**
Cong
County Mayo
☎ 092 46542

ℹ **Galway**
Aras Failte
Forster Street
Galway
County Galway
☎ 091 537700

ℹ **Oranmore**
Oranmore
County Galway
☎ 091 790811

ℹ **Oughterand**
Main Street
Oughterand
County Galway
☎ 091 552808

ℹ **Salthill**
Salthill
Galway
County Galway
☎ 091 520500

ℹ **Tuam**
Mill Museum
Tuam
County Galway
☎ 093 25486 / 24463

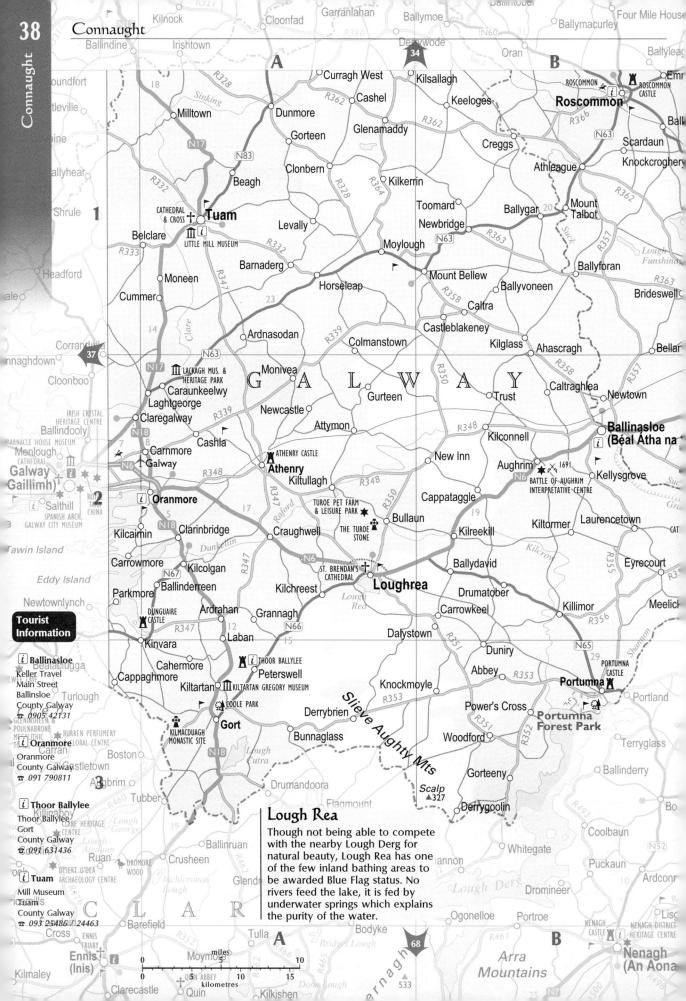

Lough Rea

Though not being able to compete with the nearby Lough Derg for natural beauty, Lough Rea has one of the few inland bathing areas to be awarded Blue Flag status. No rivers feed the lake, it is fed by underwater springs which explains the purity of the water.

Tourist Information

ℹ **Ballinasloe**
Keller Travel
Main Street
Ballinsloe
County Galway
☎ 0905 42131

ℹ **Oranmore**
Oranmore
County Galway
☎ 091 790811

ℹ **Thoor Ballylee**
Thoor Ballylee
Gort
County Galway
☎ 091 631436

ℹ **Tuam**
Mill Museum
Tuam
County Galway
☎ 093 25486 / 24463

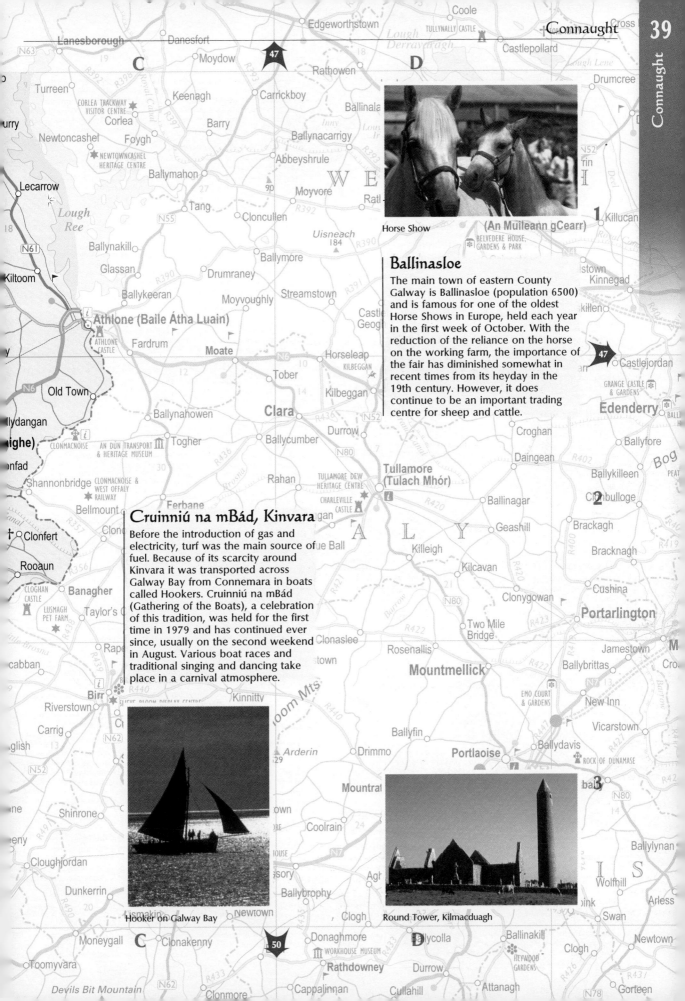

Horse Show   (An Muileann gCearr)

Ballinasloe

The main town of eastern County Galway is Ballinasloe (population 6500) and is famous for one of the oldest Horse Shows in Europe, held each year in the first week of October. With the reduction of the reliance on the horse on the working farm, the importance of the fair has diminished somewhat in recent times from its heyday in the 19th century. However, it does continue to be an important trading centre for sheep and cattle.

Cruinniú na mBád, Kinvara

Before the introduction of gas and electricity, turf was the main source of fuel. Because of its scarcity around Kinvara it was transported across Galway Bay from Connemara in boats called Hookers. Cruinniú na mBád (Gathering of the Boats), a celebration of this tradition, was held for the first time in 1979 and has continued ever since, usually on the second weekend in August. Various boat races and traditional singing and dancing take place in a carnival atmosphere.

Hooker on Galway Bay

Round Tower, Kilmacduagh

✦ Aran Islands Heritage Centre (Ionad Árainn) `36 B2`

Kilronan, Inishmore, Aran Islands, Co. Galway. The centre introduces the archaeology, history, landscape and geology, culture and marine traditions of the islands. The islanders traditional dress is displayed and there are examples of the world famous Aran style knitting.
☎ 099 61355

🏰 Athenry Castle `38 A2`

Athenry, Co. Galway. Surrounded by a strong defensive wall, this three storey tower house was built by Meiler de Bermingham around 1250. The entrance to the restored castle is made through a first floor carved decorative doorway and the castle contains an exhibition and audiovisual display.
☎ 091 844797 www.heritageireland.ie

🏰 Aughnanure Castle `37 C1`

Oughterard, Co. Galway. Aughnanure is a well preserved six storey Irish tower house of around 1500, probably built by de Burgos and then captured and retained by the O'Flahertys until confiscation in the 17th century, after which it fell into ruin. The castle has been restored and features of interest include a dry harbour, watch tower, unusual double bawn and bastions, a circular guard house with cupola roof and one remaining wall of a banqueting hall with floral carvings on the windows.
☎ 091 552214 www.heritageireland.ie

🏇 Ballinrobe Racecourse `37 C1`

Convent Road, Ballinrobe, Co. Mayo. National Hunt and Flat racing course with six race days a year.
☎ 092 41052/41418

✝ Ballintober Abbey `31 D3`

Ballintober, Claremorris, Co. Mayo. Founded in 1216 by Cathal O'Connor, King of Connaught, for the order of St Augustine, the abbey has been in daily use almost without interruption ever since, which makes it unique in Ireland. The church includes an ancient cloister arcade and the tomb of Theobald, son of the 'pirate queen' Grace O'Malley. Major restoration took place in 1966. Tóchar Phádraig, an ancient pilgrims' path, runs past here to the holy mountain of Croagh Patrick.
☎ 094 30930

🏰 Ballintober Castle `34 B2`

Ballintober, Roscommon, Co. Roscommon. The ruins of a massive castle, dating back to about 1300, which was the principal seat of the O'Connor dynasty from the time of the Anglo-Norman invasions until the 18th century when they moved to Clonalis. Many times besieged, rarely breached, it is without a keep, but retains its twin-towered gatehouse and corner towers.
☎ 0903 26342

🏰 Ballymote Castle `32 A3`

Ballymote, Co. Sligo. The remains of an Anglo-Norman castle built in 1300 by Richard de Burgo, the 'Red Earl' of Ulster. The Book of Ballymote, a compilation of manuscripts and documents put together in the castle in the late 14th century, has an important treatise on Ogham inscriptions, the ancient Celtic writing system of straight lines which can be seen on many standing stones.
☎ 079 62145

✦ Battle of Aughrim Interpretative Centre `38 B2`

Aughrim, Co. Galway. The centre recreates the bloody battle of Aughrim on July 12th 1691 when 9000 lives were lost. It was the last battle fought for the English throne between the Protestant forces of King William of Orange and the Jacobite forces of the deposed Catholic King, James II and resulted in an overwhelming victory for William. Audiovisuals give a soldiers acount of the battle and the history which led up to the war and the effect of the outcome is explained.
☎ 0905 73939

✝ Boyle Abbey `32 B3`

Boyle, Co. Roscommon. The impressive remains of the 12th century Cistercian abbey are on the north side of the market town of Boyle and are the burial place of Ireland's most famous medieval religious poet, Donnchadh Mor O'Daly. Although badly damaged in the 17th and 18th centuries when it housed a military garrison, the abbey is one of the best preserved in the country. The church is a fine example of the transition from Romanesque to Gothic; this is illustrated in the nave where there are rounded arches on one side and pointed arches on the other.
☎ 079 62604 www.heritageireland.ie

⚱ Carrowkeel Megalithic Cemetery `32 B3`

Castlebaldwin, Co. Sligo. A Bronze Age passage tomb cemetery with 14 chambered cairns situated on hilltops in the Bricklieve Mountains above the west shore of Lough Arrow. It is also the site of an ancient village consisting of some 70 circular huts, but it is not known if it is from the same era as the cemetery.
☎ 079 62145

⚱ Carrowmore Megalithic Cemetery `32 A2`

Carrowmore, Co. Sligo. One of the oldest and most important megalithic cemeteries in Europe and the largest in Ireland with over 40 tombs in various states of preservation clustered around a central cairn covered monument. Some archaeologists have suggested a date of around 4840 – 4370BC for their original construction and ongoing excavations on the site have provided evidence they were used for secondary burials in the late Neolithic, Bronze and Iron Ages.
☎ 071 61201 www.heritageireland.ie

❃ Cashel House Hotel & Garden `36 B1`

Cashel, Connemara, Co. Galway. A 19th century country house, now a hotel, with a 20ha (50 acre) informal garden of herbaceous flowers, flowering shrubs and woodland walks at the head of Cashel Bay. In 1919 the walled garden, once an orchard, was felled and replanted with many rare trees and shrubs including rhododendrons, azaleas and magnolias which had been brought from many parts of the world including from Tibet.
☎ 095 31001 www.cashel-house-hotel.com

✦ Cavan & Leitrim Railway `35 C2`

Station Road, Dromod, Co. Leitrim. The narrow gauge railway line has a vintage steam train and diesel railcars operational on 1km of track; work is ongoing to extend the railway 8km (5 miles) to Mohill where the station is also being restored. The railway first opened in 1887 but closed in 1959 and the ticket office and waiting room at Dromod have been restored as well as the workshops, engine shed and water tower. There is also a collection of rolling stock and vintage buses.
☎ 078 38599 homepage.eircom.net/~yarpie/clr

⚱ Céide Fields & Visitor Centre `31 C1`

Ballycastle, Co. Mayo. Céide Fields consists of an area of 1500ha (3705 acres) containing field systems, enclosures and megalithic tombs dating back 5000 years. Preserved beneath the bogland of North Mayo and now coming to light through excavation, it is the most extensive Stone Age monument in the world. The visitor centre, an award winning pyramid structure of limestone and peat, has displays and exhibitions which interpret the geology, archaeology, botany and wildlife of the area and there are guided tours of the site.
☎ 096 43325 www.heritageireland.ie

✦ Celtic Furrow, The `31 D3`

Ballintober Abbey, Ballintober, Claremorris, Co. Mayo. A visitor centre which explores Ireland's cultural heritage by tracing the development of customs and festivals from Neolithic times to the 20th century. It shows the particular importance of the winter and summer solstices and the two equinoxes and how pagan festivals were absorbed into Christian practice.
☎ 094 30934

✦ Clew Bay Heritage Centre `31 C3`

The Quay, Westport, Co. Mayo. Housed within a 19th century building, the heritage centre illustrates the history and marine traditions of Westport and the Clew Bay area from prehistoric times to the present day. Themes include Grace O'Malley and Ireland's struggle for independence. A genealogical service is also available with an extensive database which includes census returns, church and civil records, school registers, local newspapers and rent rolls.
☎ 098 26852

🏛 Clonalis House `34 B2`

Castlerea, Co. Roscommon. Ancestral home of the O'Connor clan, high kings of Ireland and Connaught, who can be traced back to 75AD. Built in 1878, Clonalis replaced an earlier 18th century house and is furnished with Sheraton and Louis XV furniture and hung with family portraits. Georgian silver and fine china are displayed in the house and exhibits include the inauguration stone of the kings of Connaught, family documents and manuscripts, costumes, uniforms and laces, as well as the 18th century harp of the Gaelic bard, Turlough O'Carolan.
☎ 0907 20014

✝ Clonfert Cathedral `39 C2`

Clonfert, Co. Galway. 12th century cathedral church on the site of a monastery founded in 557 by St Brendan the Navigator who was interred here in 577. The cathedral has a highly decorated Irish Romanesque west doorway consisting of six large arcs and the east window is an equally fine example of Romanesque architecture. Inside there is a notable carved oak pulpit and Bishop's chair.
☎ 0509 51269

✝ Cong Abbey `37 C1`

Cong, Co. Mayo. Founded in the 6th century by St Féichín and superseded by an Augustinian monastery in the 12th century founded by Turlough O'Connor, High King of Ireland. The remains of the chancel and cloister of the abbey church are to be found to the south west of the village. The abbey church has a beautiful north door but most appealing of all are the three doorways in the remaining convent buildings. The gold Cross of Cong is now in the National Museum in Dublin.
☎ 092 06542

🦌 Connemara National Park Visitor Centre `36 A1`

Letterfrack, Co. Galway. Comprising 2000ha (4949 acres) of scenic countryside including mountain, bog and grassland, the park is particularly rich in wildlife and there are herds of red deer. Part of the Twelve Bens range of mountains lies within the area and the River Polladirk runs through the Glanmore valley at the centre of the park. There are several sites of archaeological interest and two nature trails.
☎ 095 41054/41006 www.heritageireland.ie

✦ Coole Visitor Centre `38 A3`

Gort, Co. Galway. Once the home of the co-founder of the Abbey Theatre in Dublin, Lady Augusta Gregory, Coole Park is now a nature reserve and wildlife park. Coole House was demolished in the 1950s, although the ruined walls and garden with its yew walk remain and it is the stables that have been converted into the visitor centre. In the walled garden stands a copper beech known as the 'autograph tree' on which are carved the initials of Coole's famous visitors.
☎ 091 631804/563016 www.heritageireland.ie

✝ Creevelea Friary `32 B2`

Dromahair, Co. Leitrim. Creevelea was founded in 1508 by Margaret, wife of Owen O'Rourke and was the last such foundation before the suppression of the monasteries by Henry VIII. Accidentally burned down in 1536 but subsequently restored, it was occupied by the English in 1598. Standing in a picturesque setting beside the River Bonet, the ruins are well preserved and include a cloister, transept, east window and a kitchen and refectory in the north wing.
☎ 071 61201

⚱ Creevykeel Court Cairn `32 B1`

Cliffonoy, Co. Sligo. The 55m (180ft) long trapeze-shaped cairn encloses an oval courtyard, where ritual rites would have been performed, and a burial chamber of two compartments. It is one of the best examples of a court tomb in Ireland. The eastern entrance end is 25m (82ft) wide and there are additionally three single chamber tombs set in the west end of the monument.
☎ 071 61201

✱ Croagh Patrick Information Centre & Famine Monument   31 C3

Murrisk, Co. Mayo. Known locally as the Reek, Croagh Patrick rises to 762m (2515ft). St Patrick is said to have spent 40 days on the summit in 441AD, fasting and praying for the people of Ireland. Since early Christian times a pilgrimage has taken place every July when the devout climb the mountain in the footsteps of the saint. A Celtic hill fort encircles the summit and a dry stone oratory is one of the oldest stone churches in Ireland. Situated at the foot of Croagh Patrick opposite the Information Centre stands a bronze monument to the Great Famine of the 1840s sculpted by John Behan depicting a 'coffin ship' with skeleton bodies in the rigging.
☎ 098 64114   www.croagh-patrick.com

✱ Cruachan Aí   34 B2

Tulsk, Co. Roscommon. Cruachan Aí visitor centre interprets the mythology, archaeology and history of Rathcrogan, the best preserved Celtic Royal site in Europe where the kings of Connaught were inaugurated. Over an area of 518ha (1279 acres) there are countless archaeological remains from the Stone Age with 60 national monuments including ring forts, burial mounds and megalithic tombs, the most notable of which, Rathcrogan Mound is 88m (290ft) in diameter.
☎ 078 39268   www.cruachanai.com

🏛 Culkin's Emigration Museum   32 A2

Cannaghanally, Dromore West, Co. Sligo. Displays in the museum illustrate the era in Irish history when emigration was part of the every day life of the people of Ireland as many sought a better life abroad. Daniel Culkin's Shipping and Emigration Agency operated on this site from the 19th century until the 1930s; the restored office is now incorporated into the purpose built modern museum.
☎ 096 47152

✱ Dan O'Hara's Homestead   36 A1

Lettershea, Clifden, Co. Galway. The homestead is built on the original site of the cottage of Dan O'Hara who was evicted from his home and emigrated to America. O'Hara's wife and three of their children died during the journey, the four remaining children were taken into care and he ended up selling matches on the streets of New York. A tractor drawn carriage gives tours of a reconstructed 19th century farm and to several sites of archaeological interest including the 5000 year old Upland burial site and a crannog, ring fort and clochan.
☎ 095 21246

✱ Dr. Douglas Hyde Interpretative Centre   34 B2

Portahard, Frenchpark, Co. Roscommon. Dr. Douglas Hyde (1860 – 1949) was co-founder of the Gaelic League and first President of Ireland. A scholar, profoundly interested in the Irish language and culture, Hyde published many works which are acknowledged to be a major source for the Irish Literary Renaissance. Photographs, documents, letters, personal items and books of his work illustrate the political and literary contribution he made to Ireland. The Centre is housed in the church where his father was rector and Hyde's grave is in the churchyard.
☎ 0907 70016

⚑ Doonamo Fort   30 B1

Aghadoon, Co. Mayo. The remains of a prehistoric promontory fort near Erris Head with a 60m (200ft) wall across the headland that rises to a height of 5m (18ft) in some places. It contains the remains of a ring fort and three clochans.
☎ 096 70848

⚑ Drumcliffe High Cross & Round Tower   32 B2

Drumcliff, Co. Sligo. The remains of the round tower and a 10th century high cross are all that remains of a monastic settlement founded by St Colmcille (St Columba) in 574. The monastery was flourishing in the 13th century but went into decline soon afterwards. Irish poet W.B.Yeats, who spent much of his childhood in Sligo, is buried in the churchyard here.
☎ 071 44956   www.drumcliffe.ie

⚑ Dún Aengus   36 A2

Kilmurvey, Inishmore, Aran Islands, Co. Galway. The 2500 year old Dún Aengus is one of the most important prehistoric stone forts in Europe. It is spectacularly sited on a desolate clifftop with a 76m (250ft) drop to the Atlantic Ocean. There are three enclosures with dry stone walls up to 5m (18ft) high.The middle wall is defended by tall jagged limestone blocks (chevaux-de-frise) set vertically into the ground. The inner fort is 45m (148ft) in diameter and contains wall chambers, stairways and terraces. The visitor centre, about 1km away, gives information about the site.
☎ 099 61008   www.heritageireland.ie

🏰 Dunguaire Castle   37 C2

Kinvara, Co. Galway. Dunguaire Castle is a restored fortified tower house built by the O'Hynes in 1520. It was bought in 1924 by Oliver St John Gogarty, surgeon, poet and wit, who was involved with the Irish Literary Revival; W.B Yeats, Lady Gregory, George Bernard Shaw and J.M.Synge were among visitors to the castle. Now the venue for medieval banquets, the castle also has exhibits giving an insight into the lives of the people who have lived there since the 16th century.
☎ 061 360788

❁ Enniscoe Gardens   31 D2

Castlehill, Ballina, Co. Mayo. Enniscoe, situated on Lough Conn, is an 18th century Georgian house with gardens dating back to the 1840s. The walled garden contains organic vegetables and is separated from an ornamental garden by a decorative stone archway planted with hardy ferns. Paths run through the parkland to the lake and many of the trees in the Victorian pleasure gardens are 150 years old.
☎ 096 31809

✱ Foxford Woollen Mills   31 D2

St Josephs Place, Foxford, Co. Mayo. Working mills where skilled craftspeople produce tweed, rugs and blankets. The mills were founded in 1892 by a nun, Mother Agnes Morrogh Bernard, whose life story is told in the visitor centre with a three dimensional audiovisual presentation incorporating animated life size models.
☎ 094 56756

🏠 Frybrook House   32 B3

Elphin Street, Boyle, Co. Roscommon. Overlooking the River Boyle, Frybrook House is a three storey Georgian style town house and garden built around 1750 for Henry Fry, who become chief magistrate of the area. The house, with distinctive bay windows, contains an Adams fireplace and fine decorative plasterwork, whilst the grounds are laid out as a miniature landscape. Frybrook has a collection of old and modern paintings.
☎ 079 63513

✱ Galway Atlantaquaria   37 C2

Salthill, Co. Galway. Located on the promenade at Salthill, this National Aquarium of Ireland gives an insight into the deep sea world off the west coast of Ireland with a diverse collection of 170 species of marine life including lobster, rays, sea bass and conger eels. There are also tanks re-creating the habitats of native freshwater fish, touch tanks where visitors may handle creatures like crabs and starfish, a series of exhibits on the life of the Irish salmon and the 'fish-eye' view of life beneath a waterfall.
☎ 091 585100   homepage.tinet.ie/~atlantaquaria

✝ Galway Cathedral   37 C2

Cathedral Square, Galway, Co. Galway. Located by the Salmon Weir Bridge on the River Corrib, the Cathedral was completed in 1965 and is dedicated to Our Lady Assumed into Heaven and St Nicholas. The 45m (145ft) high green dome is prominent on the city's skyline.
☎ 091 563577

🏛 Galway City Museum   37 C2

Spanish Arch, Galway, Co. Galway. Located in the medieval docks area of Galway and adjoining the Spanish Arch, the museum presents the folklife and social history of Galway. Exhibits include 17th century stone carvings, farm implements and tools, military exhibits relating to the 1916 Rising and the civil war, maps, photographs and engravings. The building was built as a private house around 1800 and was once the home of sculptor, Clare Sheridan, whose wooden sculpture 'Madonna of the Quays' can be seen in the Spanish Arch.
☎ 091 567641

⚶ Galway Racecourse   37 C2

Ballybrit, Galway, Co. Galway. National Hunt and Flat racing course with 12 race days a year including the six day Summer Racing Festival meeting, one of Ireland's premier racing festivals and a time of great celebration in Galway itself.
☎ 091 753870   www.iol.ie/galway-races

✱ Granuaile Visitor Centre   31 C3

Louisburgh, Co. Mayo. An audiovisual presentation of the fascinating story of the 'pirate queen' Grace O'Malley (Granuaile). With a base on Clare island, O'Malley achieved control of the area around Clew Bay and the visitor centre explores her political, diplomatic and commercial achievements in the male-dominated society of 16th century Ireland. A woman of outstanding determination and drive, O'Malley travelled to London to meet with Elizabeth I to plea protection from the English suppression of local chieftains, a wish that was granted.
☎ 098 66341

✱ Hennigan's Heritage Centre   31 D2

St Joseph's Place, Foxford, Co. Mayo. Overlooking Creagaballa Lake, this small farm of less than 4ha (10 acres) was tilled by generations of the Hennigan family for 200 years. Visitors can see inside the original farmhouse and visit the theme farm where animals and poultry roam freely. Fishing and boating is available on the lake.
☎ 094 52505

✱ Irish Crystal Heritage Centre   37 C2

Merlin Park, Dublin Road, Galway, Co. Galway. The production of traditionally hand cut Irish lead crystal is shown in the context of the history, culture and landscape of Galway which has inspired the craftsmen. Visitors have the opportunity to see the craftsmen at work producing the intricately designed tabletop stemware and giftware; tours begin in the elegant Great Hall of Merlin Park House with its grand staircase and crystal chandeliers.
☎ 091 757311   www.galwaycrystal.ie

⚑ Kilmacduagh Monastic Site   38 A3

Kilmacduagh, Co. Galway. The remains of a monastic settlement founded in the early 7th century by St Colman with a notable 10th or 11th century round tower 33m (111ft) high which leans almost 50cm (19.5 inches) from the perpendicular. The site has extensive remains of several churches and of a small cathedral which contains two finely carved crosses. In addition, there is a two storey 13th century building known as Glebe House, thought to be the abbot's house.
☎ 091 631436

🏛 Kiltartan Gregory Museum   38 A3

Kiltartan, Gort, Co. Galway. Containing rare manuscripts, first editions, photographs and memorabilia relating to dramatist Lady Augusta Gregory of Coole Park and the Irish Literary Revival, the museum is housed in a former schoolhouse built by the Gregory family in 1892. The second of the two rooms has been recreated as an early 20th century schoolroom with desks, blackboard, maps, paintings and charts.
☎ 091 632346

🏛 Kiltimagh Town Museum   31 D3

Kiltimagh, Co. Mayo. Located in the restored old railway station office and two railway carriages dating back to 1894, the museum has a collection of many interesting artefacts which illustrate the history and folklore of the area. The old station master's house is now an art exhibition centre displaying national and international artists, while the whole of the restored station complex is set within a sculpture park.
☎ 094 81132

King House
32 B3

Boyle, Co. Roscommon. Built around 1730 for Sir Henry King, the house is a splendid Georgian mansion which has been beautifully restored and overlooks the River Boyle. Between 1788 and 1922 King House became a military barracks for the Connaught Rangers, a British army regiment, and more recently has housed the Irish army. Lively interactive exhibitions using life size models and special effects tell the story of the house and those who lived in it and give impressions of the town and surrounding area from the time of the Kingdom of Connaught.

☎ 079 63242

✝ Knock Basilica & Shrine
34 A2

Knock, Co. Mayo. One of the great Marian shrines of the world, Our Lady's Shrine at Knock attracts over 1.5 million visitors each year. An apparition of the Virgin Mary, St Joseph and St John on 21 August 1879 was witnessed by 15 local people on the south gable of the parish church of St John the Baptist. Ever since, Knock has been a place of pilgrimage. The focal point of the shrine is the gable of the apparition and the shrine Oratory. Nearby is the Basilica of Our Lady built in 1976 to accommodate the flow of pilgrims. It is the largest church in Ireland with room for up to 20,000 people. Pope John Paul II visited Knock on his tour of Ireland in September 1979.

☎ 094 88100   www.knock-shrine.ie

Knock Folk Museum
34 A2

Knock, Co. Mayo. In addition to the 1879 Apparition, the museum and also depicts the customs and lifestyle of people in rural Ireland at the time and in the century following. Displays include fishing, farming, crafts, education, housing and clothing. The museum also has a section about Monsignor James Horan, the parish priest responsible for the building of the Basilica at Knock and who initiated the invitation to Pope John Paul II to visit Ireland. Horan's dogged determination was also responsible for the construction of Knock airport.

☎ 094 88100

Kylemore Abbey & Garden
36 A1

Kylemore, Connemara, Co. Galway. Built in 1868 by a wealthy Manchester merchant, the neo Gothic house is now a monastic home and international school for girls in a picturesque lakeside setting at the foot of Duchruach Mountain. Kylemore has a restored Gothic church and a Victorian garden of more than 2ha (5 acres) surrounded by a wall 800m (1600ft) long. The garden features the original formal flower garden and kitchen garden and a vast complex of Victorian glasshouses which were used to grow exotic plants and fruit.

☎ 095 41146/41385   www.kylemoreabbey.com

Lackagh Museum & Heritage Park
38 A2

Lackagh, Turloughmore, Co. Galway. A restored 19th century traditional Irish thatched cottage with open hearth and an open dresser displaying crockery, reflecting a way of life which has almost gone. Rural artefacts on display include a spinning wheel and butter churns. Outside the cottage there is an impressive display of farm machinery.

☎ 091 797444

✷ Leenane Cultural Centre
36 B1

Leenane, Connemara, Co. Galway. An interpretative centre tracing the history of sheep and illustrating the importance of wool in north Connemara and in Ireland. Several breeds of sheep, some of them ancient western European breeds, can be seen grazing at the centre and, as well as a display of artefacts, there are demonstrations of carding, spinning, weaving, felting and dyeing with natural dyes. Local places of interest and history are featured on an audiovisual display.

☎ 095 42323   www.leenane-connemara.com

Lissadell House
32 A2

Ballinfull, Drumcliffe, Co. Sligo. Situated in conifer covered parkland overlooking Drumcliffe Bay, Lissadell House was built in Classical style in the 1830s for the patriotic Gore-Booth family. The Arctic explorer Sir Henry Gore-Booth was born here, as were his daughters Eva and Constance, who became the first female member of the British House of Commons, but who chose to sit instead in the revolutionary Dail Eireann. Constance was condemned to death for her part in the 1916 Easter Rising.

☎ 071 63150

Little Mill Museum
37 D1

Shop Street, Tuam, Co. Galway. Although closed for commercial operation in 1964, the cornmill has been restored and has an operating water wheel, the last remaining one in the Tuam area. Visitors can view the milling process and there is an exhibition of model mills in the adjacent miller's house.

☎ 093 25486

Lough Key Forest Park
32 B3

Rockingham, Boyle, Co. Roscommon. Lough Key is a beautiful lough with several wooded islands and is linked to the Shannon River system. Formerly part of the Rockingham estate and comprising 350ha (864 acres) of mixed woodland and open parkland, the forest park has a wide range of habitats which encourages a diversity of wildlife. Numerous features of archaeological and historical interest are found within the park including an observation tower built on the site of Rockingham House which was destroyed by fire, an icehouse, and underground tunnels used by servants.

☎ 079 62363

Lough Rynn Estate
35 C2

Mohill, Co. Leitrim. Set on the shores of Lough Rynn, the estate comprises 40ha (99 acres) of woodland and includes large ornamental terraced walled gardens dating back to 1859. The estate has nature trails and a number of rare and exotic trees. Lough Rynn house, built in 1832, was the former home of the Earls of Leitrim, the Clement's family. A turreted summerhouse affords beautiful views over Lough Rynn.

☎ 078 31427

✷ Mayo North Family Heritage Centre
31 D2

Enniscoe, Castlehill, Ballina, Co. Mayo. A genealogical service offers assistance to those wishing to trace their Mayo ancestry and, with the aim of developing the skills of traditional crafts, the heritage centre also provides forge and craft training. Historic local agricultural tools and household artefacts are on display.

☎ 096 31809   www.mayo.irishroots.net/centres.htm

Michael Davitt Museum
31 D3

Straide, Co. Mayo. The museum contains an extensive collection of documents, Land Acts, photographs and memorabilia relating to Michael Davitt (1846 – 1906) who was founder of the Land League, a mass movement which was to bring about land reform for Irish tenant farmers. He was also a Member of Parliament for South Mayo, author and journalist and a founding patron of the Gaelic Athletic Association (GAA). Davitt's grave is in the grounds of nearby Straide Abbey.

☎ 094 31022

✝ Moyne Abbey
31 D1

Ballina, Co. Mayo. A Franciscan friary founded in 1460; the church is cruciform in shape and has a bell tower suspended over the chancel arch. Moyne is now a ruin, destroyed by the governor of Connaught in the late 16th century.

☎ 096 70848

Museum of Country Life (National Museum of Ireland)
31 D3

Turlough Park, Castlebar, Co. Mayo. The only branch of the National Museum of Ireland to be situated outside Dublin was officially opened in September 2001. Housed in modern purpose-built exhibition galleries, the collection portrays the social history of rural Ireland with the primary focus between 1850 and 1950. The lives of the Irish people are presented in the context of history, folklore and the natural environment. The new galleries are adjacent to the restored Victorian Gothic style house of Turlough Park and overlook the lake and formal gardens.

☎ 094 31589

Nora Barnacle House Museum
37 C2

8 Bowling Green, Galway, Co. Galway. Nora Barnacle married novelist James Joyce and was the inspiration for much of his writing, including for the character of Molly Bloom in Ulysses. The small house is furnished as it would have been when Nora lived here with her mother in the early 19th century. There are also photographs, letters and memorabilia from the lives of Joyce and his wife.

☎ 091 564743

✷ Oceans Alive
36 A1

Renvyle, Connemara, Co. Galway. A sealife centre with an aquarium and an exhibition of local maritime history. The adjacent park has a pets' corner and children's play area; cruises along the Connemara coast are also available.

☎ 095 43473

Parke's Castle
32 B2

Fivemile Bourne, Co. Leitrim. An early 17th century fortified manor that was built by Robert Parke on the shore of Lough Gill and recently restored. Fortified with picturesque towers and gatehouses, the castle played a key role in the war of 1641 – 1652. There is an audiovisual presentation within the castle, a traditional 17th century style blacksmith's forge and models of the Parke family dressed in period costume. The courtyard shows evidence of an earlier 16th century tower house.

☎ 071 64149   www.heritageireland.ie

Portumna Castle & Gardens
38 B3

Portumna, Co. Galway. This early 17th century Jacobean semi-fortified house overlooking Lough Derg was built by Richard de Burgo, 4th Earl of Clanrickarde, and remained in the de Burgo family until it was gutted by fire in 1826. Although influenced by English and Renaissance houses, Portumna still has a distinctive Irish appearance. There are exhibitions in the gatehouse and in the castle, where the ground floor is open to the public.

☎ 0509 41658   www.heritageireland.ie

Portumna Forest Park
38 B3

Portumna, Co. Galway. Situated on the north shores of Lough Derg, the forest park comprises almost 600ha (1482 acres) with a wide variety of habitat including marsh, lake, grassland, coniferous forest and mixed woodland making it rich in bird and wildlife; fallow deer, pine martens, otters, mute swans and goldcrests are among the resident mammals and birds. Facilities include forest and lakeside walks with observation points, and a viewing tower on the nature trail.

☎ 0509 20110

✷ Quiet Man Heritage Cottage
37 C1

Circular Road, Cong, Co. Mayo. The Quiet Man, the 1951 film staring John Wayne and Maureen O'Hara was set in the west of Ireland and filmed around Cong. The ground floor of the thatched cottage has been designed as a replica of the film's 'White-o-Mornin' Cottage' with artefacts and furnishings representing a typical Irish cottage of the 1920s. The upstairs of the cottage houses a historical and archaeological exhibition relating to Cong and the surrounding area.

☎ 092 46089

Roscommon Castle
34 B3

Roscommon, Co. Roscommon. The substantial ruins of the castle built in 1269 by Robert de Ufford has a chequered history, taken alternatively by the English and Irish until 1690 when it was burned down and fell into ruin. The three storey castle has a quadrangular plan, twin towers at the entrance gateway and is surrounded at some distance from the curtain wall by a moat.

☎ 0903 26342

✷ Roscommon Heritage & Genealogy Centre
34 B2

Church Street, Strokestown, Co. Roscommon. Offering a family research service for people whose ancestors came from County Roscommon, the centre has a comprehensive database which includes census, land, church and civil records. It is housed in a former church built in 1819 with a unique octagonal nave.

☎ 078 33380   www.roscommonroots.com

✈ Roscommon Racecourse `34 B3`

Racecourse Road, Lenabane, Roscommon, Co. Roscommon. National Hunt and Flat racing course with eight race days a year including five evening meetings.
☎ 0903 63494

✝ Rosserk Friary `31 D1`

Ballina, Co. Mayo. The remains of a friary dating from 1441, one of the best preserved in the country, which was destroyed by the governor of Connaught in the late 16th century.
☎ 096 70848

✱ Royal Tara China Visitor Centre `37 C2`

Tara Hall, Mervue, Galway, Co. Galway. Factory tours of Royal Tara show the process of making the hand crafted fine bone china giftware and tableware at Tara Hall, formerly Merview House, a 17th century Queen Anne-Georgian style mansion and formerly the seat of the Joyce's, one of the principal tribes of Galway. The extensive showrooms are laid out in the elegant library and drawing rooms, which have original marble fireplaces and ornate plasterwork.
☎ 091 751301 www.royal-tara.com

✝ St Brendan's Cathedral `38 A2`

Loughrea, Co. Galway. Stained glass windows, sculpture, metalwork, woodcarving and textiles were created by some of Ireland's greatest craftspeople in the early 20th century, making this a treasure house of the art of the Celtic Renaissance. The architect, W.A. Scott designed the chalice, candelabra, metal work lamps and the benches. The corbels, baptismal font and nave capitals are by Michael Shorthall and the stations of the cross by E. Rhinds.
☎ 091 41006

✱ Sliabh an Iarainn Visitor Centre `33 C3`

Drumshanbo, Co. Leitrim. The story of Leitrim is told with a variety of exhibits and an audiovisual display. The history of transport in the area including the railway, canal and lakes is illustrated, as well as the iron and coal mining industry. Also included is a reconstructed sweat house traditionally used to cure aches and pains and a re-creation of a railway station ticket office and waiting room.
☎ 078 41522

✝ Sligo Abbey `32 B2`

Abbey Street, Sligo, Co. Sligo. Founded originally as a Dominican Friary around 1252 by Maurice FitzGerald, Chief Justice of Ireland, the building was accidentally burned down in 1414 and further destroyed in 1641. The well preserved ruin has the cloisters, nave and choir arched tower remaining and contains the only surviving 15th century decorated high altar in any Irish monastic church as well as a wealth of Gothic and Renaissance tombs and monuments.
☎ 071 46406 www.heritageireland.ie

✈ Sligo Racecourse `32 B2`

Cleveragh, Sligo, Co. Sligo. National Hunt and Flat racing course with six race days a year, set in a scenic location to the south of Sligo.
☎ 071 62484

✱ South Mayo Family Research Centre `37 C1`

Main Street, Ballinrobe, Co. Mayo. The centre offers a full service to people wishing to trace their ancestors from the area and has a database of over one million records including church and civil records, lists of emigrants and migrants, the 1901 census, school registers, rent rolls, police indexes and gravestone inscriptions.
☎ 092 41214 www.mayo.irishroots.net/centres.htm

✱ Spanish Arch `37 C2`

Galway, Co. Galway. Situated in the medieval docks area of Galway, the Spanish Arch, built in 1584, was probably part of an extension to the city wall designed to protect the quays. An adjacent arch is known as Blind Arch and the site of the two former inner arches is now occupied by the city museum. A map of 1610 shows a fort at this location, known as Ceann na Bhalla (end of the wall).
☎ 091 567641

✱ Spiddal Craft Centre (Ceardlann an Spidéil) `37 C2`

Spiddal, Co. Galway. A group of eight artisan workshops producing a variety of crafts including leatherwork, pottery, weaving, Celtic jewellery, woodturning, candle making and screen printing. The resident craftspeople draw their inspiration from the culture and landscape of the Irish speaking area of Connemara and there is also an art gallery exhibiting national and international artists.
☎ 091 553376/553478

✞ Srahmee Megalithic Tomb `31 C3`

Cregganbaun, Co. Mayo. Situated near to the roadside, the tomb is well preserved with double-walling, a fine large septal slab and traces of a cairn. The single large roof stone covering most of the main chamber of the gallery is over 4m (13ft) long. The site was formerly venerated as a holy well, known as 'The Altar Well' (Tobernahaltora).
☎ 098 25711

✝ Straide Friary `31 D2`

Bellavary, Co. Mayo. 13th century friary with a notable 15th century sculptured tomb in the church and other medieval tombs in the sacristy.
☎ 094 21207

⊞ Strokestown Park & Famine Museum `34 B2`

Strokestown, Co. Roscommon. Designed by Richard Cassells for the Mahon family, Strokestown Park House is a restored 18th century neo Palladian mansion and most of its original furnishings and family possessions have been retained. The grounds include the longest herbaceous border in Ireland, rose garden, large ornamental lily pond, Georgian peach house and vinery and a 17th century tower. The Famine Museum is housed in the former stable yards and has an extensive collection of estate documents including letters and pleas written by the tenants. Major Denis Mahon, landlord of Strokestown during that period, was assassinated after he had tried to clear two thirds of his destitute tenants from the estate.
☎ 078 33712 www.strokestownpark.ie

⌂ Teach an Phiarsaigh (Patrick Pearse's Cottage) `36 B2`

Ros Muc, Co. Galway. Patrick Pearse (1879 – 1916) was a teacher, statesman and nationalist. He was one of the leaders of the 1916 Easter Rising and he used this small cottage as a summer residence. Although the interior was burned during the War of Independence, the thatched cottage has been restored to how it would have been in Pearse's day and contains memorabilia and an exhibition.
☎ 091 574292 www.heritageireland.ie

🏛 Teach Dúchais Folk Museum `33 D3`

Drumeela, Carrigallen, Co. Leitrim. With the aim of creating the atmosphere of days gone by, this small museum contains an original, traditional public bar with old bottles adorning the shelves and a kitchen with open fire, cooking utensils, settle bed and delph china. Farm implements and newspaper cuttings are among other items on display.
☎ 049 4333055

♜ Thoor Ballylee `38 A3`

Gort, Co. Galway. The 13th century Norman tower house of Ballylee Castle is the Thoor Ballylee of W.B.Yeats' poems. A charming ivy clad tower on the banks of a river, Ballylee was the summer home of Yeats and his family in the 1920s and was where he wrote a volume of poems entitled 'The Tower'. After he left in 1929 the tower became a ruin once more until its restoration as a Yeats' Museum in 1965. Close by is the partially restored 17th century Ballylee Mill.
☎ 091 631436

✝ Tuam Cathedral & Cross `38 A1`

Tuam, Co. Galway. Incorporating a 12th century chancel and 14th century cathedral, St Mary's Church of Ireland cathedral in Gothic revival style by Sir Thomas Dean in 1861. The 12th century decorated high cross in the cathedral commemorates the building of the first cathedral and the appointment of Tuam Hugh O'Hession as the first archbishop.
☎ 093 24141

✱ Tullyboy Farm `32 B3`

Tullyboy, Boyle, Co. Roscommon. A mixed family-run farm with dairy cows, deer, ostriches, horses and pigs and where displays of threshing and sheep-shearing are among the visitor attractions. Farm tours include bottle feeding lambs and hand milking cows, and demonstrations of butter churning and breadmaking in the old farmhouse kitchen. The small farmhouse museum gives an insight into how the Irish famine of the 1840s affected people in this area.
☎ 079 68031

♟ Turlough Round Tower `31 D3`

Turlough, Co. Mayo. Well preserved 9th century round tower standing 21m (70ft) high which was a fortified bell tower used by monks to protect themselves and their treasures in time of attack.
☎ 094 21207

✱ Turoe Pet Farm & Leisure Park `38 A2`

Bullaun, Loughrea, Co. Galway. Features rare animals and birds as well as more common farm animals and domestic fowl in a rural setting, with a nature trail around the farm. Old farm machinery is on display and there is a sheep wash in the river which runs through woodland. Other attractions include a pets' corner, two children's playgrounds and a football pitch.
☎ 091 841580

♟ Turoe Stone, The `38 A2`

Bullaun, Loughrea, Co. Galway. Standing 1m (3ft) high, this rounded Iron Age monument, dating from around 200BC, has curvilinear La Téne style Celtic decoration carved on the granite stone and may have been used for ritual purposes. It is located within the grounds of Turoe Pet Farm and Leisure Park.
☎ 091 841580

⊞ Westport House `31 C3`

Westport, Co. Mayo. The house, built around 1730, is by Dublin based architect Richard Cassells with additions by James Wyatt in 1778. Entered from the quay at Westport, the house is the home of the Marquess of Sligo (a descendent of Grace O'Malley) and contains an ornate dual marble staircase, family paintings and other portraits, antique silver and furniture and Waterford glass. The park has an ornamental lake, a small theme park, miniature zoo and boating, fishing and golf facilities.
☎ 098 25430 /27766

✱ Woodville Farm `32 B2`

Woodville, Sligo, Co. Sligo. Farm animals, including some rare breeds, live here in natural surroundings and there are guided walks round the historic farm buildings, across fields and through mature woodland. A farm museum is housed in 19th century horse stalls and visitors may collect free range eggs and feed pet lambs and donkeys.
☎ 071 62741

🏛 Yeats Memorial Building `32 B2`

Hyde Bridge, Sligo, Co. Sligo. The Yeats Society provides information here about the Nobel poet William Butler Yeats (1865 – 1939) whose work was influenced by the culture and landscape of the county of Sligo. Among items on display are original manuscript drafts of some of Yeats' poems and landscape photographs of Sligo. Also housed within the building is the Sligo Art Gallery which presents up to 20 major exhibitions each year.
☎ 071 42693/45847 www.yeats-sligo.com/ www.sligoartgallery.com

Leinster

Leinster (population 1,924,702) is the most densely populated of the four provinces and contains not only the present day capital of Ireland, Dublin, but also the ancient capital of Tara in the county of the ancient seat of the high kings, County Meath.

It comprises the counties of Carlow, Dublin, Kildare, Kilkenny, Laois, Longford, Louth, Meath, Offaly, Westmeath, Wexford and Wicklow.

The northern and central parts of the province are predominantly flat and the landscape is mainly given over to farmland though there are vast expanses of peat bog from which turf is still cut in the traditional way. In the centre, all roads lead to Dublin as do most of the visitors as it is here that most of the nightlife, culture and history of the province is centred.

Customs House, St Patrick's Festival, Dublin

Natural History Museum, Dublin

Map pages in this region

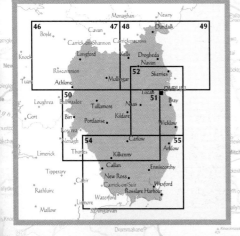

South East Regional Tourism
41 The Quay, Waterford
☎ *051 875823*   www.ireland-southeast.travel.ie

East Coast and Midlands Regional Tourism
Dublin Road, Mullingar, Westmeath
☎ *044 48761*   www.midlandseastireland.travel.ie

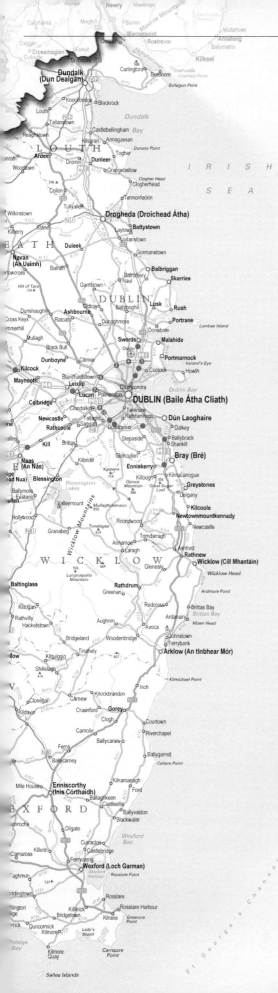

Clonmacnoise, Offaly

Ancient Monuments

Leinster is rich in ancient monuments and antiquities; Clonmacnoise is the remains of a monastic village on the banks of the Shannon, now in County Offaly, but in the Kingdom of Meath at the time of its construction in the 6th century; County Meath has the seat of the High Kings of Ireland at the Hill of Tara and also the enormous burial mounds of Newgrange, Knowth and Dowth, Four Knocks near Naul and the High Crosses at Kells; County Wicklow has the monastic village at Glendalough which is also in a magnificent setting at the foot of two lakes.

The K Club

Golf

Almost a quarter of all of the golf courses in the Republic of Ireland are within one hours travelling time of Dublin. Every variety of course is available from parkland to links and from championship to pitch & putt. The mild climate means that most courses are playable all the year round.

The K Club in County Kildare, designed by Arnold Palmer, will host the Ryder Cup in 2006, the first time it will have been held in Ireland.

Counties Wicklow & Wexford

The Wicklow Mountains are within easy reach of Dublin and as a consequence the area is frequently busy. However, once off the beaten track and onto the hill slopes, the crowds are soon left behind to be replaced by the wonderful isolation that is so often encountered in Ireland's mountains.

The southernmost county, Wexford, is rich with history being the closest to the mainland of Britain and also Europe and subsequently the first place of landing of any invaders. It is also the warmest and sunniest part of Ireland and enjoys large stretches of sandy beach along both its southern and eastern coastlines.

Glendalough, Wicklow

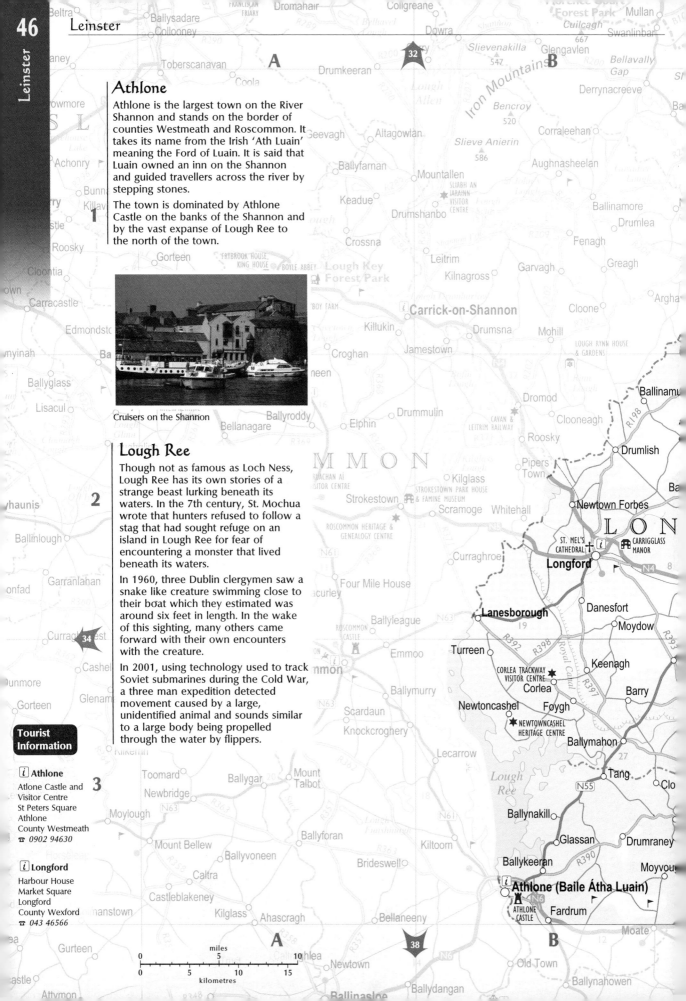

Athlone

Athlone is the largest town on the River Shannon and stands on the border of counties Westmeath and Roscommon. It takes its name from the Irish 'Ath Luain' meaning the Ford of Luain. It is said that Luain owned an inn on the Shannon and guided travellers across the river by stepping stones.

The town is dominated by Athlone Castle on the banks of the Shannon and by the vast expanse of Lough Ree to the north of the town.

Cruisers on the Shannon

Lough Ree

Though not as famous as Loch Ness, Lough Ree has its own stories of a strange beast lurking beneath its waters. In the 7th century, St. Mochua wrote that hunters refused to follow a stag that had sought refuge on an island in Lough Ree for fear of encountering a monster that lived beneath its waters.

In 1960, three Dublin clergymen saw a snake like creature swimming close to their boat which they estimated was around six feet in length. In the wake of this sighting, many others came forward with their own encounters with the creature.

In 2001, using technology used to track Soviet submarines during the Cold War, a three man expedition detected movement caused by a large, unidentified animal and sounds similar to a large body being propelled through the water by flippers.

Tourist Information

i **Athlone**

Atlone Castle and Visitor Centre
St Peters Square
Athlone
County Westmeath
☎ 0902 94630

i **Longford**

Harbour House
Market Square
Longford
County Wexford
☎ 043 46566

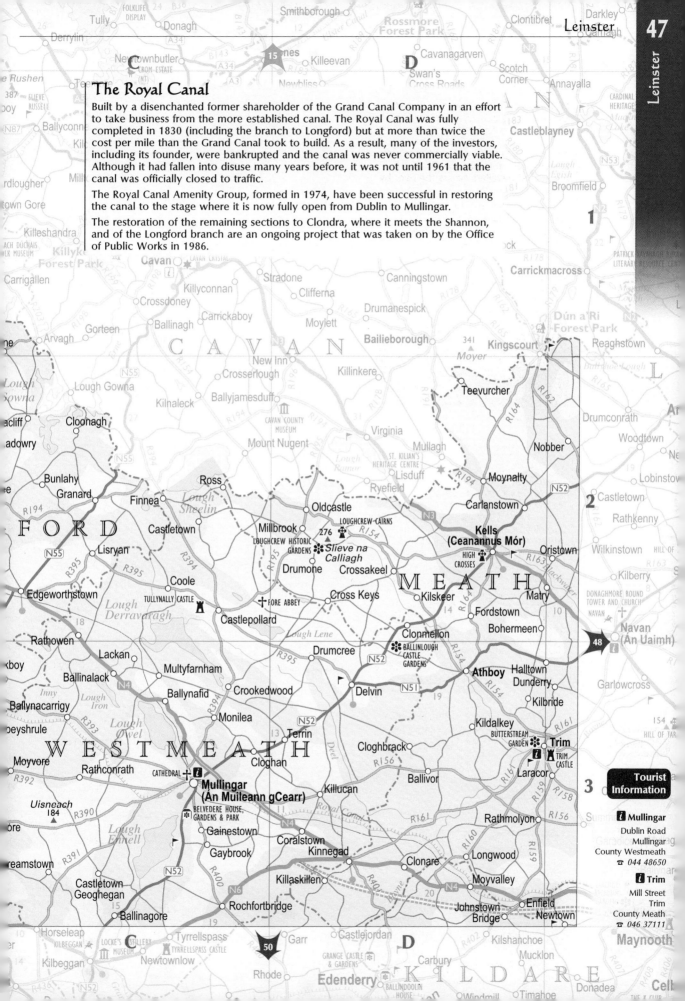

The Royal Canal

Built by a disenchanted former shareholder of the Grand Canal Company in an effort to take business from the more established canal. The Royal Canal was fully completed in 1830 (including the branch to Longford) but at more than twice the cost per mile than the Grand Canal took to build. As a result, many of the investors, including its founder, were bankrupted and the canal was never commercially viable. Although it had fallen into disuse many years before, it was not until 1961 that the canal was officially closed to traffic.

The Royal Canal Amenity Group, formed in 1974, have been successful in restoring the canal to the stage where it is now fully open from Dublin to Mullingar.

The restoration of the remaining sections to Clondra, where it meets the Shannon, and of the Longford branch are an ongoing project that was taken on by the Office of Public Works in 1986.

Tourist Information

Mullingar
Dublin Road
Mullingar
County Westmeath
☎ 044 48650

Trim
Mill Street
Trim
County Meath
☎ 046 37111

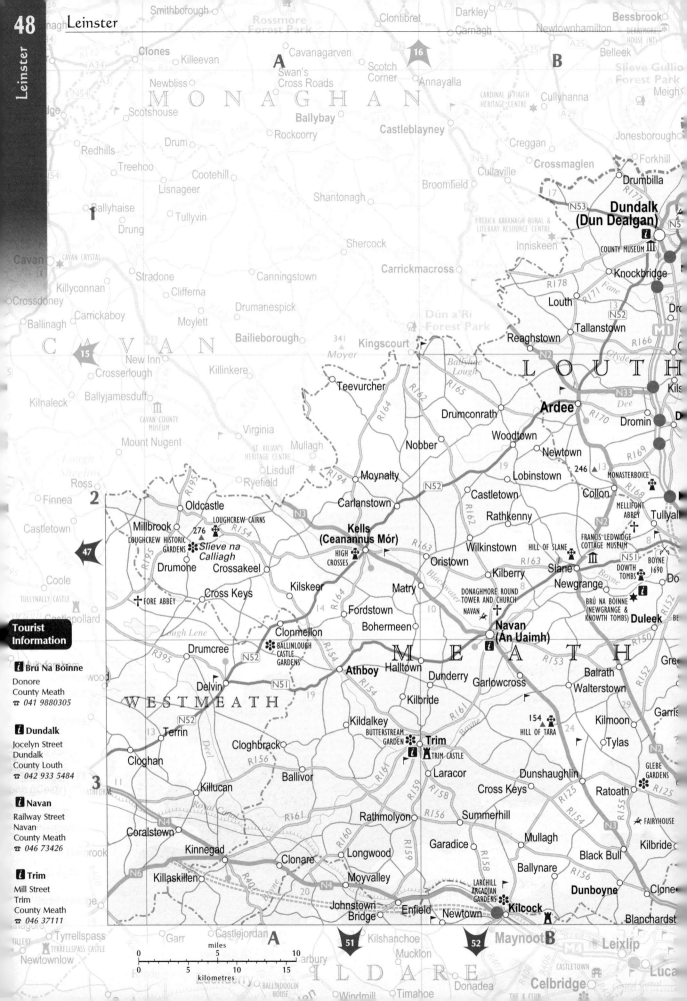

Hilltown
Newcastle
Forest Park
852

Newry
Mayobridge
MUSEUM & ARTS CENTRE
Mourne Mountains
Slieve Don 17
A2

BURREN HERITAGE CENTRE
Burren
Kilbroney Forest Park
SILENT VALLEY
Silent Valley Reservoir

Warrenpoint
Attica
CORN MILL
Mullartown
Annalong

Omeath
Rostrevor
ROSTREVOR OAKWOOD
Ballymartin

Carlingford Lough
R173
Ballymartin

Ravensdale
GREENCASTLE
Kilkeel

588
Carlingford
HOLY TRINITY HERITAGE CENTRE
KING JOHN'S CASTLE
Greencastle
Greencastle
Cranfield Point

Grange
Greenore

Rathcor
Bullagon Point

krock

Dundalk

Bay

I R I S H

ellingham

Annagassan

Dunany Point

Togher
Port

S E A

R166
Grangebellow

Clogher Head
Clogherhead

kenny
R166
Termonfeckin

R167
Baltray

Drogheda (Droichead Átha)
R150
MILLMOUNT MUSEUM
Bettystown

R108
Laytown

SONAIRTE NATIONAL ECOLOGY CENTRE
Julianstown

llewstown
N1
Gormanstown

Stamullen
Balbriggan

FOUR KNOCKS MEGALITHIC TOMB
Balrothery
Skerries

Naul
ARDGILLAN CASTLE
R127

Damastown
R128

DUBLIN
R127

Ballyboghil
LUSK HERITAGE CENTRE
Rush

bourne
Lusk
NEWBRIDGE HOUSE & FARM

hmore
R129
R126
Portrane
Lambay Island

R125
FRY MODEL RAILWAY
Donabate

Swords
N1
Malahide

GARET'S
MALAHIDE CASTLE
TALBOT BOTANIC GARDENS

Dublin
R107
Portmarnock

LY
4
3
PORTMARNOCK
Ireland's Eye
TLE
5
Coolock
Howth

O
R126
HOWTH CASTLE GARDENS

OENIX BOTANIC GARDENS
THE CAS
NATIONAL TRANSPORT
52

ston
Drumcondra
Ciontarf
WATERWAYS VISITOR CENTRE
Dublin Bay

DUBLIN (Baile Átha Cliath)

To Holyhead 3 hrs

The Royal County of Meath

So named because the Hill of Tara, south of Navan, was the seat of the High Kings of Ireland.

For centuries Meath included the area that is now County Westmeath and evidence of habitation by man has been found dating back 9000 years.

The fertility of the soil has made this an important farming area to the present day and it is only recently that the tourism potential has been realised. The Boyne Valley is not only beautiful in its own right but also contains a wealth of archaeological treasures including the Hills of Slane and Tara, the ancient tombs of Newgrange, Dowth and Knowth and Trim Castle.

Newgrange

1

2

3

Tourist Information

Birr
Castle Street
Birr
County Offaly
☎ 0509 20110

Clonmacnoise
County Offaly
☎ 0905 74134

Kilkenny
Shee Alms House
Rose Inn Street
Kilkenny
County Kilkenny
☎ 056 51500

Portlaoise
James Fintan Lawlor Avenue
Portlaoise
County Laois
☎ 0502 21178

Tullamore
Bury Quay
Tullamore
County Offaly
☎ 0506 52617

Clonmacnoise

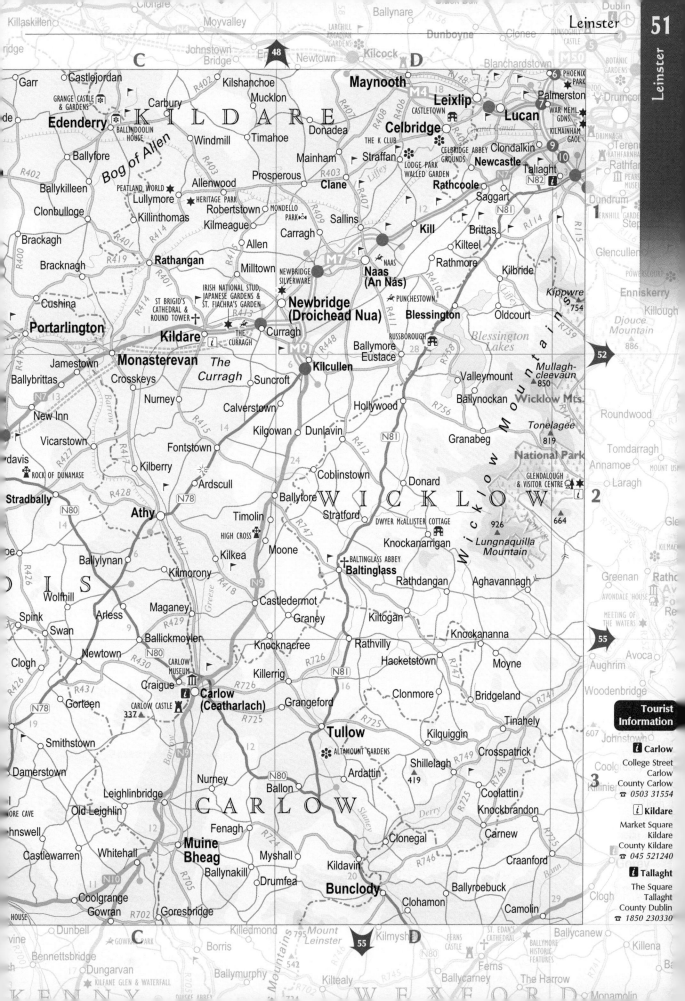

Leinster

MEATH

Halltown, Dunderry, Garlowcross, Kilbride, Bohermeen, Fordstown, Athboy, Matry, Kilberry, Newgrange, Donore, Laytown, Navan (An Uamh), Balrath, Walterstown, Kilmoon, Tylas, Ratoath, Dunshaughlin, Cross Keys, Laracor, Trim, Rathmolyon, Summerhill, Garadice, Mullagh, Ballynare, Black Bull, Kilbride, Clonee, Dunboyne, Enfield, Newtown, Kilcock, Maynooth, Mucklon

BUTTERSTREAM GARDEN, TRIM CASTLE, HILL OF TARA, GLEBE GARDENS, FAIRYHOUSE, LARCHILL ARCADIAN GARDENS

DUBLIN

Gormanstown, Stamullen, Balbriggan, Greenanstown, Ardcath, Balrothery, Skerries, Garristown, Naul, Damastown, Oldtown, Ballyboghil, Lusk, Rush, Ashbourne, Donaghmore, Swords, Donabate, Portrane, Malahide, St Margaret's, Dublin, Portmarnock, Coolock, Howth, Palmerston, Drumcondra, Clontarf, DUBLIN (Baile Átha Cliath), Phoenix Park, Zoo, Terenure, Rathfarnham, Stillorgan, Dún Laoghaire, Dalkey, Leopardstown, Ballybrack, Shankill, Bray (Bré)

FOUR KNOCKS MEGALITHIC TOMB, ARDGILLAN CASTLE, LUSK HERITAGE CENTRE, NEWBRIDGE HOUSE & FARM, Lambay Island, FRY MODEL RAILWAY, MALAHIDE CASTLE, TALBOT BOTANIC GARDENS, Ireland's Eye, HOWTH CASTLE GARDENS, NATIONAL TRANSPORT MUSEUM, Dublin Bay, THE CASINO, BOTANIC GARDENS, DUNSOGHLY CASTLE, WAR MEML GDNS, KILMAINHAM GAOL, DRIMNAGH, WATERWAYS VISITOR CENTRE, To Cherbourg, Douglas, Holyhead, Liverpool & Mostyn, To Holyhead, NATIONAL MARITIME MUSEUM, JAMES JOYCE TOWER & MUSEUM, DALKEY CASTLE & HERITAGE CENTRE, PEARSE MUSEUM, FERNHILL GARDENS, Stepaside, Glencullen, POWERSCOURT, BRAY HERITAGE CENTRE, NATIONAL SEA LIFE CENTRE, Enniskerry, KILLRUDDERY HOUSE & GARDENS, Kilmacanogue, Greystones, Delgany, NATIONAL GARDEN EXHIBITION CENTRE, Kilcoole

Leixlip, Lucan, Clondalkin, Newcastle, Tallaght, Rathcoole, Saggart, Brittas, Dundrum, Rathmines

KILDARE

Celbridge, Straffan, Clane, Mainham, Prosperous, Robertstown, Kilmeague, Carragh, Sallins, Kill, Kilteel, Rathmore, Kilbride, Naas (An Nás), Newbridge (Droichead Nua), Curragh, Kilcullen, Suncroft, Calverstown, Kilgowan, Dunlavin, Timahoe, Donadea, Timolin, Ballytore, Castledermot, Graney, Knocknacree, Rathvilly, Kiltogan

CASTLETOWN, THE K CLUB, CELBRIDGE ABBEY GROUNDS, LODGE PARK WALLED GARDEN, NEWBRIDGE SILVERWARE, MONDELLO PARK, PUNCHESTOWN, RUSSBOROUGH, Ballymore Eustace, Blessington, Oldcourt

WICKLOW

Valleymount, Ballynockan, Granabeg, Hollywood, Coblinstown, Donard, Stratford, Moone, Baltinglass, Rathdangan, Aghavannagh, Knockanarrigan, Blessington Lakes, Kippwre 754, Djouce Mountain 886, Great Sugar Loaf 506, Mullaghcleevaun 850, Wicklow Mts., Tonelagee 819, Lungnaquilla Mountain 926, 664, National Park, GLENDALOUGH & VISITOR CENTRE, DWYER McALLISTER COTTAGE, HIGH CROSS, BALTINGLASS ABBEY, Killough, Newtownmountkennedy, Roundwood, Tomdarragh, Annamoe, Laragh, Greenan, Redcross, Rathdrum, Rathnew, Glenealy, Wicklow (Cill Mhantáin), Kilbride, Ashford, MOUNT USHER GARDENS, Newcastle, Kilmacurragh, WICKLOW'S HISTORIC GAOL, AVONDALE HOUSE, Avondale Forest Park, MEETING OF THE WATERS, Brittas Bay, Wicklow Hd, Ardmore Point, Vartry Res, Mizen Hd, Ardanairy

miles 0 5 10
kilometres 0 5 10 15

Carlow (Ceatharlach)

Dublin (Population: 481,854)

Dublin, derived from the Irish 'Dubh Linn' meaning Black Pool, originated south of the River Liffey and it is here where most of the historic attractions can be found. The main shopping areas are around O'Connell Street and Grafton Street where street theatre is commonplace.

The Cultural Quarter of the Temple Bar area was first developed in the 19th century and is a collection of pubs, restaurants, music venues and the more alternative shops. It is now rejuvenated and would take several days to explore thoroughly.

There are numerous festivals – the Theatre Festival held in late September to mid October, the Film Festival in March, the Writers Festival in June, Art Ireland Exhibition in November – all of which inject even more life into the city.

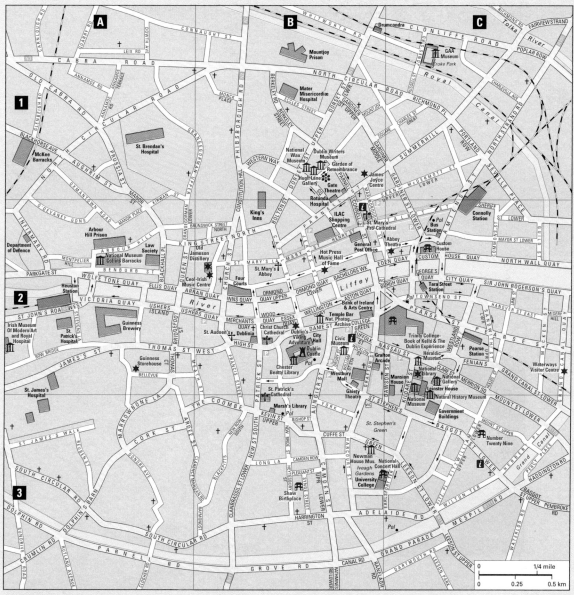

Index to street names

Tourist Information

Dublin Tourism
☎ 1850 230230
(from Rep of Ire)
☎ 08000 397 000
(from UK)

𝑖 O'Connell St

𝑖 Suffolk St

𝑖 Bord Failte
(Irish Tourist Board)
Baggot St Bridge
☎ 01 602 4000

LAOIS

Borris-In-Ossory
Aghaboe
Ballybrophy
ABBEYLEIX HERITAGE HOUSE
Abbeyleix
Wolfhill
Maganey
Knock
Newtown
Ballacolla
Clogh
Spink
Swan
Arless
Knocknacree

A 50 51 **B**

Errill
Donaghmore
WORKHOUSE MUSEUM
Rathdowney
Ballycolla
Durrow
Ballinakill
HEYWOOD GARDENS
Clogh
Newtown
Ballickmoyler
CARLOW MUSEUM
Craigue
Carlow (Ceatharlach)
Kille

Clonmore
Cappalinnan
Cullahill
Attanagh
R426
Gorteen
R431
CARLOW CASTLE
337

1

Templetuohy
Galmoy
Lisdowney
Castlecomer
Ballyragget
Smithstown
Damerstown
Leighlinbridge
Nurney
CAR

Crosspatrick
Johnstown
Freshford
Mohil
DUNMORE CAVE
Johnswell
Old Leighlin
Whitehall
Fenagh
Muine Bheag
Ballynakill

Urlingford
Tubbrid
Sieveardagh Hills
LORY MEAGHER HERITAGE CENTRE
Kilkenny (Cill Chainnigh)
Castlewarren
Coolgrange
R702
Goresbridge
Killedmo

Twomileborris
Tullaroan
KILKENNY CASTLE
ST. CANICE'S CATHEDRAL
ROTHE HOUSE
Dunbell
Gowran
GOWRAN PARK
Borris

Littleton
Ballycallan
Grevine
Bennettsbridge
Dungarvan
Ballymurphy

New Birmingham
Kilmanagh
Grange
Burnchurch
KILFANE GLEN & WATERFALL
DUISKE ABBEY

RARY
Ballingarry
Ballymack
KILKENNY
R703
Graiguenamanagh

Ballynunty
Killenaule
Callan
Kells
Stoneyford
MOUNT JULIET
Thomastown
519
Glynn

Ballinure
Dually
Drangan
Mullinahone
KELLS PRIORY
Dunnamaggan
JERPOINT ABBEY
Brandon Hill
WOODSTOCK GARDENS
Inistioge
Drummin

2

Fethard
Killamerry
Knocktopher
Newmarket
Ballyhale
Coolroebeg

Rosegreen
Cloneen
Windgap
R701
Kilmaganny
Boolyglass
Listerlin
Tullogher
BERKELEY COSTUME & TOY MUSEUM

Poulnamucky
Ahenny
AHENNY HIGH CROSSES
Lukeswell
Rosbercon
DUNBRODY SHIP
New Ross
BALLYLANE FARM

i **Carlow**
College Street
Carlow
County Carlow
☎ 0503 31554

i **Hook Head**
Fethard
County Wexford
☎ 051 397502

i **Kilkenny**
Shee Alms House
Rose Inn Street
Kilkenny
County Kilkenny
☎ 056 51500

i **New Ross**
The Quay
New Ross
County Waxford
☎ 051 421857

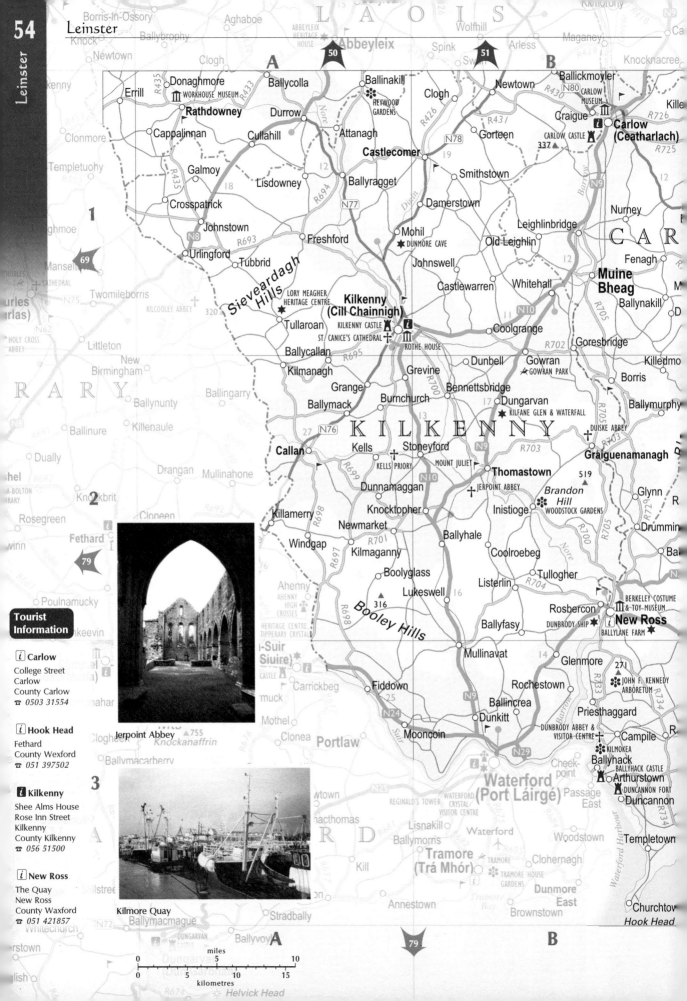

Jerpoint Abbey

Kilmore Quay

HERITAGE CENTRE, TIPPERARY CRYSTAL
(Suir Siuire)
Booley Hills
316
Ballyfasy
Mullinavat
Glenmore
271
JOHN F. KENNEDY ARBORETUM

3

Knockanaffrin 755
Clonea
Portlaw
Fiddown
Rochestown
Priesthaggard
Campile

Mothel
Dunkitt
Ballincrea
DUNBRODY ABBEY & VISITOR-CENTRE
KILMOKEA
Ballyhack
BALLYHACK CASTLE

Ballymacarberry
Mooncoin
N29
Waterford (Port Láirge)
Passage East
Arthurstown
DUNCANNON FORT
Duncannon

Lisnakill
Ballymorris
Waterford
Woodstown
Templetown

REGINALD'S TOWER
WATERFORD CRYSTAL VISITOR CENTRE
Tramore (Trá Mhór)
Clohernagh
Dunmore East

Cheekpoint

Annestown
Brownstown
Churchtow
Hook Head

Stradbally
Ballymacmague

DUNGARVAN CASTLE
Ballyvoy

A 79 **B**

miles
0   5   10

0   5   10   15
kilometres

Helvick Head

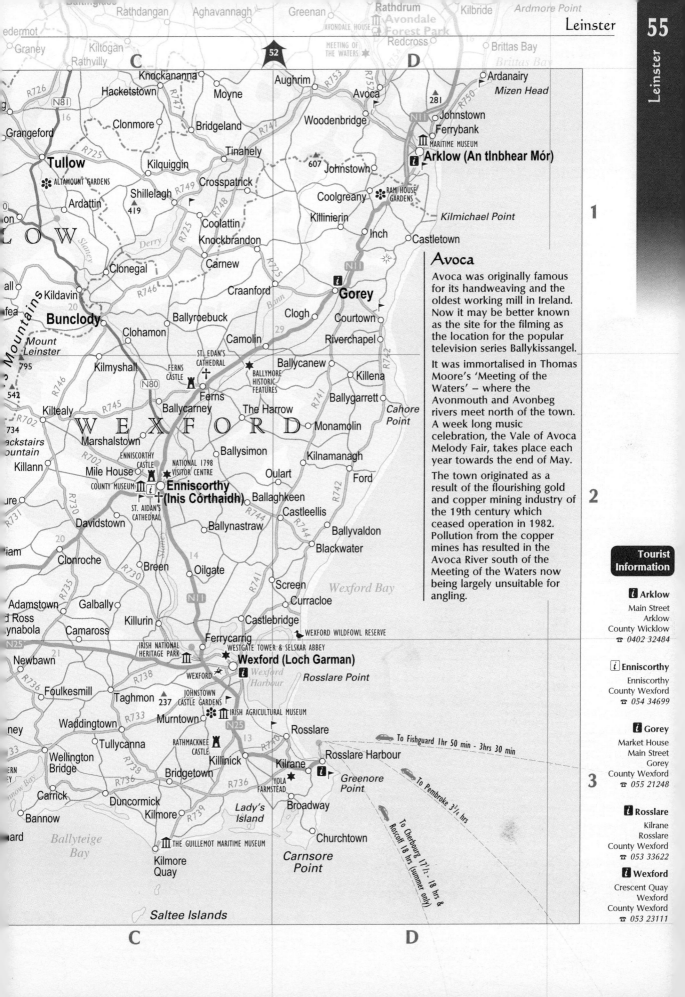

Avoca

Avoca was originally famous for its handweaving and the oldest working mill in Ireland. Now it may be better known as the site for the filming as the location for the popular television series Ballykissangel.

It was immortalised in Thomas Moore's 'Meeting of the Waters' – where the Avonmouth and Avonbeg rivers meet north of the town. A week long music celebration, the Vale of Avoca Melody Fair, takes place each year towards the end of May.

The town originated as a result of the flourishing gold and copper mining industry of the 19th century which ceased operation in 1982. Pollution from the copper mines has resulted in the Avoca River south of the Meeting of the Waters now being largely unsuitable for angling.

Tourist Information

ℹ Arklow
Main Street
Arklow
County Wicklow
☎ 0402 32484

ℹ Enniscorthy
Enniscorthy
County Wexford
☎ 054 34699

ℹ Gorey
Market House
Main Street
Gorey
County Wexford
☎ 055 21248

ℹ Rosslare
Kilrane
Rosslare
County Wexford
☎ 053 33622

ℹ Wexford
Crescent Quay
Wexford
County Wexford
☎ 053 23111

✷ Abbey Theatre `53 C2`
26 Lower Abbey Street, Dublin, Co. Dublin. Ireland's National Theatre, founded by Lady Gregory and W.B. Yeats in 1904. The Abbey quickly became world renowned, staging plays by J.M. Synge and Sean O'Casey, and played a significant role in the renaissance of Irish culture. The present theatre was built in 1966 to replace the previous building which had been destroyed by fire. The Abbey stages classic Irish plays, while the Peacock theatre downstairs presents new and experimental drama.
☎ 01 887 2200   www.abbeytheatre.ie

🏛 Abbeyleix Heritage House `50 B2`
Abbeyleix, Co. Laois. Abbeyleix Heritage House is located in a restored 1884 school building in the village of Abbeyleix. It tells the story of the village, which was built by the de Vesci family in the mid 1700s, as well as explaining much of the history of the county. The interior of the Abbeyleix carpet factory, which made carpets for the Titanic ship, has also been re-created here.
☎ 0502 31653

❀ Altamont Gardens `51 D3`
Tullow, Co. Carlow. Altamont Gardens contain trees planted in the mid 18th century, plus many exotic and native shrubs and trees planted since. The 40ha (100 acre) estate was inherited by Corona North in 1983, who restored and developed the gardens to their present splendid state. They include a formal garden adjacent to the house, a man made lake excavated in 1845, surrounded by rhododendrons and magnolias, a wild garden and an ice age glen with walks alongside the River Slaney. The gardens are now managed by Duchas.
☎ 0503 59444

🏛 An Dún Transport & Heritage Museum `50 A1`
Doon, Ballinahown, Athlone, Co. Offaly. Vintage, post war and classic cars, trucks, bikes and tractors are on display here. Other exhibits include restored agricultural machinery, household utensils, industrial artefacts and horse drawn transport. There is also a model railway and cable car display, with a buyers corner.
☎ 0902 30106

✾ Ardgillan Castle `52 B1`
Balbriggan, Co. Dublin. Dating from 1738, this restored country manor house with 'castellations' includes a permanent exhibition of the Down Survey colour maps and text of 1658. The gardens comprise a formal garden, which has been restored to the layout of 1865 and a 1ha (2 acre) walled garden, an Irish garden and a 20 alcove free standing fruit wall.
☎ 01 849 2212

🏛 Arklow Maritime Museum `55 D1`
St Mary's Road, Arklow, Co. Wicklow. There has been a permanent port at Arklow since Viking times and, by the 20th century, Arklow was the premier fishing port of Ireland. The museum displays the port's maritime history, especially boat building, fishing and its life boat traditions. There are photographs from the mid 19th century, a working model of the wheelhouse controls of a trawler and models of vessels built in Arklow, including one of Gypsy Moth III.
☎ 0402 32868

♖ Athlone Castle `46 B3`
St Peter's Square, Athlone, Co. Westmeath. Built at a strategic fording point on the River Shannon, this 13th century castle has seen much action over the centuries, especially during the Cromwellian and Jacobite wars of the 17th century. It now contains exhibitions and presentations including the military history and Siege of Athlone and the history and ecology of the River Shannon.
☎ 0902 92912

🏛 Avondale House & Forest Park `52 B3`
Rathdrum, Co. Wicklow. Avondale House was built in 1777 and is a museum dedicated to the memory of one of Ireland's most famous political leaders, Charles Stewart Parnell, who was born here. The Estate is 200ha (494 acres), bordering the west bank of the Avonmore river. It contains miles of forest trails through a great variety of tree species, some of which are as old as the house.
☎ 0404 46111

♖ Ballaghmore Castle `50 B2`
Dublin Road, Borris-in-Ossory, Co. Laois. Originally built by the Gaelic Chieftan MacGoillaphadraig (changed to Fitzpatrick by order of Henry VIII) in the late 15th century, Ballaghmore Castle was partially destroyed by the armies of Oliver Cromwell in the mid 1600s. The castle was restored in 1836 but was not lived in and was used as a granary, after which it fell into disuse until the present owners bought and restored it in 1990.
☎ 0505 21453   www.castleballaghmore.com

▦ Ballindoolin House & Garden `51 C1`
Edenderry, Co. Offaly. The Georgian house was built in the early 1820s and contains original features, along with some unique furniture which was specifically designed for the house. The 1ha (2 acre) 19th century walled garden has been restored to include a working kitchen garden which supplies the restaurant. The rest of the gardens comprise of 200 year old trees, a Victorian rockery, many flowers and shrubs and woodland containing a nature trail, a tree folklore trail a limekiln and an iron age mound.
☎ 0405 31430   www.ballindoolin.com

❀ Ballinlough Castle Gardens `47 D3`
Clonmellon, Co. Westmeath. These restored gardens contain a 1.2ha (3 acre) walled garden which includes an orchard, lily pond, rose garden and herbaceous borders. There are walks through woodland, around the lakes and through a Water Garden which has an 18th century 'Rockbridge' and summerhouse.
☎ 046 33135

♖ Ballyhack Castle `54 B3`
Ballyhack, Co. Wexford. Overlooking Waterford Estuary, this tower house castle is thought to have been built by the Knights Hospitallers of St John in 1450. Some of the building has been renovated to contain a small museum.
☎ 051 389468

✷ Ballylane Visitor Farm `54 B2`
New Ross, Co. Wexford. This is a 60ha (150 acre) working farm with a 1.5 hour walk, safe for children, through fields of crops and farm animals, a nature reserve, woods, ponds and historical artefacts. There is a visitor centre, restaurant, and play area.
☎ 051 425666

🏛 Ballymore Historic Features `55 C2`
Ballymore, Carolin, Co. Wexford. This museum is located in several buildings on a large family farm. There is a 1798 Exhibition, a 'Family' museum (the Donovans have lived here for 300 years) which includes old farm accounts, a picture gallery and a display of old farm equipment. Other features on the farmland which can be visited include an old church, a holy well, a mill pond and a Norman motte.
☎ 054 83189

✝ Baltinglass Abbey `51 D2`
Baltinglass, Co. Wicklow. Dermot McMurrough, King of Leinster founded this Cistercian Abbey in 1148, on the banks of the River Slaney just north of the town. The 12th century remains include a run of beautiful Gothic arches along the nave, supported on alternate round and square decorated pillars. The fragments of cloisters and church are from this period, as are the three west windows and a doorway on the south side of the cloister. The Abbey ceased to be a monastery in the 16th century. The tower was erected in the middle ages but replaced with a Gothic style one in the 19th century.
☎ 0404 69117

⚔ Battle of the Boyne `48 B2`
Obelisk Centre, Drybridge, Drogheda, Co. Louth. This famous battle took place on the 1st July 1690, between James II of Ireland and William of Orange, King of England, at Oldgrange near Drogheda on the banks of the River Boyne. The site of the battle can be seen from a viewing point accessed by some steps opposite the Tullyallen turn off the N51. Today, the battle is recalled on the 12th of July, as eleven days were lost when the change was made to the Gregorian calendar.
☎ 041 984 1644

🐎 Bellewstown Racecourse `48 B2`
Bellewstown, Co. Meath. Bellewstown has an annual three day meeting with a carnival-like atmosphere. Flat and National Hunt racing.
☎ 01 289 2888

✾ Belvedere House, Gardens & Park `47 C3`
Mullingar, Co. Westmeath. Belvedere House was the 18th century home of Robert Rochfort, Earl of Belvedere. It has been beautifully restored and is open to the public. The Estate covers 65ha (160 acres) on the shores of Lough Ennell and includes a walled garden and several follies – the 'Jealous Wall' is the largest man-made folly in Ireland. The visitor centre tells the story of the cruel imprisonment of the Earl's second wife and the scandalous seduction of Lady Cloncurry.
☎ 044 49060   www.belvedere-house.ie

🏛 Berkeley Costume & Toy Museum `54 B3`
New Ross, Co. Wexford. Housed in the property of George Berkeley is a collection of 18th and 19th century rare dolls, toys, embroidered textiles and toy carriages. The small but attractive garden can also be visited.
☎ 051 421361

❀ Birr Castle Demesne `50 A2`
Birr, Co. Offaly. Birr Castle has been occupied by the Parsons family since 1620 when Sir Laurence Parsons built most of the current building. Twice beseiged in the late 17th century, the Gothic façade was added in the 19th century. Although the castle is only occasionally opened to the public, the gardens are open daily and consist of a beautifully restored collection of trees and shrubs, the tallest box hedge in the world, and a kitchen garden, all set around a lake and waterfalls. An unusual feature is the case of the Great Telescope, built in the 1840s by the 3rd Earl of Rosse and the largest in the world until 1917.
☎ 0509 20336   www.birrcastle.com

✷ Bray Heritage Centre `52 B2`
Old Courthouse, Lower Main Street, Bray, Co. Wicklow. This Old Court House, originally built in 1841, now houses a permanent exhibition on the history of the town. Downstairs is a re-creation of the insides of 12th century Bray Castle, whilst upstairs is a railway theme, commemorating the work of the engineer William Dargan.
☎ 01 286 7128

**✷ Brú na Bóinne Visitor Centre
(Knowth & Newgrange Tombs)** `48 B2`
Donore, Drogheda, Co. Meath. Access to the Newgrange and Knowth tombs, both World Heritage Sites, is by guided tour from the Visitor Centre only. The Centre includes a full size replica of the chamber at Newgrange, which is naturally lit by the sun during the Winter Solstice, a time so popular that bookings need to be made in advance.
☎ 041 988 0300/982 4488   www.knowth.com

❀ Butterstream Garden `48 B3`
Trim, Co. Meath. This inspiring 1ha (2.5 acres) garden was started in the 1970s by the owner, Jim Reynolds. It is a remarkable achievement in the best traditions of the Vita Sackville-West principle of 'the strictest formality of design, with the maximum informality in planting'. Hedges of yew, beech and thorn enclose different but interlinked areas containing a rose garden, a wild garden, a pool garden, an herbaceous garden and many others.
☎ 046 36017

♖ Carlow Castle `51 C3`
Carlow, Co. Carlow. This Norman castle was built in 1208 by William Marshall, Earl of Pembroke. Half the keep still remains but originally there would have been outer curtain walls, perhaps two towered gate buildings with other associated towers and buildings, with a basement and a great hall on the first floor.
☎ 0503 31554

🏛 Carlow Museum   `51 C3`

Town Hall, Carlow, Co. Carlow. Currently located in the Town Hall, this museum is run by the old Carlow Society. Exhibits of 19th and early 20th century domestic and commercial life in the Carlow area, are imaginatively displayed in shop layouts.
☎ 0503 40730

⊞ Carrigglas Manor   `46 B2`

Longford, Co. Longford. The original Manor was built in the early 1600s. In 1837 it was rebuilt for the French Huguenot Lefroy family by the architect Daniel Robertson, who added the Tudor Gothic turrets in the early romantic style, which can still be seen today. The Lefroy family are still in residence and give guided tours of the house, which includes a collection of Waterford crystal as well as period furniture, paintings and artefacts. There is also a 263ha (650 acre) estate, stableyards built in 1790 and a Robinsonian style woodland and water garden.
☎ 043 45165

⊞ Casino, The   `52 B2`

Malahide Road, Marino, Dublin, Co. Dublin. A miniature 18th century neo-classical masterpiece designed by Sir William Chambers. Casino means 'small house'. It is a compact building containing 16 rooms, with many interesting architectural features. The interior circular hall, ringed by columns, is crowned by a coffered dome. The graceful roof urns disguise chimneys while the columns conceal drainpipes.
☎ 01 833 1618

⊞ Castletown   `51 D1`

Celbridge, Co. Kildare. Just outside the Liffeyside village of Celbridge, Castletown, built in 1722 for the Speaker of the Irish House of Commons, William Connolly, is perhaps the largest private house in Ireland. Consisting of a central block flanked by colonnades, Castletown was designed by the Florentine, Alessandro Galilei, and Edward Pearce, architect of the Dublin Parliament. The house has been restored through the work of the Irish Georgian Society.
☎ 01 628 8252

❋ Celbridge Abbey Grounds   `51 D1`

Clane Road, Celbridge, Co. Kildare. The abbey was built in 1697 by Bartholomew Van Homrigh. His daughter Vanessa planted the grounds, which are situated on the rivers Liffey and Millrace, for her friend Jonathan Swift. The St John of God Order are developing the grounds for the public to enjoy; they include a garden centre, model railway, tea rooms, theme walks, children's playground, crafts and gifts and woodland gardens.
☎ 01 627 5508

✹ Ceol, Irish Traditional Music Centre   `53 B2`

Smithfield Village, Dublin, Co. Dublin. An interactive museum which explores and celebrates the history and personalities of traditional Irish music, song and dance. Ceol – the Irish word for music – shows how important traditional music has been to the cultural life of Ireland, and its relevance to the social and political history of the country. Among the displays are musical instruments of the Irish tradition including Uilleann pipe, fiddle, flute, and button accordion. The highlight of the centre is a film about present day musicians from various parts of Ireland, shown in a 180 degree widescreen auditorium. There is also a dedicated area for children to experience and enjoy Irish Music
☎ 01 817 3820   www.ceol.ie

⚔ Charleville Castle   `50 B1`

Tullamore, Co. Offaly. Built in the late 18th century, this is regarded as the finest neo-Gothic house in Ireland. It has many turrets and spires along with 55 rooms and a gallery which runs the full length of the building. The 12ha (30 acres) of grounds include a medieval grotto, an oak tree reputed to be 700 years old and five avenues flanked with Irish Yews radiating from the house.
☎ 0506 23040

🏛 Chester Beatty Library   `53 B2`

The Clock Tower Building, Dublin Castle, Dublin, Co. Dublin. Reopened in 2000 in a purpose designed home in the Clock Tower building of Dublin Castle, the library is a treasure of manuscripts, books, prints and textiles collected by American scholar Sir Alfred Chester Beatty. It has some of the rarest original manuscripts still in existence. With many Early Christian papyri, the library is a major resource for the study of the Old and New Testaments.
☎ 01 407 0750   www.cbl.ie

✝ Christ Church Cathedral   `53 B2`

Christchurch Place, Dublin, Co. Dublin. The Cathedral was established by Strongbow and Archbishop Laurence O'Toole in 1173 on the site of the cathedral founded around 1030 by the Norse King Sitric Silkenbeard. Lambert Simnel, pretender to the English throne, was crowned here as Edward VI in 1487. It was extensively restored between 1871 – 78 by George Edmund Street and is one of the best examples in Ireland of early Gothic architecture. The medieval crypt is one of the oldest and largest in Ireland.
☎ 01 677 8099   www.cccdub.ie

⚔ Cloghan Castle   `50 A1`

Banagher, Co. Offaly. Cloghan Castle consists of a well-preserved tower and 17th century bawn where there is a plaque in memory of those members of the Boleyn family exiled here after the execution of Anne Boleyn, wife of Henry VIII.
☎ 0509 51650   www.cloghancastleoffaly.com

✝ Clonmacnoise   `50 A1`

Shannonbridge, Co. Offaly. The remains of one of Ireland's first and most holy monasteries sit on a ridge on the banks of the Shannon. Founded in 545 by St Kiaran, a few months before his death, his tomb became an object of pilgrimage and the monastery grew to become a centre of Irish art and literature. Clonmacnoise has endured many fires and numerous pillagings by Irish, Viking and English. The remains consist of two fine High Crosses, 400 memorial slabs from the 8th, 9th and 10th centuries, two Round Towers and eight churches. The 10th century West cross, with its frieze depicting St Kiaran and the local king from whom he obtained the monastery land, and the magnificently carved doorway of the Cathedral church are of particular interest.
☎ 0905 74195

✹ Clonmacnoise & West Offaly Railway   `50 A1`

Blackwater Works, Shannonbridge, Co. Offaly. This train runs on a 9 km (5.5 mile) circular route through Blackwater Raised Bog. On the guided tour learn about the 6000 year old bog oaks and the past, present and future of the area, in terms of industry and ecology. There is a stop to see traditional turf cutting methods.
☎ 0905 74114

✹ Corlea Trackway Visitor Centre   `46 B3`

Kenagh, Co. Longford. This Visitor Centre is built on a raised bog and houses an 18m (58ft) section of the largest Iron Age Oak Bog Road in Europe. It has been dated to 148BC and is preserved in the Centre in climatically controlled conditions. A display tells its story. The road continues in the surrounding bog which is being conserved by Bord na Mona and the Heritage Service to make sure it remains wet.
☎ 043 22386

🏇 Curragh Racecourse, The   `51 C1`

The Curragh, Kildare, Co. Kildare. The headquarters of Irish Flat Racing, this 3.2km (2 mile) course hosts meetings between March and November, almost every fortnight. Classic races include the 1000 Guineas and the 2000 Guineas in May, followed by The Derby, The Oaks and the St Leger.
☎ 045 441205/441105   www.curragh.ie

⊞ Custom House   `53 C2`

Custom House Quay, Dublin, Co. Dublin. An architectural masterpiece designed by James Gandon and completed in 1791. Exhibits relate to James Gandon and the history of the Custom House itself, with illustrations of how the building was restored after it was gutted by fire in 1921. The building is best viewed from the south bank of the River Liffey.
☎ 01 878 7660

⚔ Dalkey Castle & Heritage Centre   `52 B2`

Castle Street, Dalkey, Co. Dublin. This 15th century castle with its battlements, turrets and garderobe even includes a murder hole! It has been restored to include a heritage centre, showing the development of the town from medieval to Victorian times. There is also information on notables such as Shaw and Joyce, and modern day writers who live in this area. The centre frequently houses exhibitions of art and crafts from the best artists in Ireland.
☎ 01 285 8366

✝ Donaghmore Round Tower & Church   `48 B2`

Navan, Co. Meath. The Round Tower is probably 10th century and in good condition, having been restored in the 19th century. The ruined 15th century church is built on the site of an earlier structure, where St Patrick is said to have founded the first monastery, leaving it the care of his disciple St Cassanus.
☎ 041 988 0305

⚰ Dowth Tomb   `48 B2`

Dowth, Co. Meath. This passage tomb is thought to have been built around 5000 years ago and is the oldest of its type in the Boyne Valley. Although much plundered and damaged over the centuries, the mound is still impressive, being about 85m (290ft) in diameter and 15m (49ft) high. It contains two prehistoric tombs and an early Christian chamber. The name 'Dowth' translates as 'darkness' and the main chamber faces the setting sun. At the winter solstice, the rays of the sun shine into the tomb..
☎ 041 988 0300/982 4488   www.knowth.com/dowth.htm

⚔ Drimnagh Castle   `52 B2`

Long Mile Road, Drimnagh, Dublin, Co. Dublin. Ireland's only castle with a flooded moat. This Norman castle has a fully restored Great Hall, medieval undercroft and 17th century style formal garden.
☎ 01 450 2530

⚔ Dublin Castle   `53 B2`

Dame Street, Dublin, Co. Dublin. Originally built between 1204 – 1228, the Record Tower is the principal remnant of the 13th century Anglo-Norman fortress and has walls 5m (16ft) thick but what remains today is largely the result of 18th and 19th century re-building. The 15th century Bermingham Tower was once the state prison and was rebuilt in the 18th century. Within the State Apartments are the magnificent throne room and St Patrick's Hall, 25m (82ft) long with a high panelled and decorated ceiling which are now used for Presidential Inaugurations and state receptions. In the undercroft can be seen the remains of a Viking fortress and parts of the original moat and old city walls.
☎ 01 677 7129

🏛 Dublin Civic Museum   `53 B2`

58 South William Street, Dublin, Co. Dublin. Housed in the former Georgian City Assembly House, the museum illustrates the history of Dublin and has a large collection of maps, prints and newspapers. Among the artefacts is the head of the statue of Lord Nelson, blown off its pillar in O'Connell Street in an IRA explosion in 1966.
☎ 01 679 4260

🏛 Dublin Writer's Museum   `53 B1`

18 Parnell Square North, Dublin, Co. Dublin. Tracing the history of Irish literature from its earliest times to the 20th century. Writers and playwrights including Jonathan Swift, George Bernard Shaw, Oscar Wilde, W.B. Yeats, James Joyce and Samuel Beckett are brought to life through personal items, portraits, their books and letters. There is also a room dedicated to children's authors. The museum is housed in a restored 18th century Georgian mansion with decorative stained-glass windows and ornate plaster-work.
☎ 01 872 2077

Ⓨ Dublin Zoo   `52 B2`

Phoenix Park, Dublin, Co. Dublin. The Zoo is well known for its captive-breeding programme and is committed to the conservation and protection of endangered species. The zoo doubled in size in 2000 and an African Plains area has been developed providing greater space and freedom for giraffe, hippo, rhino and other African animals and birds. Other attractions include a zoo train, discovery centre, and 'meet the keeper' programme.
☎ 01 677 1425   www.dublinzoo.ie

✷ **Dvblinia** `53 B2`

Christ Church, Dublin, Co. Dublin. A multimedia re-creation of Dublin life in medieval times from the Anglo-Norman arrival in 1170 to the dissolution of the monasteries in 1540. There is a scale model of the medieval city, a life size reconstruction of a merchant's house and numerous Viking and Norman artefacts from excavations at nearby Wood Quay. The building is the old Synod Hall and is linked to Christ Church Cathedral by an ornate Victorian pedestrian bridge which spans the road.

☎ 01 679 4611   www.dublinia.ie

✷ **Dublin's Viking Adventure** `53 B2`

Essex West Street, Temple Bar, Dublin, Co. Dublin. A reconstruction of the sights, sounds and smells of life in Viking Dublin 1000 years ago, along with a fascinating exhibition of artefacts discovered in the area. A guide leads visitors through the narrow streets of the Viking town of Dyflin to observe daily life and work.

☎ 01 679 6040

✝ **Duiske Abbey** `54 B2`

Graignamanagh, Co. Kilkenny. Built at the start of the 13th century, this Cistercian Abbey was the largest of its kind in Ireland. Restored in the late 1970s, it contains exhibitions of local artefacts, contemporary Christian art and a large carved Norman knight. In the grounds there are two crosses, dating from the 8th and 9th centuries. The Abbey takes its name from the local river Duiske, which means 'Black Water'. Guided tours are available on request.

☎ 0503 24238

✝ **Dunbrody Abbey & Visitor Centre** `54 B3`

Dunbrody Park, Arthurstown, Co. Wexford. The ruins of this Cistercian Monastery date back to the late 12th century and are reputedly the finest example of medieval architecture in the county. The visitor centre includes a small museum with a dolls house. There is also a hedge maze, golf pitch and putt and a craft gallery.

☎ 051 388603

✷ **Dunbrody Ship** `54 B3`

New Ross, Co. Wexford. At the quayside in New Ross is a full scale sea-going replica of a three masted barque famine ship of the 19th century. Visitors can board the ship, explore it, and look through the huge database of passengers recorded as having sailed from Ireland during this time. An interactive exhibition shows shipboard life as it would have been 150 years ago and traces the success stories of families such as the Kennedys.

☎ 051 425239   www.dunbrody.com

🏰 **Duncannon Fort** `54 B3`

Duncannon, Co. Wexford. Located on a promontory in Waterford Harbour, this star shaped 16th century military fort is one of four in Ireland. Its purpose was to defend against an attack by the Spanish Armada. Of interest is the grisly story of the 'Croppy Boy', the dry moat and the massive exterior walls. It now houses an art gallery and studio, craft centre and marine museum.

☎ 051 389454

🏇 **Dundalk Racecourse** `48 B1`

Dowdallshill, Dundalk, Co. Louth. This one mile and two furlong course hosts both Flat and National Hunt racing.

☎ 042 933 4419

✷ **Dunmore Cave** `50 B3`

Ballyfoyle, Co. Kilkenny. These limestone caves contain magnificent calcite formations along almost a quarter of a mile of passageways. Many of these are now lit and stairs and walkways have been installed for visitors (guided tours). In 928AD, the cave was the site of a Viking massacre and the bones of 44 individuals have been identified. In late 1999, 43 silver and bronze artefacts dating to around 970AD were found by a tour guide in the caves. The caves are a National Monument and the visitor centre houses exhibitions and displays.

☎ 056 67726

🏰 **Dunsoghly Castle** `52 B1`

Dunsoghly, Co. Dublin. Dunsoghly Castle consists of a stately residential keep-like tower on three floors buttressed by rectangular corner turrets. It was built in the 15th century by Thomas Plunkett, Chief Justice of the King's Bench, whilst the nearby chapel was built in 1573 by Sir John Plunkett, also Chief Justice but for the Queen's Bench.

☎ 01 605 7755

🏠 **Dwyer McAllister Cottage** `51 D2`

Derrynamuck, Knockanarrigan, Co. Wicklow. This is an excellent example of a traditional thatched Irish cottage, built of local stone and now whitewashed outside and in. It was from here that the famous Irish rebel Michael Dwyer escaped from British troops in 1799.

☎ 0404 45325/45352

✺ **Emo Court & Gardens** `50 B2`

Emo, Co. Laois. Emo Court is a neo-classical style building designed by James Gandon for the Earl of Portarlington in 1790. Subsequently owned by the Jesuits, it was acquired by Mr. Cholmeley-Harrison in 1960 and extensively restored. The gardens contain formal lawns, parkland and woodland walks, with fine trees and shrubs, along with a 9ha (22 acre) lake and a 1.5km (1 mile) tree lined avenue dating from the late 19th century.

☎ 0502 26573

🏰 **Enniscorthy Castle** `55 C2`

Enniscorthy, Co. Wexford. This Norman castle is a well preserved example of its kind. In spite of several onslaughts and alterations in the 16th century, it retained its three distinctive round towers. Overlooking the Slaney River, in the centre of the town, it now houses the County Wexford Historical and Folk Museum. There are two rooms containing memorabilia from the 1798 and 1916 uprisings.

☎ 054 35926

🏇 **Fairyhouse Racecourse** `48 B3`

Ratoath, Co. Meath. Fairyhouse has hosted the Irish Grand National since the late 1900s. 19km (12 miles) north west of Dublin, there are frequent fixtures for both National Hunt and Flat Racing.

☎ 01 825 6167/8/9   www.fairyhouseracecourse.ie

✺ **Fernhill Gardens** `52 B2`

Sandyford, Co. Dublin. Overlooking Dublin Bay, these 16ha (40 acres) of gardens, laid out in a 'Robinsonian' style, contain many fine Himalayan trees and shrubs, spring bulbs, ferns and heathers, as well as a kitchen garden, water garden and numerous other features. The original layout was created in the mid 17th century.

☎ 01 295 6000

🏰 **Ferns Castle** `55 C2`

Ferns, Co. Wexford. Half of this Norman castle remains, with two towers and some curtain wall still standing, one of which contains a lovely circular chapel, several fireplaces and a vaulted basement.

☎ 054 34699

✝ **Fore Abbey** `47 C2`

Fore, Co. Westmeath. Originally built as a monastery in 630AD, by St Fechin, the remains seen today are of the nearby 13th century Benedictine priory, with 15th century fortifications. The ruins of the church of St Fechin are 11th and 13th century and above this is an anchorite's cell, occupied by hermits until the 17th century. Associated with these ruins are the 'Seven Wonders of Fore'.

☎ 044 48650

⚱ **Fourknocks Megalithic Tomb** `49 C3`

Naul, Co. Meath. Built around 5000 years ago, Fourknocks Passage Chamber Tomb contains a rare example of the image of a human face, just inside the entrance.

☎ 01 849 5208

🏛 **Francis Ledwidge Cottage Museum** `48 B2`

Janeville, Slane, Co. Meath. The local poet Francis Ledwidge was born in this labourer's cottage, at Janeville near Slane, in 1887. Before he was killed in the First World War in 1917, he wrote many poems, several of which are displayed in this museum.

☎ 041 9824544

✷ **Fry Model Railway** `52 B1`

Malahide Castle, Malahide, Co. Dublin. Covering 233 sq m (2500 sq ft) this is one of the world's largest working miniature railways. Besides the track, the railway has stations, bridges, trams, buses and barges and includes the Dublin landmarks of Heuston station and O'Connell Bridge. On display are the hand constructed models of Irish trains by Cyril Fry, draughtsman and railway engineer.

☎ 01 846 3779

🏛 **GAA Museum** `53 C1`

New Stand, Croke Park, Dublin, Co. Dublin. The Gaelic Athletic Association (GAA) is Ireland's largest sporting and cultural organisation and is dedicated to promoting the games of hurling, Gaelic football, handball, rounders and camogie. The museum is at Croke Park, home of Irish hurling and football, and traces the history of Gaelic sports and their place in Irish culture right up to the present day. Interactive exhibits allow visitors the chance to try out the skills of the games for themselves.

☎ 01 855 8176

✺ **Garden of Remembrance** `53 B1`

Parnell Square East, Dublin, Co. Dublin. The Garden of Remembrance, opened in 1966, is dedicated to all those who died in the cause of Irish Freedom. There is a sculpture by Oisín Kelly representing the Irish legend, Children of Lir.

☎ 01 874 3074

✺ **Glebe Gardens** `48 B3`

Ratoath, Co. Meath. There are two gardens here. 'Glebelands' was created in 1813 and consists of low retaining walls with mature native trees along the boundaries, all set in gently rolling countryside. 'Glebewood', influenced by Lutyens, was only constructed in 1990. It required much sculpting to reflect the characteristics of the older garden, and aims to create a relaxing and interesting atmosphere.

☎ 01 825 6015

✷ **Glendalough & Visitor Centre** `52 B3`

Glendalough, Bray, Co. Wicklow. Glendalough is a 6th century Christian monastic site founded by St Kevin. There are some interesting remains, namely the impressive 31m (100 ft) high round tower, several stone churches and decorated crosses. The Visitor Centre is set at the gateway to Glendalough Valley and the new national park. It contains a model of the site as it would have appeared in 1080 and an audiovisual presentation.

☎ 0404 45325/45352

🏇 **Gowran Park** `54 B2`

Mill Road, Gowran, Co. Kilkenny. This course is 13kms (8 miles) from Kilkenny. It hosts both Flat and National Hunt racing and is home to the Thyestes Chase, a Group 1 Steeplechase.

☎ 056 26120

🏠 **Grange Castle & Gardens** `51 C1`

Grange, Co. Kildare. Originally built as a Tower House by the Bermingham family in the late 15th century, ornamental battlements and Jacobean chimneys were added in the mid 17th century. The grounds contain many old trees including beech and oak. It is currently owned by the Tyrrell family who have granted a 99 year lease to the Tyrrell Trust for the continuing development of the site.

☎ 0405 33316   www.ils.ie/grange

🏛 Guillemot Maritime Museum, The `55 C3`
Kilmore Quay, Co. Wexford. The lightship Guillemot is the last Irish Lights Vessel. Now beached at Kilmore Quay, it contains all of its original features. Also on board are many interesting nautical artefacts, model ships and a collection of pictures. Both the Hook and Barrels lights can be seen from the deck, as well as excellent views of the Saltee Islands.
☎ 051 561144

✱ Guinness Storehouse `53 A2`
St James's Gate, Dublin, Co. Dublin. This attraction tells the story of Guinness from its beginnings in 1759, how it is made and the advertising campaigns used to make it internationally famous. Recently rehoused in St James's Gate Brewery, on six floors, the entrance is through a pint glass shaped atrium capable of holding 10,000 pints!
☎ 01 408 4800   www.guinnessstorehouse.com

🏛 Heraldic Museum `53 C2`
Kildare Street, Dublin, Co. Dublin. The first permanent Heraldic Museum in the world was set up in 1909 and moved to its present location in 1987. The development and application of heraldry is traced throughout Ireland and Europe.
☎ 01 603 0200

❊ Heywood Gardens `50 B2`
Ballinakill, Co. Laois. These gardens comprise parkland and interlinked elements designed by Sir Edwin Lutyens in the early 20th century. There is a formal lawn with herbaceous borders and several pools with associated features, such as a hidden pergola and a pavilion with planted terraces. Other planted areas are enclosed with yew hedges.
☎ 0502 33563/056 51863

✱ Hill of Slane `48 B2`
Slane, Co. Meath. This site is most famous for its 5th century legend. St Patrick lit a fire here at Easter, which was against the pagan law of the time, as the High King of Tara had decreed that no fire should be lit until the one on the Hill of Tara was ablaze. Luckily, St Patrick was able to convert the King to Christianity by daybreak. There are ruins of buildings from various dates here, including those of a 16th century church with a tower that can still be climbed; the views are magnificent.
☎ 041 988 0305

✝ Hill of Tara `48 B3`
Navan, Co. Meath. In the late stone age, a passage tomb was built here and later, an Iron age hill fort. It is best known, however, for being the seat of the legendary 'Kings of Ireland', reaching the height of its success with Cormac MacAirt in the third century. Its importance gradually declined with the coming of Christianity, although it was not finally abandoned until the 11th century. Excavations continue and there are guided tours and a visitor centre.
☎ 046 25903

✱ Holy Trinity Heritage Centre `49 C1`
Teach Eolais, Old Quay Lane, Carlingford, Co. Louth. The Heritage Centre is located in the Church of the Holy Trinity. It was restored in 1804 and has recently been refurbished to house an exhibition, including video presentations, showing how the town has developed from Norman times.
☎ 042 937 3454/3888

✱ Hot Press Irish Music Hall of Fame `53 B2`
Abbey Street Middle, Dublin, Co. Dublin. The Hall of Fame Tour is an interactive multimedia tour through the history of Irish music with particular emphasis on 20th century rock music. The building is also used as a concert venue.
☎ 01 878 3345

❊ Howth Castle Gardens `52 B2`
Howth, Co. Dublin. Howth Castle has been the seat of the Lawrence family since the 16th century although the family had settled in the area some 400 years previously. The private castle dates from 1564 and the beautiful gardens, for which soil had to be brought by the sackful by the castle staff in 1850, are renowned for their azaleas and 2000 varieties of rhododendrons.
☎ 01 832 2624   www.deerpark-hotel.ie

🏛 Hugh Lane Gallery `53 B1`
Charlemont House, Parnell Square North, Dublin, Co. Dublin. 19th and 20th century paintings, mainly Impressionist works, bequeathed by Sir Hugh Lane who was drowned in the Lusitania in 1915, form the nucleus of this collection. The Lane Collection is split with the Tate Gallery in London; each half is alternated between the galleries every five years. The exhibition area includes the London studio of Dublin-born artist Francis Bacon, which was carefully dismantled and reconstructed here.
☎ 01 874 1903   www.hughlane.ie

🏛 Irish Museum of Modern Art & Royal Hospital `53 A2`
Military Road, Kilmainham, Dublin, Co. Dublin. Opened in 1991 in the building and grounds of the 17th century Royal Hospital, the museum is an important institution for the collection of modern and contemporary art. A wide variety of work by major established 20th century figures and that of younger contemporary artists is presented in an ever changing programme of exhibitions, drawn from the museum's own collection and from public and private collections world-wide.
☎ 01 612 9900   www.modernart.ie

🏛 Irish National Heritage Park `55 C3`
Ferrycarrig, Co. Wexford. This Park traces the social development of the Irish people from 7000BC to the Norman Conquest. It does this by means of full size reconstructions of homes, farmsteads, places of worship and burial grounds on this 14ha (35 acre) site of woodland, open fields and other appropriate environments. There is an audiovisual introduction to the site and in summer, there are demonstrations of tasks such as spinning and cookery .
☎ 053 20733   www.inhp.com

✱ Irish National Stud, Japanese Gardens & St Fiachra's Garden `51 C1`
Tully, Kildare, Co. Kildare. The 400ha (1000 acre) farm has been used as stud farm since the turn of the century. Guided tours run throughout the day and there is a museum and video showing the birth of a foal. The Japanese Gardens were completed in 1910 and symbolise the 'Life of Man' and are a realistic re-creation of the type of gardens being produced in Japan at that time. St Fiachra's Garden was created as a millennium project to celebrate the Irish landscape in its most natural state and contains woods, wetlands, lakes and islands.
☎ 045 521617/522963   www.irish-national-stud.ie

✱ James Joyce Centre `52 B1`
35 North Great George's Street, Dublin, Co. Dublin. A museum in a restored Georgian town house, built in 1784, devoted to the great novelist and run by members of his family. The centre hosts readings, lectures and debates on all aspects of Joyce and his literature and conducts guided city tours.
☎ 01 878 8547   www.jamesjoyce.ie

🏛 James Joyce Tower & Museum `52 B2`
The Joyce Tower, Sandycove, Co. Dublin. The museum is housed in the Martello Tower which Joyce used as the setting for the opening chapter of Ulysses, his great work of fiction which immortalised Dublin. Joyce stayed here briefly in 1904 and the living room and view from the gun platform remains much as he described it in the novel. The museum collection includes personal possessions, letters, photographs, first editions and items that reflect the Dublin of Joyce.
☎ 01 280 9265/872 2077

✝ Jerpoint Abbey `54 B2`
Thomastown, Co. Kilkenny. The remains of Jerpoint Abbey are a superb example of Cistercian monastic life, in that many of the domestic areas are still recognisable. Founded in the late 12th century, it had its own gardens, kitchens, infirmary, watermills, granary and cemetery (which is still used today). The Irish-Romanesque transepts and chancel are the oldest parts, where faded wall paintings can still be seen. The central tower is a 15th century addition. The cloister piers have been restored and show carvings representative of drawings found in Medieval manuscripts.
☎ 056 24623

❊ John F. Kennedy Arboretum `54 B3`
New Ross, Co. Wexford. Dedicated to the memory of John Fitzgerald Kennedy, this arboretum covers 252ha (622 acres) and contains over 4500 species of trees and shrubs, all planted in botanical sequence. The many paths and nature trails lead to 200 forest plots grouped by continent and several picnic areas. There is a lake, miniature railway, visitor centre with audiovisual presentations and a tea room.
☎ 051 388171/2

❊ Johnstown Castle Gardens & Irish Agricultural Museum `55 C3`
Murntown, Co. Wexford. The impressive Gothic Revival Johnstown Castle itself is not open to the public but the 20ha (50 acres) of gardens are. They contain lakes, hot houses, woodland (which includes the ruins of Rathlannon Castle), a walled garden and masses of rhododendrons. The Museum is housed in the castle's farm buildings and depicts all aspects of Irish rural and agricultural life. There is a permanent exhibition telling the story of the potato and of the Great Famine of 1845 – 47.
☎ 053 42888

⚑ K Club, The `51 D1`
Straffan, Co. Kildare. Designed by Arnold Palmer and opened in 1991. Home to the European Open and venue for the 2006 Ryder Cup.
☎ 01 601 7300   www.kclub.ie

✝ Kells High Crosses `48 A2`
Kells, Co. Meath. There are five crosses here, decorated with biblical scenes and regarded by many as the most important in Ireland. Apart from the Market Cross, at the crossroads of Castle Street and John Street, the rest are in the churchyard of St Columba. The oldest is 9th century (the South Cross), a 10th century cross (the West Cross) has the best decoration, the East Cross has incomplete carvings, known as 'the unfinished' cross and only the base remains from the North Cross.
☎ 041 988 0305

✝ Kells Priory `54 B2`
Stoneyford, Kells, Co. Kilkenny. In 1193 a priory was founded in Kells, for Canons Regular of St Augustine from Bodmin in Cornwall. The impressive remains are divided into two courts by a branch of the river, in the northernmost of which are the remains of the church, with traces of medieval paving tiles, and the ruined claustral buildings. Substantial medieval fortified walls surround the site, with mostly complete 15th century dwelling towers.
☎ 056 28255

🏇 Kilbeggan Racecourse `50 B1`
Loughnagore, Kilbeggan, Co. Westmeath. Situated 1.6kms (1 mile) from Kilbeggan, National Hunt racing takes place here during the summer.
☎ 0506 32176

✱ Kilfane Glen & Waterfall `54 B2`
Thomastown, Co. Kilkenny. Listed as an Irish Heritage Garden, this is an excellent example of a romantic garden, dating from the late 18th century. At that time it was designed to provide 'VIPs' with a setting for tea parties and outings. There are winding woodland paths, seats, bridges, fountains, a grotto, and a thatched summerhouse (cottage orne). The beautiful 9m (30 ft) waterfall was created by diverting a stream to a rock face. In the upper garden are commissioned works of art.
☎ 056 24558   www.nicholasmosse.com/garden.htm

♜ Kilkenny Castle `54 A1`

The Parade, Kilkenny, Co. Kilkenny. A wooden tower was built on this site by Richard de Clare in 1172, followed by a stone castle constructed twenty years later by his son-in-law. In the late 14th century, the castle was bought by the powerful Butler family, the Earls of Ormonde, who lived there until 1935. They restored it after damage in the mid 17th century and it was significantly rebuilt by the Victorians in the early 19th century. Bought by the state in 1967 for £50, it now includes a Long Gallery which has brightly painted ceilings and portraits of the Butler family, a library, drawing room and bedrooms. The Butler Gallery hosts art exhibitions and the old kitchens now serve teas in summer.

☎ 056 21450

❖ Kilmacurragh `52 B3`

Rathdrum, Co. Wicklow. This arboretum was planted by curators of the National Botanic Gardens in Glasnevin, in the 19th century. The soil and climate at Kilmacurragh was very favourable for many of the less hardy conifers from around the World for which this garden is famous.

☎ 01 661 6764

✦ Kilmainham Gaol `52 B2`

Inchicore Road, Dublin, Co. Dublin. After its closure in 1924 Kilmainham re-opened in 1966 as a museum dedicated to the Irish patriots imprisoned there from 1792 – 1924. Patrick Pearse and James Connolly were executed in the prison yard and Eamon de Valera, later Prime Minister and then President of Ireland, was one of the last inmates. It is one of the largest unoccupied gaols in Europe with tiers of cells and overhead catwalks. Access is by guided tour only and features an exhibition and audiovisual show.

☎ 01 453 5984

❖ Kilmokea `54 B3`

Great Island, Campile, Co. Wexford. Many rare and tender trees and shrubs grow in these 2.8ha (7 acres) of frost free gardens. Divided into two parts, a formal walled garden and a woodland garden, there are features such as an Italian loggia and pool, topiary, herbaceous borders and woodland walks with a lake, rhododendrons, magnolias and the giant borage.

☎ 051 388109   www.kilmokea.com

▥ Kilruddery House & Gardens `52 B2`

Bray, Co. Wicklow. This early 17th century house was remodelled in the 1820s and reduced in size in the 1950s to its current proportions. It is one of the earliest Elizabethan-Revival mansions in Ireland, and is still home to the Earls of Meath. The statue gallery contains a collection of mid 19th century Italian statuary. The gardens are the oldest in Ireland and are still largely in their original 17th century style. There are a pair of canals, 170m (550 ft) long with the house at one end and an avenue of lime trees at the other. To the left of the canals are radiating walks (The Angles) flanked by hedges of beech, hornbeam and lime. On the other side is the only known Sylvan Theatre in Ireland, with terraced banks and a high bay hedge. Finally, there is an 18m (60ft) diameter pond with a French style fountain in the centre.

☎ 01 286 2777/3405

♜ King John's Castle `49 C1`

Carlingford, Co. Louth. The castle remains, strategically located to command the quay, dating back to the late 12th century, played host to King John who stayed here on his way to attack Hugh de Lacy, at Carrickfergus. It has an unusual D-shape while the west gateway was designed to allow the entry of only one horseman at a time. The remains of an earlier castle include the southwest tower and the west wall.

☎ 042 933 5484

❖ Larchill Arcadian Gardens `52 A1`

Kilcock, Co. Kildare. This mid 18th century garden is unique in being the only surviving example of an Arcadian (ornamental farm) garden in Ireland or Europe. In the 26ha (64 acres) of parkland there are 10 follies situated around a 40 minute circular walk. There are also gazebos and a walled garden plus a 3ha (7.4 acres) lake with a Greek temple. The parkland is stocked with the largest number of rare breeds in Ireland.

☎ 01 628 7354

♜ Leap Castle `50 A2`

Roscrea, Co. Offaly. Built in 1250 by the Princes of Ely, the O'Carrolls, to guard the pass from the Slieve Bloom mountains to Munster, this is supposedly the most haunted castle in Ireland. It harbours a ghost with an obnoxious smell! During the civil unrest of 1922 it was badly burnt but the remains are still standing.

☎ 0509 31115

⛷ Leopardstown Racecourse `52 B2`

Foxrock, Dublin, Co. Dublin. One of the top European racetracks, Leopardstown is 10kms (6 miles) from Dublin. It hosts 22 race meetings per year of both Flat and National Hunt Racing.

☎ 01 289 3607   www.leopardstown.com

▦ Locke's Distillery Museum `50 B1`

Kilbeggan, Co. Westmeath. The original distillery closed in 1957, after 200 years of production. In 1982 restoration of the buildings commenced, and they now house the last working example of a small pot still distillery in Ireland. The whole process of making the whiskey can be seen and working conditions in the 19th century appreciated. At the end of the tour, there is a complimentary tasting of the product and home made food can be sampled in the restaurant.

☎ 0506 32134   www.lockesdistillerymuseum.com

❖ Lodge Park Walled Garden `51 D1`

Straffan, Co. Kildare. Restoration work on this 18th century walled garden started in 1980. A superb south facing shrub and perennial border edged with clipped box and topiaried yews runs the length of the garden, while the other compartments, which include flowers, vegetables and fruit, are divided by beech hedging. The orchard is entered through a beautiful rosery. There is a steam museum adjacent.

☎ 01 627 3477   www.steam-museum.ie

✦ Lory Meagher Heritage Centre `54 A1`

Curragh House, Tullaroan, Co. Kilkenny. This is the home of the Kilkenny Gaelic Athletic Association (GAA) Museum. The two storey 17th century thatched mansion was the home of the 1920s hurling hero, Lory Meagher. It has been beautifully restored and shows the lifestyle of a well-to-do Irish farming family of the time. The museum is housed in an adjoining restored stone building and contains all kinds of hurling mementos, trophies, reports and a section for clubs.

☎ 056 69202/69107

✝ Loughcrew Cairns `48 A2`

Corstown, Oldcastle, Co. Meath. There are many cairns on the hills in this area, known as the Hills of the Witch. The main concentrations are on three peaks, Cairnbane, Sliabh na Cailli and Patrickstown and comprise of Neolithic passage tombs about 5000 years old. One of the largest is Cairn T on Cairnbane, which contains a cruciform chamber and some wonderful Neolithic art.

☎ 049 854 2009   www.knowth.com/loughcrew.htm

❖ Loughcrew Historic Gardens `48 A2`

Old Castle, Co. Meath. Started in 1660, the Naper family have continuously developed these gardens whilst retaining their historical setting. They include a medieval motte and St Oliver Plunkett's Family Church and Tower House; from the 17th century, there is a magnificent yew walk. The gardens have been carefully redeveloped in the 19th and 20th centuries to include rockeries, follies, watergardens, woodland walks, watermill, vistas with hidden fairies, giant bugs and spiders in trees!

☎ 049 854 1922   www.loughcrew.com

▥ Louth County Museum `48 B1`

Jocelyn Street, Dundalk, Co. Louth. The role of the County Museum is to show the social, natural and archaeological history of the County from prehistoric times to today. It achieves this through a series of changing exhibitions using local artefacts, models and interactive displays. The ground floor houses the only permanent display showing the industrial and agricultural history of Louth. This beautifully restored 18th century warehouse also has a 72 seater audiovisual theatre. There are many artistic events, lectures and workshops throughout the year.

☎ 042 932 7056/7

✦ Lullymore Heritage Park `51 C1`

Lullymore, Rathangan, Co. Kildare. Designed to tell the story of the Irish people and boglands, this heritage park is located on a mineral island in the Bog of Allen, the largest bogland in Ireland. There is a reconstruction of a neolithic farmstead, a replica of Newgrange and visitor centre. Other features include theme gardens, a fairy bower, exhibitions of the 1798 rebellion and the Famine, an adventure park, crazy golf, tea rooms and a craft/souvenir shop.

☎ 045 870238

✦ Lusk Heritage Centre `52 B1`

Lusk, Co. Dublin. This centre comprises a church built in the 19th century, with an older round tower and a medieval belfry. An exhibition about medieval churches in North County Dublin is housed in the belfry, along with the 16th century effigy tomb of Sir Christopher Barnewall and Marion Sharl, his wife.

☎ 01 843 7683/833 1618

✦ Lusmagh Pet Farm `50 A1`

Banagher, Co. Offaly. This farm has a large selection of farm and other animals including ostriches and emus. There is also a nature trail and a display of old farm machinery.

☎ 0509 51233

♜ Malahide Castle `52 B1`

Malahide, Co. Dublin. Originally built in 1185, it was the seat of the Talbot family until 1973 when the last Lord Talbot died; the history of the family is detailed in the Great Hall alongside many family portraits. Malahide also has a large collection of Irish portrait paintings, mainly from the National Gallery, and is furnished with fine period furniture. Within the 100ha (250 acres) of parkland surrounding the castle is the Talbot Botanic Gardens, largely created by Lord Milo Talbot between 1948 and 1973.

☎ 01 846 2184

♜ Maynooth Castle `52 A1`

Maynooth, Co. Kildare. Built in 1175, the home of the Earls of Kildare, much of the original building still stands, including the keep which is one of the largest of its type in Ireland. In the 15th century it was the stronghold of the Great Earl of Kildare, Garret Mór Fitzgerald. It had fallen into disrepair by the early 17th century but was renovated by the Earl of Cork. It now forms an impressive entrance to Maynooth College, founded in the late 18th century.

☎ 01 647 2493/2503

✦ Meeting of the Waters `52 B3`

Avoca, Co. Wicklow. The Rivers Avonmore and Avonbeg meet about 4km (2.5 miles) north of the village of Avoca to form the River Avoca. At this meeting point, the poet Thomas Moore is said to have sat on the root of a tree in the form of a 'rustic' seat and written the words to the Irish melody Sweet Vale of Avoca.

☎ 0404 69117

✝ Mellifont Abbey `48 B2`

Tullyallen, Drogheda, Co. Louth. Mellifont was Ireland's first Cistercian abbey. Founded in 1140 by the King of Uriel, at the instigation of St Malachy, who had been inspired by St Bernard's work at Clairvaux, the abbey became the home of the Moore family after its suppression in 1539. Though scattered, the remains are of great interest and include portions of the Romanesque cloister arcade, the 13th century chapter house extension, and the octagonal washroom.

☎ 041 982 6459

Millmount Museum　49 C2

Millmount, Drogheda, Co. Louth. The museum is housed in a former military complex, built in the early 19th century. The main attraction here is an exhibition of trade banners painted in the 1700s to mid 1800s; those depicting the broguemakers, carpenters and weavers are the only Guild banners left in Ireland. Other historical artefacts from the area are also on display here. The Martello Tower was built by the British army in the 18th century, as a defence in the Napoleonic wars. It was damaged in the Irish Civil War in 1922 but has been recently restored to house a military museum.
☎ 041 983 3097/6391

Monasterboice　48 B2

Collon, Co. Louth. Just north of Drogheda is the early 6th century ruin of Monasterboice (meaning 'Buite's monastery'). Although a small site, there is a Round Tower in excellent condition and two of the finest 10th century High Crosses in Ireland. The Cross of Muiredach is 5.2m (17ft) high and although not the tallest, the carvings on it are remarkably clear.
☎ 041 983 7070

Mondello Park　51 D1

Donore, Naas, Co. Kildare. Hosting many types of motor racing, both cars and motorbikes, this is Ireland's premier racing circuit. In June 2001 it was the first circuit outside the UK to host a round of the British Touring Car Championship. It has now moved into motorsport entertainment and members of the public can experience driving performance cars on this superb track.
☎ 045 860200　　www.mondellopark.ie

Moone High Cross　51 C2

Moone, Co. Kildare. Located in Moone Abbey churchyard, on the site of an early Columban monastery, the 7th century Moone High Cross stands over 5m (16ft) high. It is made of granite and contains 51 sculptured panels. It was discovered in pieces in the late and mid 19th century and finally reconstructed in 1893.
☎ 045 522696

Mount Juliet Golf Club　54 B2

Thomastown, Co. Kilkenny. Designed by Jack Nicklaus and opened in 1992, the Irish Open was held here in 1993 – 95 and was extended to over 7000 yards in preparation for the World Golf Championship in 2002. It was also host to the 4th National Putting Championships in 2001.
☎ 056 73000　　www.mountjuliet.com

Mount Usher Gardens　52 B2

Ashford, Co. Wicklow. Charmingly located by the River Vartry, the gardens of Mount Usher are made up of 8ha (20 acres) planted with over 5000 species of flora. Including many sub-tropical plants, the naturalised gardens, laid out in 1868 by Edward Walpole, of a Dublin family of linen manufacturers, are famous for the Eucalyptus and Eucryphia collections and offer some fine woodland walks.
☎ 0404 40205/40116　　www.mount-usher-gardens.com

Mullingar Cathedral　47 C3

Mullingar, Co. Westmeath. This Roman Catholic cathedral, dedicated as Cathedral of Christ the King, was built in 'modernised Renaissance' style, with a dome and twin towers, just before World War II. Above the Sacristy is a museum of interesting ecclesiastical exhibits.
☎ 044 48338/48402

Naas Racecourse　51 D1

Tipper Road, Naas, Co. Kildare. This 2.4km (1.5 mile) racecourse is about 40km (25 miles) from Dublin City, in the heart of the thoroughbred county of Kildare. It hosts both National Hunt and Flat race meetings throughout the year.
☎ 045 897391　　www.naasracecourse.com

National Botanic Gardens　52 B2

Glasnevin, Dublin, Co. Dublin. Established in 1795, these magnificent gardens occupy an area of 20ha (49 acres) and contain a fabulous collection of plants, shrubs and trees. Many of the plants come from tropical Africa and South America and are housed in large Victorian glasshouses. Features include a rose garden, rockery and wall plants, herbaceous borders, vegetable garden and arboretum.
☎ 01 837 7596/4388

National Concert Hall　53 B3

Earlsfort Terrace, Dublin, Co. Dublin. Home of the National Symphony Orchestra of Ireland, but also a venue for international artists and orchestras, jazz, contemporary and traditional Irish music. The classical building was designed for the Great Exhibition of 1865, then became the centrepiece of University College Dublin before opening as Ireland's National Concert Hall in 1981.
☎ 01 475 1666　　www.nch.ie

National Gallery of Ireland　53 C2

Merrion Square, Dublin, Co. Dublin. Paintings by illustrious 20th century European artists such as Morrisot, Bonnard, Picasso and Monet hang in the National Gallery as well as the work of Old Masters including Titian, Caravaggio, Rembrandt and Vermeer. There is the National Collection of Irish art, a room dedicated to the work of Jack B. Yeats, English paintings, and over 250 sculptures. William Dargan organised the 1853 Dublin Exhibition on this site and used the proceeds to found the collection; his statue stands on the lawn.
☎ 01 661 5133　　www.nationalgallery.ie

National Garden Exhibition Centre　52 B3

Kilquade, near Kilpedder, Co. Wicklow. Kilquade is the home of the National Garden Exhibition Centre. It started as a nursery 25 years ago and now has at least 19 different gardens of all shapes, sizes and styles designed by some of the best garden designers and contractors in Ireland. Some of the gardens are permanent and include a herb knot, an acid garden, a woodland and water garden. There is also the unique Irish designed Le Batre Fountain Clock. Refreshments are available and there is a plant sales area.
☎ 01 281 9890　　www.clubi.ie/calumet

National Library of Ireland　53 C2

Kildare Street, Dublin, Co. Dublin. Offers over half a million books, a vast collection of maps, prints and manuscripts and an invaluable collection of Irish newspapers and periodicals. The impressive Victorian building has been home to the Library since 1890, and there is a large domed reading room.
☎ 01 603 0200　　www.nli.ie

National Maritime Museum　52 B2

Haigh Terrace, Dun Laoghaire, Co. Dublin. A former Mariner's Church is home to the museum which features a French Longboat sent to Bantry Bay in support of the United Irishmen in 1796. There are models of the Irish Fleet, a lifeboat display and an exhibit about Robert Halpin, captain of the Great Eastern steamship which laid the first transatlantic telegraph cable in 1866.
☎ 01 280 0969

National Museum of Ireland (Archaeology & History)　53 C2

Kildare Street, Dublin, Co. Dublin. Houses a fabulous collection of national antiquities, including prehistoric gold ornaments, and outstanding examples of Celtic and medieval art. The 8th century Ardagh Chalice and Tara Brooch are amongst the treasures. The entire history of Ireland is reflected in the museum with 'The Road to Independence Exhibition' illustrating Irish history from 1916 – 1921. There is also an Ancient Egypt exhibition.
☎ 01 677 7444

National Museum of Ireland (Decorative Art & History)　53 A2

Collins Barracks, Benturb Street, Dublin, Co. Dublin. Ireland's museum of decorative arts and economic, social, political and military history, based in the oldest military barracks in Europe. Major collections include Irish silver, Irish country furniture and costume jewellery and accessories. The work of museum restoration and conservation is explained and the Out of Storage gallery provides visitors with a view of artefacts in storage.
☎ 01 677 7444

National Museum of Ireland (Natural History)　53 C2

Merrion Street, Dublin, Co. Dublin. First opened in 1857 and hardly changed since then, the museum houses a large collection of stuffed animals and the skeletons of mammals and birds from both Ireland and the rest of the world. The exhibits include three examples of the Irish Great Elk which became extinct over 10,000 years ago and the skeleton of a Basking Shark. Fascinating glass reproductions of marine specimens, known as the Blaschka Collection, are found on the upper gallery.
☎ 01 677 7444

National Photographic Archive　53 B2

Meeting House Square, Temple Bar, Dublin, Co. Dublin. Established in 1998, it has over a million photographs recording people, political events, and scenes of Irish cities, towns and countryside. Images from the collection are always on view. There is also a reading room and darkrooms.
☎ 01 603 0371　　www.nli.ie

National Sea Life Centre　52 B2

Strand Road, Bray, Co. Wicklow. Features marine life from the seas around Ireland including stingrays, conger eels, and sharks; also freshwater fish from Irish rivers and streams. A touch pool gives children the opportunity to pick up small creatures such as starfish, crabs and sea anemones. By way of contrast is the fascinating 'Danger in the Depths' tank with many sea creatures from around the world which have proved harmful or fatal to humans.
☎ 01 286 6939

National 1798 Visitor Centre　55 C2

Mill Park Road, Enniscorthy, Co. Wexford. The centre tells the story of the 1798 rebellion and gives an insight into the beginnings of modern democracy in Ireland. The latest technology is employed to provide interactive displays and audiovisual information and visitors can choose their own pace to travel through the unfolding story.
☎ 054 37596　　www.1798centre.com

National Transport Museum　52 B2

Howth, Co. Dublin. A collection of buses, trams, trucks, tractors and fire engines, some dating back to 1880, along with other memorabilia from the transport industry.
☎ 01 848 0831/847 5623

National Wax Museum　53 B1

Granby Row, Parnell Square, Dublin, Co. Dublin. Over 300 life-size wax figures of well-known people and personalities from the past and present ranging from Eamon De Valera to Elvis Presley. Also a dimly lit Chamber of Horrors.
☎ 01 872 6340

Navan Racecourse　48 B2

Proudstown, Navan, Co. Meath. 48kms (30 miles) north of Dublin, Navan was founded in the 1920s. It hosts top class racing and many famous National Hunt horses have competed here, including Arkle. It now includes an 18 hole golf course.
☎ 046 21350

Newbridge House & Farm　52 B1

Donabate, Co. Dublin. Built in 1737 for Archbishop Charles Cobbe, and still the residence of his descendants, Newbridge has one of the most beautiful period manor house interiors in Ireland and is set within 142ha (350 acres) of parkland. A fully restored 18th century farm lies on the estate together with dairy, forge, tack room, and estate worker's house.
☎ 01 843 6534

Newbridge Silverware　51 D1

Cutlery Lane, Newbridge, Co. Kildare. Since 1934, silverware has been produced here by craftsmen using traditional skills. Today, the range includes cutlery, jewellery, kitchenware giftware and executive giftware.
☎ 045 431301　　www.newbridgecutlery.com

✦ Newman House — 53 B3

85-86 St Stephen's Green, Dublin, Co. Dublin. Newman House is made up of two splendid 18th century Georgian mansions, which were once part of the buildings of the Catholic University of Ireland and named after Cardinal Newman, the first rector of the university. There is a classroom furnished as it would have been when James Joyce was a pupil here from 1899 – 1902. A guided tour explains the history and heritage of the house and how it was restored.
☎ 01 706 7422

✹ Newtowncashel Heritage Centre — 46 B3

Newtowncashel, Co. Longford. Located in a cottage on the main street, the Heritage Centre shows what life was like here in the early 1900s. The kitchen, parlour and bedroom house artefacts from this period and outside there is a display of farm machinery.
☎ 043 25306 /25021

✦ Number Twenty Nine — 53 C3

Lower Fitzwilliam Street, Dublin, Co. Dublin. This elegant four-storey house has been restored and furnished exactly as it would have been between 1790 – 1820 by any well-to-do middle class family. Everything in the house is authentic with period items from the National Museum. The wallpaper was hand-made for Number 29 using 18th century techniques. Among the rooms in the house are a kitchen, pantry, governess' room, nursery and boudoir.
☎ 01 702 6165

✹ Old Jameson Distillery — 53 B2

Bow Street, Smithfield, Dublin, Co. Dublin. The art of Irish Whiskey making shown through an audiovisual presentation, working models of the distilling process, and guided tour of the old distillery which was in use between 1780 – 1971.
☎ 01 807 2355

🏛 Pearse Museum — 52 B2

St Enda's Park, Grange Road, Rathfarnham, Dublin, Co. Dublin. Housed in the former school run by nationalist Patrick Pearse from 1910 – 1916, it includes an audiovisual presentation and a nature study room with displays on Irish flora and fauna. Pearse was executed in 1916 for his part in the Easter Rising.
☎ 01 493 4208

✹ Peatland World — 51 C1

Lullymore, Rathangan, Co. Kildare. Based at Lullymore in Rathangan, this fascinating centre has a museum, housed in a restored 19th century courtyard, with a series of trails around it where guided walks can be offered to visitors. The museum explains the history, development, ecology, exploitation and future importance of bogs. There is also a craft centre and restaurant.
☎ 045 860133

✹ Phoenix Park Visitor Centre — 52 B2

Phoenix Park, Dublin, Co. Dublin. The visitor centre illustrates the history and wildlife of the park with an audiovisual display, a variety of fascinating exhibits and temporary exhibitions. Adjoining the centre is a restored medieval tower house, Ashtown Castle. On Saturdays there are free guided tours to the Irish President's House which is situated in the Park.
☎ 01 677 0095

⚑ Portmarnock Golf Club — 52 B1

Strand Road, Portmarnock, Co. Dublin. One of the oldest and finest links courses in Ireland and host to several Irish Opens as well as the 1992 Walker Cup.
☎ 01 846 2968

❉ Powerscourt Gardens & Waterfall — 52 B2

Enniskerry, Co. Wicklow. A disastrous fire in the 1970s has left only the shell of Powerscourt House, built in 1730 for Viscount Powerscourt by the Huguenot architect Richard Cassels and then enlarged and altered in the 19th century. Its mountain setting is magnificent, however, as are the gardens with their handsome 19th century terraces, Monkey Puzzle Avenue, and Japanese Garden, added in 1908. In the grounds, and approachable by a separate car entrance, is a spectacular 120m (400ft) waterfall.
☎ 01 204 6000
www.powerscourt.ie

⚰ Proleek Dolmen — 48 B1

Aghnaskeagh, Ballymascanlon, Co. Louth. Proleek is the site of the so called 'Giant's Load', a tomb that is the legendary grave of Para Bui Mor Mhac Seoidin, the Scottish giant who challenged Finn MacCool. A trio of smaller upright stones supporting a larger capstone, the tomb dates back to 3000BC. It is thought that the capstone was hauled into position by means of a vanished earthen ramp.
☎ 042 933 5484

⚐ Punchestown Racecourse — 51 D1

Naas, Co. Kildare. This 3.2km (2 mile) course was founded in 1793 and is regarded as the home of National Hunt racing. It is renowned for its double bank and stone walls but now includes bush fences and hurdles, with Flat Racing also taking place. The largest race is the four day National Hunt Festival, run every April.
☎ 045 897704
www.punchestown.com

❉ Ram House Gardens — 55 D1

Coolgreany, Gorey, Co. Wexford. Situated in Coolgreany village, this small delightful garden is divided into garden 'rooms' and features, amongst other things, a stream, woodland glade, ponds, lawns and over 70 varieties of clematis. There are even refreshments available.
☎ 0402 37238

♜ Rathfarnham Castle — 52 B2

Rathfarnham, Dublin, Co. Dublin. Dating from around 1583, this castle has 18th century interiors by Sir William Chambers and James Stuart and is presented to visitors as a castle undergoing conservation.
☎ 01 493 9462

♜ Rathmacknee Castle — 55 C3

near Murntown, Wexford, Co. Wexford. This late medieval castle was probably built by John Rosseter, Seneschal of the Liberties of Wexford in 1451. Although now lacking a roof and floors, this is still a remarkably well preserved building. The five storey tower stands at the south east corner of the five sided bawn, the wall of which is 1.2m (4 ft) thick and 7m (24ft) high. There is a round turret on the north east corner and a smaller square one on the north west corner, making this castle almost complete.
☎ 053 23111

♜ Rock of Dunamase — 51 C2

Portlaoise, Co. Laois. Close to Portlaoise, on the Stradbally road, a large ruined castle sits on top of this 46m (150ft) rock, all that remains of what was a considerable fortress, destroyed in the Cromwellian wars. Through the marriage of the daughter of the King of Leinster, it had moved into Anglo Norman hands in the late 12th century, and was twice rebuilt, in 1250 and at the end of the 15th century. There are fine views to be had from the summit of the rock where the remains of the gatehouse, walls and 13th century keep are still in evidence.
☎ 0502 21178

🏛 Rothe House — 54 A1

Parliament Street, Kilkenny, Co. Kilkenny. Built in the late 16th century by a wealthy merchant, John Rothe, this is a typical Tudor middle class house. The three stone buildings are now owned by the Kilkenny Archaeological Society and contain a collection of period costumes, the city and county museum, a genealogical research centre and some impressive oak furniture and pictures. The third building has been recently restored and houses the brewhouse, bakery and great kitchen.
☎ 056 22893

✦ Russborough — 51 D1

Blessington, Co. Wicklow. One of Ireland's foremost Palladian houses was built for a Dublin brewer, Joseph Leeson, 1st Earl of Milltown, by Richard Cassels and Francis Bindon in the 1740s. A granite exterior conceals an interior coated in extravagant stucco work and bearing a fine painting collection.
☎ 045 865239

✝ St Aidan's Cathedral — 55 C2

Main Street, Enniscorthy, Co. Wexford. Recently restored, this cathedral was originally designed by A.W. Pugin. It was dedicated in 1860 but the spire was not completed until 1873. The paints used in the restoration of the decorative stencilling, are replicas of the original paintwork, reproduced from paint samples found in the cathedral.
☎ 055 21248

✝ St Audoen's Church — 53 B2

Cornmarket, High Street, Dublin, Co. Dublin. Dublin's only surviving medieval parish church, with a 12th century font and portal. The bell tower, restored in the 19th century, has three 15th century bells. The guild chapel has an exhibition on the importance of the church in the life of the medieval city. Dublin's only surviving city gate, known as St Audoen's Arch, stands nearby.
☎ 01 677 0088

✝ St Brigid's Cathedral & Round Tower — 51 C1

Kildare, Co. Kildare. This 13th century protestant cathedral, restored by the Victorians, is built on the 5th century site of a religious centre founded by the patron Saint of Ireland, St Brigid. The centre then housed both monks and nuns. In the grounds a restored fire pit is visible. This pagan feature used to contain a perpetually burning fire, tended by virgins, until the dissolution of the monasteries in the 16th century. The cathedral contains the tomb of the 16th century Bishop of Kildare, Walter Kellesley and in the graveyard are the earls and dukes of Kildare. The Round Tower, built near the cathedral, is 12th century.
☎ 045 521229

✝ St Canice's Cathedral — 54 A1

Kilkenny, Co. Kilkenny. The city actually takes its name from St Canice who founded a monastery here in the 6th century, upon the site of which stands the current cathedral. Much restored in the 19th century, it is the second largest medieval cathedral in Ireland. Inside is the finest display of burial monuments in the country whilst the high round tower adjacent to the cathedral is the only substantial relic from the monastery. The building is essentially 13th century and the oldest tomb is also from this period, although the oldest decipherable slab is that of Jose Kyteler, the father of Alice Kyteler, tried for witchcraft in 1323.
☎ 056 64971

✝ St Edan's Cathedral — 55 C2

Ferns, Co. Wexford. The original cathedral was built here in the early 13th century, although a church had stood here since the 8th century. The medieval building was burnt down in the reign of Elizabeth the First and little remains. It was not until the 19th century that it was rebuilt again.
☎ 054 66124

⚐ St Margaret's Golf Club — 52 B1

St Margaret's, Co. Dublin. This 7000 yard long course has played host to the Irish Seniors Open and also the Ladies Irish Open Championships.
☎ 01 864 0400
www.st-margarets.net

✝ St Mary's Abbey — 53 B2

Chapter House, Meetinghouse Lane, off Capel Street, Dublin, Co. Dublin. Established originally as a Benedictine foundation in 1139, it became Cistercian eight years later. The remains include a fine vaulted Chapter House of 1190 and there is an interesting exhibition about the history of the abbey.
☎ 01 872 1490

✝ St Mary's Pro-Cathedral — 53 B2

Marlborough Street, Dublin, Co. Dublin. A Greek Doric style building designed by John Sweetman and built between 1815 and 1825, with the interior modelled on the Church of St Philippe de Roule in Paris. St Mary's is Dublin's most important Catholic Church and is used on State occasions. Tenor John McCormack was once a member of the Palestrina choir that sings a Latin mass every Sunday.
☎ 01 874 5441
www.procathedral.ie

† **St Mel's Cathedral**   `46 B2`
Longford, Co. Longford. Built of grey limestone, in the Renaissance style, St Mel's Cathedral dates from the 1840s. 24 columns of local stone support the roof and the tall dome is visible from outside the town. The museum at the rear of the building contains the 10th century St. Mel's Crozier.
☎ 043 46465

† **St Patrick's Cathedral**   `53 B3`
St Patrick's Close, Dublin, Co. Dublin. The National Cathedral of the Church of Ireland, it was built in the late 12th century on the site of the pre-Norman parish church of St Patrick. Architect John Semple added a spire in 1749 and St Patrick's was fully restored in the 19th century with finance from the Guinness family. The massive west tower houses the largest ringing peel of bells in Ireland. The cathedral is full of memorial brasses, busts and monuments to famous Irishmen.
☎ 01 453 9472   www.stpatrickscathedral.ie

🏠 **Shaw Birthplace**   `53 B3`
33 Synge Street, Dublin, Co. Dublin. This delightful Victorian terrace home was the birthplace of one of Ireland's four Nobel prize-winners for literature, George Bernard Shaw. Restored to give the feeling that the Shaw family is still in residence, the home provides an insight into the domestic life of Victorian Dubliners.
☎ 01 475 0854/872 2077

★ **Slieve Bloom Display Centre**   `50 A2`
Roscrea Road, Birr, Co. Offaly. Located at Birr, this is an information centre for the Slieve Bloom Mountain area. Using illustrations, photographs and maps, the natural history, geology, archaeology and history of the mountains are explained.
☎ 0509 20110

★ **Sonairte National Ecology Centre**   `49 C2`
Laytown, Co. Meath. Based at Laytown, Sonairte is a registered charity which aims to promote awareness of environmental issues and sustainable living. On the seven acre site there are examples of renewable energy systems, nature conservation and organic growing with restored farm buildings providing shops and offices. There is also a nature trail alongside the River Nanny.
☎ 041 982 7572/7854

❇ **Talbot Botanic Gardens**   `52 B1`
Malahide Castle, Malahide, Co. Dublin. Covering 8ha (20 acres) and part of the Malahide Castle grounds, these gardens were created by Milo, the seventh Lord Talbot de Malahide, within the 101ha (250 acre) park now managed by Dublin County Council. Milo planted around 5000 plants largely of Australian and South American origin during the middle part of the 20th century. There is also a four acre walled garden.
☎ 01 872 7777

† **Tintern Abbey**   `54 B3`
Saltmills, New Ross, Co. Wexford. This fine 13th century Cistercian Abbey (named after its Welsh counterpart) was built here by William Marshall, Earl of Pembroke, after he was blown ashore during a storm; he vowed he would build an Abbey if he was saved. After 1541 it was partially converted into living quarters and the same family occupied it from the 16th century to the 1960s. The substantial remains include the nave, tower, chancel, cloister and chapel.
☎ 051 562650

🏰 **Trim Castle**   `48 B3`
Trim, Co. Meath. Located in the centre of Trim, this is the largest Anglo-Norman castle in Ireland. Hugh de Lacy first started construction in the 1170s, although the central keep – a three storey, 20 sided tower – was not completed until the 1220s. The massive curtain walls can still be seen today, largely intact. Trim was conquered three times, the most recent in 1649 by Cromwell's army. More recent fame was found in its use as a setting for the film 'Braveheart'.
☎ 046 38618

🏠 **Trinity College**   `53 C2`
University of Dublin, Dublin, Co. Dublin. The original Elizabethan college was founded in 1592 but the present building was largely built between 1755 – 1759. The oldest surviving part of the college is the red brick apartment building from 1700 known as The Rubrics. The Library has over a million books and a magnificent collection of early illuminated manuscripts, including the famous Book of Kells. Edmund Burke, Oliver Goldsmith and Samuel Beckett are among former Trinity College students.
☎ 01 608 2320/2308   www.tcd.ie

★ **Tullamore Dew Heritage Centre**   `50 B1`
Bury Quay, Tullamore, Co. Offaly. This attraction is located in a canalside warehouse in the centre of the town. There are models, displays and many interactive activities explaining the history of the town and its links to the canal. There is also the story of Tullamore Dew Irish Whiskey and Liqueur, with a complimentary tasting after your visit.
☎ 0506 25015   www.tullamore-dew.org

❄ **Tullynally Castle**   `47 C2`
Castlepollard, Co. Westmeath. Originally a 17th century tower house, this structure was extensively remodelled in the early 1800s, by the second Earl of Longford, in the Gothic Revival style, to become one of Ireland's largest castles. Owned and lived in by the Packenhams since its construction, it contains fine portraits and Irish furniture. The grounds date from the 19th century and cover almost 12ha (30 acres). They include a walled garden, two ornamental lakes, a Chinese garden, Tibetan garden and an avenue of Irish Yews some 200 years old.
☎ 044 61159

🏰 **Tyrrellspass Castle**   `50 B1`
Tyrrellspass, Co. Westmeath. Dating from 1411, this restored defensive tower house castle still contains an original spiral staircase and a roof beam dating from 1280. The Tyrrells built many castles in Ireland but this was the only one left standing after the Cromwellian wars. During the 19th century, it was renovated and housed English troops for a time. More recently, a highly successful licensed restaurant has been established here.
☎ 044 23105   www.tyrrellspasscastle.ie

❇ **War Memorial Gardens**   `52 B2`
Islandbridge, Dublin, Co. Dublin. Dedicated to the memory of the Irish soldiers who died in the First World War, these gardens include a sunken rose garden and herbaceous borders. They were designed by Sir Edward Lutyens. The names of the 49,400 soldiers who died between 1914 – 1918 are contained in the granite bookrooms in the gardens, access to which is only by arrangement with the management.
☎ 01 677 0236

★ **Waterways Visitor Centre**   `53 C2`
Grand Canal Quay, Dublin, Co. Dublin. A modern centre built on piers over the Grand Canal, housing an exhibition about Ireland's inland waterways. Working models of various engineering features are displayed and there is an interactive multimedia presentation.
☎ 01 677 7510

✝ **Westgate Tower & Selskar Abbey**   `55 C3`
Wexford, Co. Wexford. The 12th century Selskar Abbey was founded by Alexander de la Roche and is built on what is thought to be the oldest place of worship in the County, a pre-Christian temple dedicated to Odin. It is said that Henry II did penance here for the murder of Thomas a' Becket. The Abbey was largely ruined during the Cromwellian wars. Westgate tower, built in the early 1300s, houses the Westgate Heritage Centre.
☎ 053 46506

🏛 **Wexford County Museum**   `55 C2`
Castle Hill, Enniscorthy, Co. Wexford. Located in a 13th century Norman castle in Enniscorthy, the history of County Wexford is dramatically told through artefacts and displays from agriculture, the military, the church, seafaring and industrial occupations.
☎ 054 35926

🏇 **Wexford Racecourse**   `55 C3`
Wexford, Co. Wexford. Just outside Wexford, this course hosts both flat and National Hunt racing.
☎ 051 421681   www.wexfordraces.ie

🐦 **Wexford Wildfowl Reserve**   `55 D2`
North Slob, Wexford, Co. Wexford. The North Slobs mudflats are the overwintering home for between one third and half of the total world population of Greenland White Fronted Geese. This reserve has excellent facilities, including hides, an observation tower and visitor centre with audiovisual information, for observing these geese and many other species of birds.
☎ 053 23129

🐾 **Wicklow Mountains National Park**   `52 B3`
Upper Lake, Glendalough, Co. Wicklow. Established in 1991, the total area managed is now 20,000ha (49,400 acres), with a core area based around the lakes at Glendalough. The Park includes Liffey Head Bog and the Gleneal Valley Heath and Bog as well as various wooded areas with old coppiced Sessile Oaks. The Wicklow Mountains themselves are granite and hold high concentrations of lead, tin, copper, iron and zinc, all of which have been mined in the past. Most of Ireland's mammals can be found here; various species of deer, foxes, badgers, brown and Irish hares, red squirrels, birds of prey, red grouse and many other birds and fish. The Park Information Office is near the Upper Glendalough lake.
☎ 0404 45425/45338

★ **Wicklow's Historic Gaol**   `52 B3`
Kilmantin Hill, Wicklow, Co. Wicklow. The old County gaol has been here since 1702 and it was in service until 1924. Now it has been developed into a centre to tell the story of the thousands of people of all ages, both innocent and guilty, who passed through its doors. By using a combination of audiovisual material, displays and actor-interpreters, this history is brought to life through the eyes of the inmates. The fate of those who were transported can be experienced by visiting a reconstruction of the prison ship Hercules.
☎ 0404 61599

❇ **Woodstock Gardens**   `54 B2`
Inistioge, Co. Kilkenny. The gardens were designed by Lady Louisa Tighe during the 19th century and were one of the finest examples of a Victorian garden. They gradually became overgrown but 20ha (50 acres) of formal gardens, arboretum and woodland are now being restored to their former glory. The Arboretum was planted between 1750 and 1900 and contains many rare, mature trees. There are many walks from which the terraced flower garden, bathhouse, walled garden, rose garden, dovecote, ice-house and several follies can be seen.
☎ 056 52699

🏛 **Workhouse Museum**   `50 B3`
Donaghmore, Co. Laois. Originally built in the 1850s, this workhouse could, and did, take up to 400 people at any one time, following the famine years of 1845 to 1849. Today, there is an agricultural museum displaying artefacts which were in use by the rural community during the 19th and 20th centuries. Life in the workhouse has also been depicted by the renovation of the original dormitories and workrooms.
☎ 0505 46212

★ **Yola Farmstead Folk Park**   `55 D3`
Tagoat, Rosslare, Co. Wexford. This restored 18th century farmstead complex shows life as it was in the 1700s. It features a farmhouse, school, forge, working windmill, church, aviary, thatched cottages and farm animals. Refreshments are available in 'Granny's Kitchen' with its authentic open fire. Yola Park is also a County Genealogy Centre.
☎ 053 32610

Munster

Munster (population 1,033,903) is the largest of the four provinces of Ireland having an area of 24,000 sq kms but a population less than that of County Dublin.

It comprises counties Clare, Kerry, Limerick, Tipperary, Waterford and Cork which is the largest county in Ireland having an area of 7457 sq kms.

The Ring of Kerry and the Dingle Peninsula are two of the most frequented areas in Ireland and can be extremely busy in the summer months.

Gaeltacht (Irish speaking) areas include the Dingle Peninsula, parts of the Iveragh Peninsula, the Muscerry Gaeltacht west of Macroom in County Cork, Clear Island and the area around Ring in County Waterford.

Great Blasket Island

Cork Kerry Regional Tourism

Aras Fáilte, Grand Parade, Cork
☎ 021 273251

Shannon Development

Shannon, Co Clare
☎ 061 361555   www.shannon-dev.ie/tourism

South East Regional Tourism

41 The Quay, Waterford
☎ 051 875823   www.ireland-southeast.travel.ie

Map pages in this region

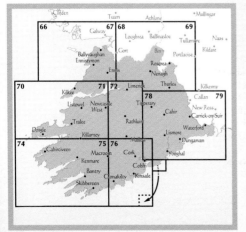

Primroses in Ballyheigue

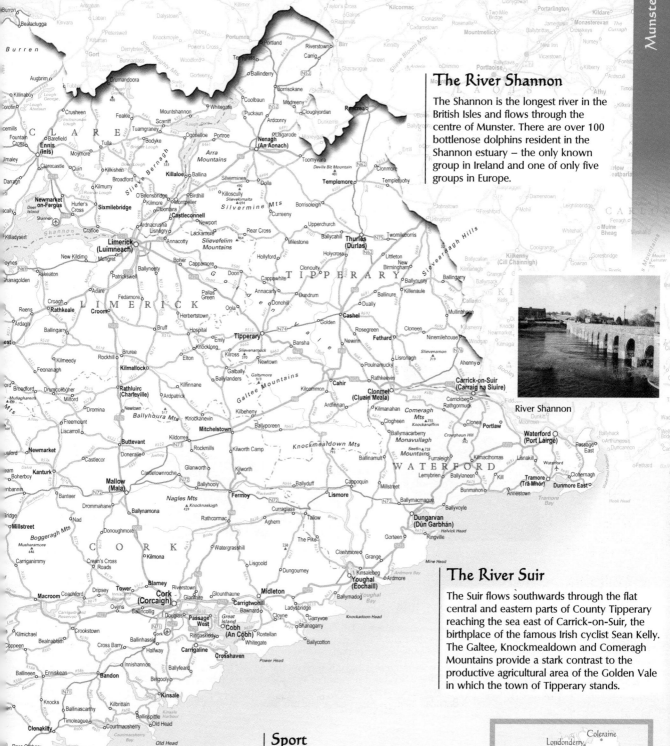

The River Shannon

The Shannon is the longest river in the British Isles and flows through the centre of Munster. There are over 100 bottlenose dolphins resident in the Shannon estuary – the only known group in Ireland and one of only five groups in Europe.

River Shannon

The River Suir

The Suir flows southwards through the flat central and eastern parts of County Tipperary reaching the sea east of Carrick-on-Suir, the birthplace of the famous Irish cyclist Sean Kelly. The Galtee, Knockmealdown and Comeragh Mountains provide a stark contrast to the productive agricultural area of the Golden Vale in which the town of Tipperary stands.

Sport

Sport is an important part of life throughout Ireland and nowhere more so than in Munster. Limerick, in particular, is a big rugby area and hurling and gaelic football are popular throughout the province – a common sight during each season are the county flags being hung from windows and flagposts particularly when the all-Ireland championships reach their respective climaxes at Croke Park in Dublin, usually in September. Hurling is the world's oldest field game which has been chronicled in Irish history for over 2000 years.

Hurling

Munster

Romance in Lisdoonvarna

Lisdoonvarna is a small spa town famous for its annual Matchmaking Festival which runs throughout September and into October, mainly concentrated at weekends. Matchmaking originated by the desire of rich landowners that their children marry into a similar family. The Festival culminates in the selection of Mr and Miss Lisdoonvarna and also Queen of the Burren.

The Cliffs of Moher

Doolin

The Clare Coastline

County Clare is home to some spectacular, rugged coastline stretching from Loop Head past the Cliffs of Moher and further north towards Doolin and Black Head, where the limestone pavement of the Burren, stretches out into the sea.

There are evocative names to coastal features such as Mal Bay, Hag's Head (see page 70), and Spanish Point, so called because of its association with the ships of the Spanish Armada, which foundered nearby. Many of the survivors were massacred by High Sheriff Boethius Mac Clancy and are buried near the shore.

Tourist Information

ⓘ **Cliffs of Moher**
Cliffs of Moher
Liscannor
County Clare
☎ 065 708 1171

ⓘ **Kilkee**
The Square
Kilkee
County Clare
☎ 065 905 6112

ⓘ **Kilrush**
Town Hall
Kilrush
County Clare
☎ 065 905 1577

miles
0 5 10

0 5 10 15
kilometres

The Burren

The Burren

The Burren (*boireann* meaning rocky place), is one of Ireland's most unique areas, being the largest area of Karst limestone in Europe. It almost resembles a lunarscape in its most isolated areas and is a stark contrast to the mountains or lush green landscape most associated with Ireland. Apart from being of great interest to botanists and geologists, a wealth of archaeological interest is to be found in the Burren including the famous Poulnabrone Dolmen south of Ballyvaughan dating back to 2500BC.

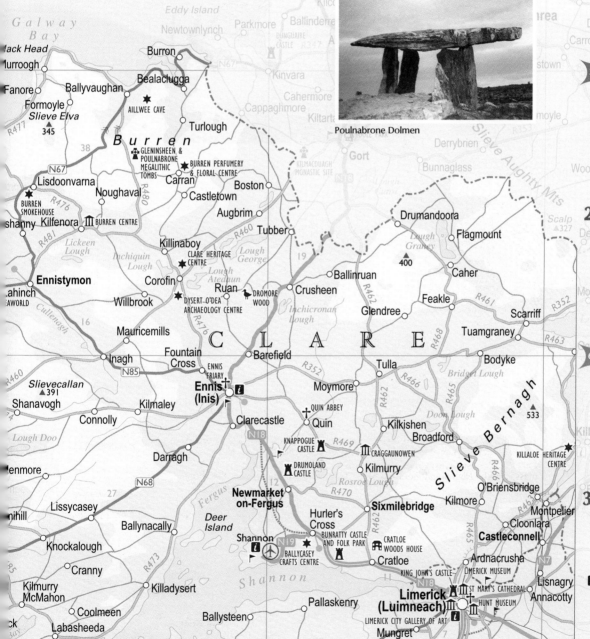
Poulnabrone Dolmen

Tourist Information

🛈 **Ennis**
O'Connell Street
Ennis
County Clare
☎ 065 682 8366

🛈 **Limerick**
Arthur's Quay
Limerick
County Limerick
☎ 061 317522

🛈 **Shannon Airport**
Arrivals Hall
Shannon Airport
Shannon
County Clare
☎ 061 471664

Munster

Lough Derg

The vast expanse of Lough Derg is the largest lake on the River Shannon which runs through Counties Clare, Limerick and Tipperary.

The scenery around the lake changes from being flat, though not without its attraction, in the north, to being surrounded by the wooded mountains of Slieve Bernagh and the Arra Mountains in the south.

Portumna, Mountshannon and Killaloe are the main boating centres for the exploration of Lough Derg.

Lough Derg

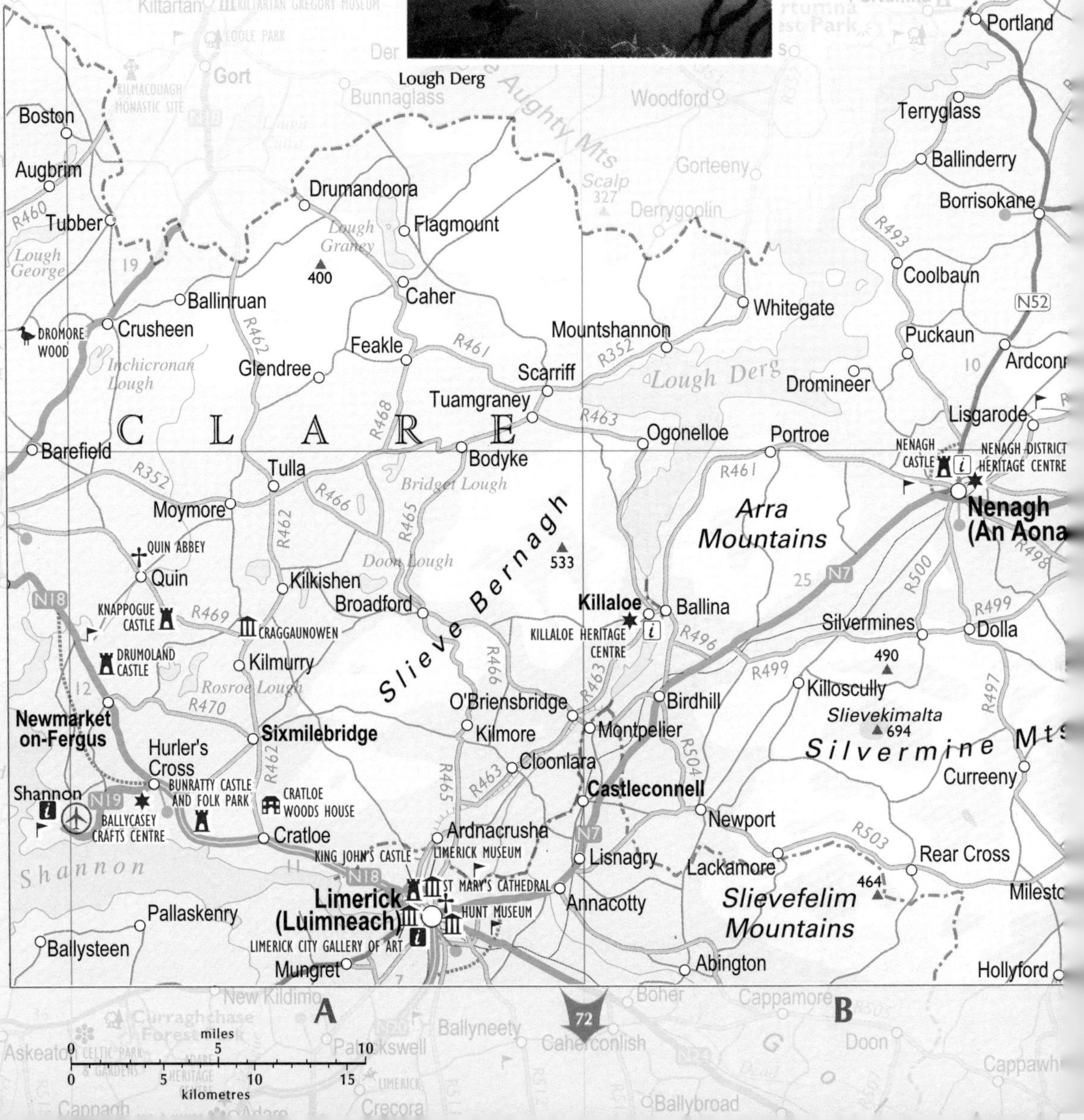

Tourist Information

i **Killaloe**
Heritage Centre
Killaloe
County Clare
☎ 061 376866

i **Limerick**
Arthur's Quay
Limerick
County Limerick
☎ 061 317522

i **Nenagh**
Connolly Street
Nenagh
County Tipperary
☎ 067 31610

i **Shannon Airport**
Arrivals Hall
Shannon Airport
Shannon
County Clare
☎ 061 471664

miles
0   5   10

0   5   10   15
kilometres

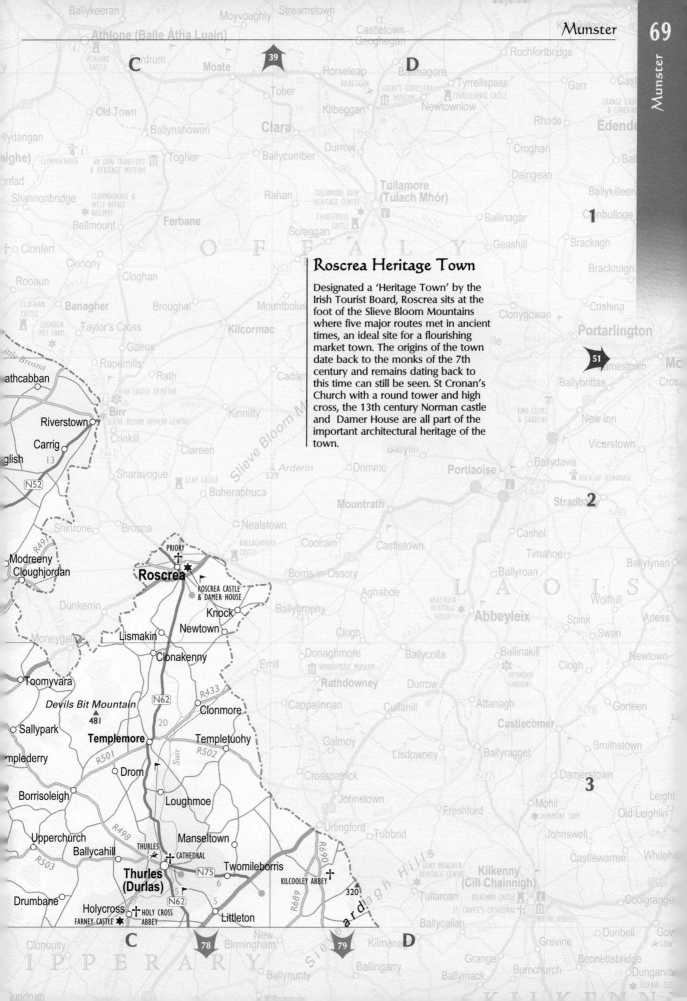

Roscrea Heritage Town

Designated a 'Heritage Town' by the Irish Tourist Board, Roscrea sits at the foot of the Slieve Bloom Mountains where five major routes met in ancient times, an ideal site for a flourishing market town. The origins of the town date back to the monks of the 7th century and remains dating back to this time can still be seen. St Cronan's Church with a round tower and high cross, the 13th century Norman castle and Damer House are all part of the important architectural heritage of the town.

A **B**

The Legend of Loop Head

The Clare coastline is spectacular and nowhere more so than at Loop Head, which has the advantage of being off the tourist routes and is relatively quiet. Loop Head (Ceann Léime) gets its name from Cúchulainn who leapt the chasm between the headland and the offshore rock in order to escape the pursuing hag, Mal. In trying to follow she fell to her death in the sea below. Her body was washed ashore further north in Mal Bay and her head at Hag's Head just south of the Cliffs of Moher.

Loop Head

1

Irish National Folk Theatre

2

Tralee

Race Week and the Rose of Tralee Festival are held in Tralee (population 21,000) every August. The Rose of Tralee beauty pageant has been held every year since 1959 and attracts entrants of Irish birth or ancestry from all over the world.

Tralee is also the headquarters of Ireland's National Folk Theatre (Siamsa Tire) which presents performances of Irish culture throughout the year.

3

Tourist Information

ⓘ **Dingle**

The Pier
Dingle
County Kerry
☎ 066 915 1188

Feeard

Kilbaha

Loop Head

Mo

Ballynaskreen

Dreenagh
Kerry Hd
▲ 217
Ballyheigue

R55

Ballyheigue Bay

R55

ARDFERT CATHEDRAL
Ardfert

The Seven Hogs or Magharee Islands

Brandon Head
Brandon

Fahamore

Rough Pt

Tralee Bay

Fenit
FENIT SEAWORLD ★
Spa
R5

Ballydavid Head
Tiduff
765 ▲
Brandon Mountain
953 ▲

Ballyquin

Brandon Bay

Castlegregory

TRALEE & DIN
STEAM RAIL

Camp
R560
Derrymore
Baurtregaum
Caherconree ▲
827 ▲ 852

N86

Smerwick Harbour
Feohanagh

Cloghane

Beenoskee
827

Stradbally

Dingle

Smerwick

Sybil Point

✝ GALLARUS (ORATORY)
R559

Slievanea
618

Lougher

Boottee
R561

Aughils Bridge

Slieve Mish Mt

Anascaul

Inch

Castlemaine Harbour

Inishtooskert

THE BLASKET CENTRE ★
Ventry
Milltown

OCEANWORLD
★ **Dingle**
ⓘ

N86

Lispole

Great Blasket I.

Dunquin
R559

Doonmanagh

Cromane

Killorglin

Slea Head

Tearaght Island

miles
0   5   10

0   5   10   15
kilometres

Inishvickillane

Glenbeigh

🏛 KERRY BOG VILLAGE

494

N70

Seefin

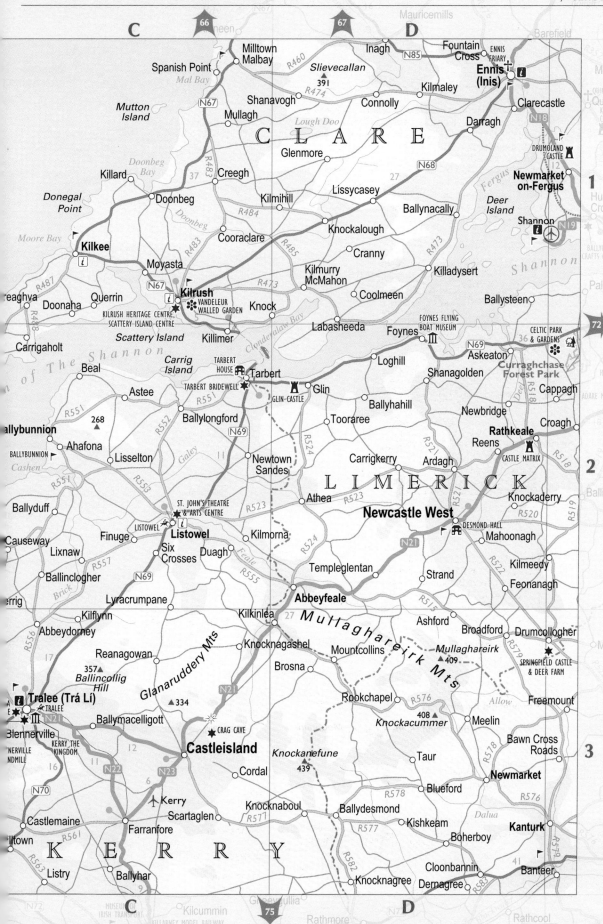

66 · 67 · 72 · 75

Tourist Information

Ennis
O'Connell Street
Ennis
County Clare
☎ 065 682 8366

Kilkee
The Square
Kilkee
County Clare
☎ 065 905 6112

Kilrush
Town Hall
Kilrush
County Clare
☎ 065 905 1577

Listowel
St John's Church
The Square
Listowel
County Kerry
☎ 068 22590

Shannon Airport
Arrivals Hall
Shannon Airport
Shannon
County Clare
☎ 061 471664

Tralee
Denny Street
Ashe Hall
Tralee
County Kerry
☎ 066 712 1288

68

68

71

76

78

Tourist Information

i **Adare**
Adare Heritage Centre
Main Street
Adare
County Limerick
☎ 061 396255

i **Killaloe**
Heritage Centre
Killaloe
County Clare
☎ 061 376866

i **Limerick**
Arthur's Quay
Limerick
County Limerick
☎ 061 317522

i **Nenagh**
Connolly Street
Nenagh
County Tipperary
☎ 067 31610

i **Shannon Airport**
Arrivals Hall
Shannon Airport
Shannon
County Clare
☎ 061 471664

i **Tipperary**
James Street
Tipperary
County Tipperary
☎ 062 51457

Limerick (Population: 52,039)

Christian settlements had been established in the 5th century on the island later to become known as King's Island. It was here that Limerick developed during the reign of King John of England 1199 – 1216, after whom the island is named.

Limerick loves its sport especially Horse Racing, Gaelic Football, Hurling and, perhaps most of all, Rugby. The high kick followed by the charge to recapture the ball is named after the Garryowen Rugby Club, alleged to have been the first to use it.

Frank McCourt, based his Pulitzer Prize winning book *Angela's Ashes* on his upbringing in Limerick.

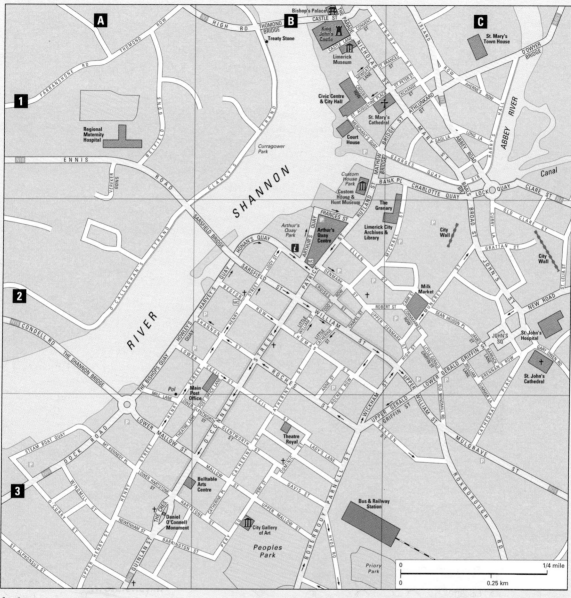

Index to street names

Tourist Information

i **Limerick City**
Arthurs Quay
☎ 061 317522

A   B

Inishtooskert
THE BLASKET CENTRE   (ORATORY) OCEANWORLD
Great Blasket I.   Slea Head   Dunquin   Ventry   Milltown   Dingle   N86   Lispole   Anascaul   Aughils Bridge
                                                                                      Inch
                                                                                      Slieve

Tearaght Island

Inishvickillane

70   Doonmanagh   Killorglin

Dingle Bay

N70

Glenbeigh   494   KERRY BOG VILLAGE MUSE
R561   Seefin   Lough Caragh   Shanacashel   Carr
                                    Bealalaw Bridge   Maghanlawa
Ring of Kerry   Darby's Bridge   Coomacarrea   Colly   Macgilly
Knocknadober   691   Kells   774   688
                                    Iveragh
1
Doulus Head   HERITAGE CENTRE   The Pocket   774   K
Knightstown   Cahirciveen   Foilclough   Lissatinning Bridge   Derreendaragh
Valencia Island   Chapeltown   N70   500
SKELLIG EXPERIENCE   R565   Knocknagullion
Clynacartan   Agnagar Bridge   Inny   Mastergeehy   Derriana Lough   Letterfinish   415
Portmagee   R566   Saliahig   Cloonaghlin Lough   R568
Bray Head   Teeranearagh   R567   Waterville   Lough Currane   Sneem   RING OF KERRY   Tahilla
St Finan's Bay   Ballinskelligs   Ballybrack   39   Parknasilla   Kenmare River
Bolus Head   Ballinskelligs Bay   STAIGUE STONE FORT   R573
Skellig Rocks   DERRYNANE HOUSE   Castlecove   DERREEN GARDEN
                 Derrynane   Catherdaniel   Collorus   Laur
2   Nat. Hist. Park   N70   B e
   Lamb's Head   Ardgroom   Glanmore Lake
Lakes of Killarney   Scariff Island   R571   Hungry Hil   686
                     Cod's Head   Eyeries   Glenbeg Lough   Castletown   Curryglas
                                    Allihies   Bere   Ballynakilla
                     Ballydonegan   Slieve Miskish Mts   R572   Rerrin
Ballynacallagh   Garnish   R575
Dursey Island   Cahermore   Bear Island
Dursey Head   Ballyroo

Monterivary or Sheep's Head

Three Castle Head   Crookha

MIZEN VISION
3   Mizen Head

Muckross House

Gap of Dunloe

A   B

miles
0   5   10
0   5   10   15
kilometres

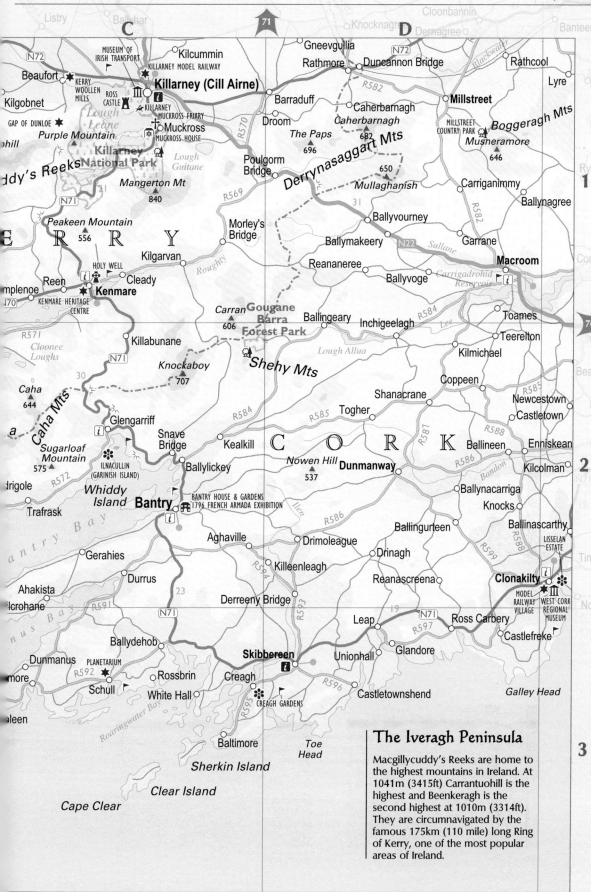

The Iveragh Peninsula

Macgillycuddy's Reeks are home to the highest mountains in Ireland. At 1041m (3415ft) Carrantuohill is the highest and Beenkeragh is the second highest at 1010m (3314ft). They are circumnavigated by the famous 175km (110 mile) long Ring of Kerry, one of the most popular areas of Ireland.

71
76

Tourist Information

i **Bantry**
The Old Courthouse
The Square
Bantry
County Clare
☎ 027 50229

i **Clonakilty**
25 Ashe Street
Clonakilty
County Cork
☎ 023 33226

i **Glengarriff**
Eccles Car Park
Glengarriff
County Cork
☎ 027 63084

i **Kenmare**
Heritage Centre
Kenmare
County Kerry
☎ 064 41233

i **Killarney**
Beech Road
Killarney
County Kerry
☎ 064 31633

i **Macroom**
Castle Gates
The Square
Macroom
County Cork
☎ 026 43280

i **Skibbereen**
Town Hall
Skibbereen
County Cork
☎ 028 21766

Map labels

Kanturk · Ballyclough · Castletownroche · Lyrenac

Banteer · Mallow (Mala) · Killavullen · Ballyhooly · Clondulane

Fermoy

N72 · N72

A · B

Drommahane · Ballynamona · Burnfoot · Knocknaskagh 429 · Castlelyons

Lyre · Nad · Rathcormac · R628 · Aghern · Ballynoe

Donoughmore · Bottlehill · Glenville · Bride · Britway

C O R K · Watergrasshill · Ardglass

Kilmona · Whitechurch · Leamlara · Lisgoold · Dungourney

Crean's Cross Roads · 22 · Knockraha · R626

Rylane Cross

Ballynagree · Matehy · N8

Aghabullogue · R619 · BLARNEY HOUSE · **Blarney** · Riverstown · RIVERSTOWN HOUSE · BARRYSCOURT CASTLE

Coachford · Dripsey · **Tower** · DUNKATHEL · ASHBOURNE HOUSE · Glounthaune · **Midleto**

BLARNEY CASTLE · **Cork (Corcaigh)** · Glanmire · FOTA ISLAND · Carrigtwohill · JAMESON HERITAGE

Inniscarra Reservoir · Ovens · Ballincollig · CATHEDRAL · CORK HERITAGE PARK · FOTA WILDLIFE PARK & ARBORETUM · Bawnard

Carrigadrohid Reservoir · BALLINCOLLIG GUNPOWDER MILLS · CORK CITY GAOL, CORK PUBLIC MUSEUM · Great Island · THE QUEENSTOWN STORY · Cloyne

N22 · 23 · Aherla · Douglas · N52

Crookstown · Waterfall · N71 · N27 · **Passage West** · **Cobh (An Cóbh)** · R630

R590 · Raheen · Cork · Ringaskiddy · R613 · Rostellan

Bealnablath · Ballinhassig · **Carrigaline** · R612 · Whitegate · Churchto

Cross Barry · Halfway · **Crosshaven** · Gyleen

Newcestown · R589 · 19 · Minane Bridge · For continuat see below

Castletown · R586 · Innishannon · WEST CORK HERITAGE CENTRE · Ballyfeard · To Roscoff 14 hrs (summer only) · To Swansea 10 hrs

Enniskean · Belgooly · Nohoval

Ballineen · Kilcolman · N71 · **Bandon** · R605 · KINSALE 1601 · DESMOND CASTLE · KINSALE MUSEUM

Knocks · 13 · Ballinadee · R606 · **Kinsale** · CHARLES FORT · Oysterhaven

Ballinascarthy · R602 · R603 · Kilbrittain · R600 · Kinsale Harbour

R588 · TIMOLEAGUE ABBEY · Ballinspittle · Old Head

Clonakilty · LISSELAN ESTATE · Timoleague · Courtmacsherry · Lispatrick

MODEL RAILWAY VILLAGE · WEST CORK REGIONAL MUSEUM · North Ring · R601 · Courtmacsherry Bay · Old Head of Kinsale

Butlerstown · Seven Heads

Clonakilty Bay

Galley Head

Tourist Information

ℹ Blarney
Blarney
County Cork
☎ 021 438 1624

ℹ Clonakilty
25 Ashe Street
Clonakilty
County Cork
☎ 023 33226

ℹ Cork
Tourist House
Grand Parade
Cork
County Cork
☎ 021 425 5100

ℹ Kinsale
Pier Road
Kinsale
County Cork
☎ 021 477 2234

ℹ Midleton
Jameson Heritage
Centre
Distillery Walk
Midleton
County Cork
☎ 021 461 3702

Lusitania Monument

Cobh

Cobh (pronounced Cove) was renamed Queenstown after a visit by Queen Victoria in 1849 though it reverted to its original name in 1921. One of the world's largest natural harbours, it was a major departure point for emigrants especially during the famine years of the 1840s.

On the promenade stands a monument to the victims of the Lusitania, torpedoed by a German submarine off the Kinsale coast in 1915. Cobh was also the last port of call for the Titanic before sinking in the Atlantic in 1912.

The Royal Cork Yacht Club (formerly The Water Club of the Harbour of Cork) was established in 1720 and is the world's oldest sailing club.

Midleton inset
ℹ **Midleton** · N25 · R633 · Ballymadog

JAMESON HERITAGE CENTRE · Castlemartyr · Ladysbridge · Ballymacoda

Bawnard · R633 · R632

Cloyne · R629 · Garryvoe

R630 · Shanagarry · BALLYMALOE COOKERY SCHOOL GARDENS

Churchtown · Ballycotton

Scale

miles
0 · 5 · 10

0 · 5 · 10 · 15
kilometres

Cork (Population: 127,187)

Cork is Ireland's third city behind Belfast and Dublin. The Irish form is Corcaigh, meaning marshy place, though the marshes are no longer in evidence. The city was originated in the 7th century by St Fin Barre to the south on the site of the 19th century St Fin Barre's Cathedral. However, the centre is now on the island between the two arms of the River Lee which give the city a continental feel with the many bridges that cross the river.

The River Lee is popular with salmon anglers and sea angling is available out of nearby Cobh, Crosshaven and Monkstown.

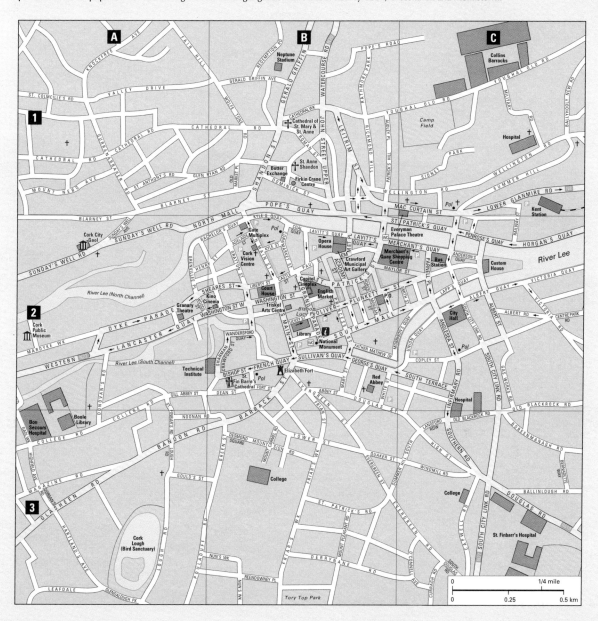

Index to street names

Tourist Information

i **Cork City**
Grand Parade
☎ 021 427 3251

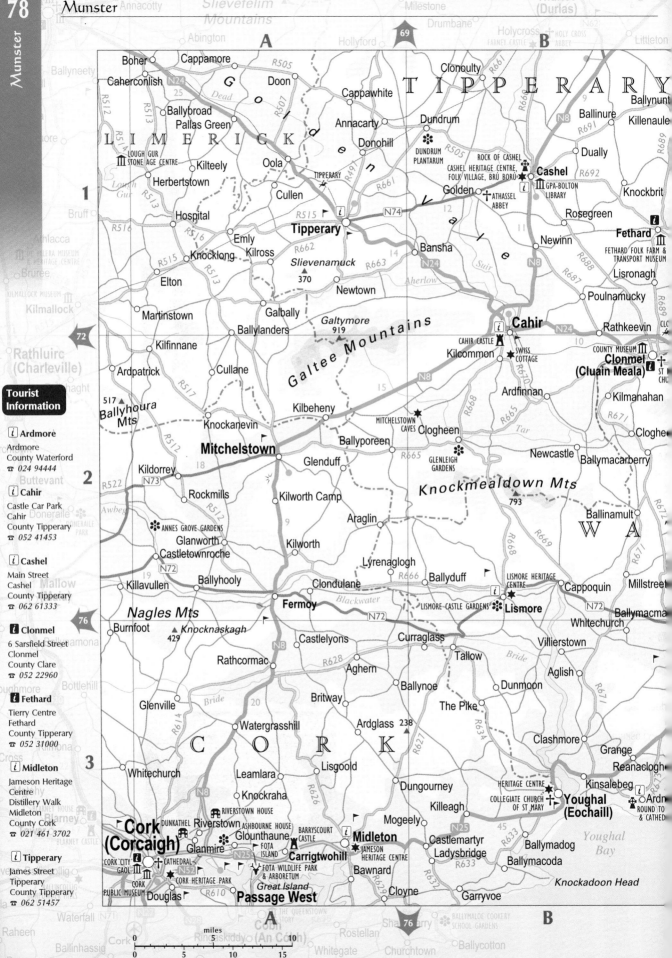

Tourist Information

i **Ardmore**
Ardmore
County Waterford
☎ 024 94444

i **Cahir**
Castle Car Park
Cahir
County Tipperary
☎ 052 41453

i **Cashel**
Main Street
Cashel
County Tipperary
☎ 062 61333

i **Clonmel**
6 Sarsfield Street
Clonmel
County Clare
☎ 052 22960

i **Fethard**
Tierry Centre
Fethard
County Tipperary
☎ 052 31000

i **Midleton**
Jameson Heritage
Centre
Distillery Walk
Midleton
County Cork
☎ 021 461 3702

i **Tipperary**
James Street
Tipperary
County Tipperary
☎ 062 51457

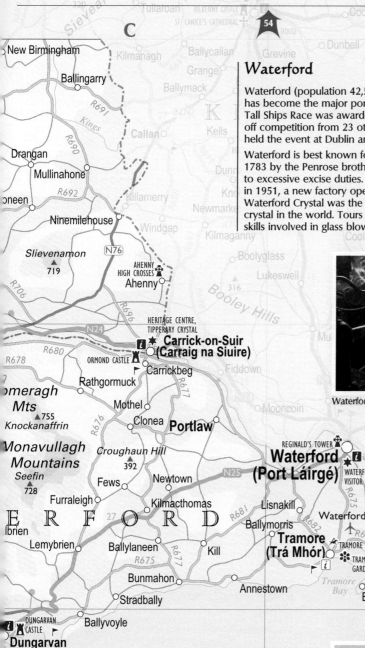

Waterford

Waterford (population 42,540) at the head of the Suir estuary, has become the major port in South East Ireland. The annual Tall Ships Race was awarded to Waterford for 2005 after fighting off competition from 23 other locations. Ireland has previously held the event at Dublin and Cork.

Waterford is best known for its crystal which was founded in 1783 by the Penrose brothers but forced to close in 1851 due to excessive excise duties. However the crystal was relaunched in 1951, a new factory opened in the 1960s and by the 1980s. Waterford Crystal was the largest producers of hand crafted crystal in the world. Tours of the factory give an insight into the skills involved in glass blowing and cutting.

Waterford Crystal

Rock of Cashel

Tourist Information

i **Carrick-on-Suir**

Heritage Centre
Carrick-on-Suir
County Tipperary
☎ 051 640 200

i **Dungarvan**

Gratton Square
Dungarvan
County Waterford
☎ 058 41741

i **Tramore**

Railway Square
Tramore
County Waterford
☎ 051 381572

i **Waterford**

41 The Quay
Waterford
County Waterford
☎ 051 875823

i **Waterford**

Waterford Crystal
Visitor Centre
Kilbarry
Cork Road
Waterford
County Waterford
☎ 051 358397

✴ Adare Heritage Centre — 72 A2

Adare, Co. Limerick. Situated beside the River Maguire, the picturesque village of Adare once belonged to the Kildare Fitzgeralds and then the Earls of Dunraven; the story of Adare from the arrival of the Normans is told at the centre through audiovisual displays and models. Several buildings of historic interest in the village are witness to its heritage; the remains of a 16th century Franciscan Friary, medieval Desmond castle and 19th century Adare Manor.
☎ 061 396666/396924

❋ Adare Manor — 72 A2

Adare, Co. Limerick. A Gothic Revival manor house built by the 2nd Earl of Dunraven in 1832 to his own design with additional work by James Pain and A.W. Pugin; the interior contains a handsome rococo staircase and distinctive arched entrance hall. Situated beside the River Maguire, the manor has 336ha (830 acres) of formal gardens and ornamental parkland.
☎ 061 396566   www.adaremanor.com

✝ Ahenny High Crosses — 79 C1

Ahenny, Co. Tipperary. A pair of intricate high crosses dating from the 8th century carved in interlacing traditional Celtic patterns rather than the more usual style depicting Biblical stories.
☎ 051 640200

✴ Aillwee Cave — 67 C2

Ballyvaughan, Co. Clare. Aillwee Cave was discovered in 1940 by a local shepherd. Well over 2 million years old, the 1km long tunnel is filled with stalagmites and stalactites and has an illuminated underground river and waterfall.
☎ 065 707 7036   www.aillweecave.ie

❋ Annes Grove Gardens — 78 A2

Castletownroche, Co. Cork. This 12ha (30 acre) garden was transformed to its current layout in 1907. It comprises a walled garden, water garden, the glen and the riverside garden. Rhododendron seeds collected by Kingdon Ward in the Himalayan region are a major feature of the woodland garden, and the riverside garden, set in a limestone gorge, has an island and bridges which were constructed before WWI by soldiers stationed at Fermoy.
☎ 022 26145   www.gardensireland.com

✝ Ardfert Cathedral — 70 B3

Ardfert, Co. Kerry. 'The Great Navigator' St Brendan, who, folklore has it, discovered America 900 years before Columbus, founded a monastery on this site in the 6th century. Today there are remains of two medieval churches, a friary and the Cathedral which dates from the 12th century. It has a well-preserved Romanesque doorway, interesting carvings and a row of nine lancets.
☎ 066 713 4711   www.heritageireland.ie

✝ Ardmore Round Tower & Cathedral — 78 B3

Ardmore, Co. Waterford. Dominating the coastline, 12th century Ardmore Round Tower stands 29m (95ft) high on a monastic site which includes the ruins of a 12th century cathedral with a 9th century chancel. The west gable of the cathedral is decorated with a Romanesque frieze of carved figures depicting Biblical scenes and there are stones inscribed with Ogham writing, the first written Celtic language. Close by is a small stone church or oratory, possibly dating back to the 8th century, and reputed to be the site of St Declan's grave.
☎ 024 94444

❋ Ashbourne House & Gardens — 76 B1

Glounthaune, Co. Cork. A 2.5ha (6 acre) Robinsonian style garden originated by Richard Henrik Beamish at the start of the 20th century which includes a bog garden, an arched Irish Yew Walk and a woodland garden.
☎ 021 435 3319

✝ Athassel Abbey — 78 B1

Golden, Co. Tipperary. Built in the 12th century and burnt down in 1447, it is believed to be the largest medieval priory in Ireland. The original cloisters, gatehouse and chapter house are still standing as well as the 15th century tower.
☎ 052 41453

✴ Ballincollig Gunpowder Mills — 76 A1

Ballincollig, Co. Cork. One of the largest industrial complexes in the area in the mid 19th century covering over 50ha (130 acres). The mills fell into disuse after the end of the Boer War in 1902. Restoration began in the 1980s and the site was opened to the public in 1993 and now includes an informative Heritage Centre.
☎ 021 487 4430   indigo.ie/~ballinco

⛳ Ballybunnion Golf Club — 71 C2

Sandhill Road, Ballybunnion, Co. Kerry. A links course described by Tom Watson as 'one of the best and most beautiful tests of links golf anywhere in the world'. The Irish Professional, the Irish Matchplay and the Irish Open Championships have all been held here.
☎ 068 27146   www.ballybuniongolfclub.ie

✴ Ballycasey Crafts Centre — 72 A1

Ballycasey, Shannon, Co. Clare. Only a few minutes from Shannon Airport, craftsmen can be observed making Aran knitwear, pottery, ironwork and jewellery in the courtyard of the 18th century Ballycasey House.
☎ 061 362105

❋ Ballymaloe Cookery School Gardens — 76 B3

Shanagarry, Midleton, Co. Cork. Set on a working organic farm with its own animals. Most of the vegetables and herbs used in the school are grown in the adjoining gardens which are open to the public. The herb garden is the largest in Ireland and there is also a shell house, fruit and water gardens and a celtic maze.
☎ 021 464 6785   www.ballymaloe-cookery-school.ie

⊞ Bantry House & Gardens — 75 C2

Bantry, Co. Cork. Home of the White family since 1765 and magnificently sited to overlook Bantry Bay. On display is furniture and art collected on the European travels of the 2nd Earl of Bantry. He was also responsible for the gardens which are in the process of being restored.
☎ 027 50047   www.bantryhouse.ie

♜ Barryscourt Castle — 76 B1

Carrigtwohill, Co. Cork. Barryscourt Castle was the seat of the Barry family for 500 years until the 17th century. The Tower house dates from the 15th century though it was added to in the 16th century. An exhibition of the history of the castle and of the arts in Ireland during the time of the Barrys is on the ground floor of the Keep.
☎ 021 488 2218   www.heritageireland.ie

⚔ Battle of Kinsale — 76 A2

Kinsale, Co. Cork. The struggle for independence was dealt an ultimately terminal blow when the Irish forces, led by Hugh O'Neill and Hugh O'Donnell, and their Spanish allies were defeated at the Battle of Kinsale in 1601. The Spanish landed at Kinsale and were surrounded by the English meaning that the Irish had to make a long march south to come to their aid. Despite having the greater numbers, the alliance was defeated and for many this signalled the end and the migration to the Americas began.
☎ 021 477 2234   www.kinsale1601.com

⌂ Bishop's Palace — 73 B1

Church Street, King's Island, Limerick, Co. Limerick. Formerly the home of the Protestant Bishops of Limerick, the English Palladian style building with classical façade is now occupied by the Limerick City Trust.
☎ 061 313399

♜ Blarney Castle — 76 A1

Blarney, Co. Cork. The keep, standing on a rocky outcrop, amid 18th century parkland, was built in 1446. The Blarney Stone lies just beneath the battlements. According to the rhyme 'A stone that whoever kisses, O he never misses to grow eloquent' but the origin of this bizarre piece of hokum is unknown, although it is said that Dermot MacCarthy was expert in using honeyed language to keep the English at bay in the 16th century.
☎ 021 438 5353   www.blarneycastle.ie

⌂ Blarney House — 76 A1

Blarney, Co. Cork. Situated next to Blarney Castle, Blarney House is as good an example of a Scottish baronial mansion as can be found. The landscaped gardens include an arboretum and views of Blarney Lake.
☎ 021 438 5252

✴ Blasket Centre, The (Ionad an Bhlascaid Mhóir) — 70 A3

Dunquin, Dingle, Co. Kerry. The Centre at Dunquin (Dún Chaoin) tells the story of the Blasket Islands off the tip of the Dingle Peninsula which were abandoned in 1953. The rich literary history and the traditional Irish culture of the islands are told and there are regular boat trips to Great Blasket in the summer, weather permitting.
☎ 066 9156444/9156371   www.heritageireland.ie

✴ Blennerville Windmill — 71 C3

Blennerville, Tralee, Co. Kerry. Built in the late 18th century by Sir Rowland Blennerhasset, the windmill was restored in 1984 and is the largest working windmill in Ireland at 21.5m (70 ft) high. The visitor is guided through the flour making process and the visitor centre has audiovisuals and exhibitions giving an insight into the history of the industry and of the area.
☎ 066 712106

✴ Brú Ború Heritage Centre — 78 B1

Cashel, Co. Tipperary. Located at the foot of the Rock of Cashel, the Centre is named after Brian Ború, the 10th century king of Ireland. Many facets of Irish life including music, dance, theatre and genealogy are celebrated.
☎ 062 61122

♜ Bunratty Castle & Folk Park — 72 A1

Bunratty, Co. Clare. The magnificent keep has been restored to how it looked at the time of its construction in 1460. Widely admired in its heyday, the three storeyed keep retains its corner towers and massive arches. Inside is the vaulted entrance hall, with so-called 'sheela-na-gig' (female fertility figure) in the wall, chapel and cellars with 16th century stucco work. Many rooms contain period furniture whilst mock banquets regularly evoke the castle's colourful past. The nearby folk park has examples of traditional Irish houses and agricultural machinery and demonstrations of ancient skills.
☎ 061 360788   www.castlesireland.com

⛪ Burren Centre — 67 C2

Kilfenora, Co. Clare. An introduction to the rich diversity of flora, fauna and geology of the Burren (boirreen in Gaelic meaning rocky place) which has created the magnificent landscape of limestone pavement into which numerous ruins, monuments and megalithic tombs blend quite naturally.
☎ 065 708 8030

✴ Burren Perfumery & Floral Centre — 67 C2

Carron, Co. Clare. The oldest working perfumery in Ireland producing such fragrances as Man of Aran, Fronde, Fraoch and Ilaun. The distillation and blending processes can be observed and a herb garden has recently been opened.
☎ 065 708 9102   www.burrenperfumery.com

✴ Burren Smokehouse — 67 C2

Kincora Road, Lisdoonvarna, Co. Clare. The processing of fresh Atlantic salmon, mackerel, trout and eels can be seen including the sorting, salting and smoking over oak chips. The Visitor Centre gives an overview of the whole process in several languages and a craft shop sells locally produced goods.
☎ 065 707 4432   www.burrensmokehouse.ie

♜ Cahir Castle `78 B2`

Castle Street, Cahir, Co. Tipperary. A pretty town, Cahir boasts this impressive castle, the largest of its type in the country, which sits on a rocky outcrop in the middle of the River Suir at the foot of the Galty Mountains. It dates back to the 15th century and was inappropriately restored in 1840. However, behinds its walls are a huge keep, a furnished great hall and two courts. Notwithstanding its solid appearance it was frequently overrun and in 1650 surrendered to Cromwell without coming to battle.

☎ 052 41011   www.heritageireland.ie

✹ Cahirciveen Heritage Centre `74 A1`

The Barracks, Cahirciveen, Co. Kerry. Housed in the unusual conical tower of the Royal Irish Constabulary Barracks constructed in the 1870s. The building would not be out of place in India and it has been said that an Irish Police Station stands on the Indian North West frontier after the plans were accidentally switched! A variety of exhibits show the history of the town and of the building.

☎ 066 947 2777

✹ Carrick-on-Suir Heritage Centre `79 C2`

Main Street, Carrick-on-Suir, Co. Tipperary. The converted former Protestant church of St Nicholas of Myra which includes many interesting gravestones, amongst the many exhibits of local interest and a celebration of basketmaking which was once commonplace in the area.

☎ 051 640200

✹ Cashel Folk Village `78 B1`

Dominick Street, Cashel, Co. Tipperary. A reconstruction of a traditional thatched village including a butchers, public house and a blacksmiths. There are also exhibitions about the Great Famine, traditional trades including turf cutting and the 1916 Rising and the War of Independence.

☎ 062 62525

✹ Cashel Heritage Centre `78 B1`

Town Hall, Main Street, Cashel, Co. Tipperary. There is a scale model of Cashel in the 1640s and a multimedia presentation. The craft shop sells locally produced products including pottery, carvings, cheeses, preserves and woollen clothing.

☎ 062 62511

♜ Castle Matrix `71 D2`

Rathkeale, Co. Limerick. Built in 1440 by the 7th Earl of Desmond, the castle contains original furnishings, objets d'art, a fine library and historic documents. Walter Raleigh is reputed to have met Edmund Spencer here in the 1580s and begun a lifelong friendship. During the 17th century the castle was taken by Irish rebels and then in 1642 by Cromwell's forces. The castle has been fully restored and is now a venue for banquets and conferences.

☎ 069 64284

✝ Cathedral of St Mary & St Anne `77 B1`

Cathedral Street, Cork, Co. Cork. The Cathedral was built in 1808 and features a 55m (180ft) high tower built over the Great West Door. It was extensively renovated in 1996, the reordination of which was the last public function performed by Bishop Michael Murphy before he died 8 days later. The funeral of former Taoiseach Jack Lynch was held in the Cathedral in October 1999.

☎ 021 430 4325   www.iol.ie/~thefold/cath.html

❊ Celtic Park & Gardens `72 A2`

Kilcornan, Co. Limerick. Situated on the site of an original Celtic settlement, Celtic Park and Gardens was a renowned estate in the 17th century. Now re-created with authentic features such as stone circles, dolmens, cooking sites, and an early ring fort which give a perspective on the way of life of the pre-Christian Celts. Meanwhile, the classic style gardens with roses, flowering shrubs, lily ponds, and herbaceous beds afford panoramic views of the surrounding countryside, and the adjoining parkland is home to a variety of wild orchids.

☎ 061 394243

♜ Charles Fort `76 B2`

Summer Cove, Kinsale, Co. Cork. A classic 17th century example of a star-shaped fort which has five bastions, two of which face the sea. It was built by the English to protect the harbour but was poorly protected from landward attack and was taken by the forces of William of Orange in 1690. It remained in service until 1922 and was declared a National Monument in 1973.

☎ 021 477 2263   www.heritageireland.ie

✝ Church of St Anne Shandon `77 B1`

Church Street, Cork, Co. Cork. A landmark visible from most of the city with a distinctive salmon weather vane and a clock on all four sides of the tower. Built on the site of a medieval church in 1722 from a combination of red sandstone and limestone taken from the ruins of Shandon Castle and a Franciscan Friary nearby. A climb up the 120 steps to the top of the tower is rewarded with good views of the city and visitors get the opportunity to ring the Shandon bells.

☎ 021 450 5906   www.shandonsteeple.com

✹ Clare Heritage Centre `67 C2`

Church Street, Corofin, Co. Clare. Housed in the former St Catherine's Church which was previously an old barn before being converted in 1715. The original Tau Cross is on display and the 19th century Irish history of famine, disease and mass emigration is explored in some detail.

☎ 065 683 7955

✹ Cliffs of Moher & O'Brien's Tower `66 B2`

Liscannor, Co. Clare. The hustle and bustle of the car park and visitor centre 5kms (3 miles) north of Liscannor are a marked contrast to the spectacular cliffs a short walk away which rise to 200m (660ft) and extend for 8kms (5 miles). Seabirds nest on the numerous ledges on the headlands and stacks that have been created from the constant pounding of the Atlantic. The 19th century O'Brien's Tower is a Victorian viewpoint on the highest point of the cliffs near the visitor centre.

☎ 065 708 1171

✗ Clonmel Racecourse `78 B2`

Powerstone Park, Clonmel, Co. Tipperary. National Hunt and Flat racing course of 2kms (1.2 miles) with 12 race days a year including two evening meetings.

☎ 052 25719

✝ Collegiate Church of St Mary `78 B3`

Youghal, Co. Cork. Alleged to have been founded by St Declan in the 5th century it was rebuilt in the 13th century and has been substantially altered since then. Contains the grave and a monument to Sir Richard Boyle, Earl of Cork, who died in 1643 and a 14th century stone font.

☎ 024 94444

🏛 Cork City Gaol `77 A2`

Convent Avenue, Sunday's Well, Cork, Co. Cork. The Gaol closed after the Civil War in 1923 and is now a museum with furnished cells and life size figures showing the life of the inmates during the 19th and 20th century. The Radio Museum Experience is located in the Governor's House which housed the original studios of the 6CK radio station set up in 1927.

☎ 021 430 5022

🏛 Cork Heritage Park `76 B1`

Bessboro Road, Blackrock, Co. Cork. Set in 2.5ha (6 acres) of grounds originally part of the estate of the prominent Pike family in the 19th century. There are audio tours of the history and development of Cork, fire fighting and maritime exhibitions.

☎ 021 435 8854

🏛 Cork Public Museum `77 A2`

Fitzgerald Park, Cork, Co. Cork. The history of Cork is traced and archaeological finds from recent digs around the town walls are on display. Letters exchanged between Michael Collins and Kitty Kiernan are a recent addition to the exhibits.

☎ 021 427 0679

✗ Cork Racecourse `72 A3`

Navigation Road, Mallow, Co. Cork. A round, right handed, National Hunt and Flat racing course with 17 race days a year.

☎ 022 50207   www.corkracecourse.ie

✹ Crag Cave `71 C3`

Castleisland, Co. Kerry. Not far from Tralee, Crag Cave is really a network of limestone caves some 4kms (2.5 miles) in length, only discovered 1983. Over a million years old, they are festooned with stalactites and stalagmites, many of which have joined to form curtains and pillars. The Crystal Gallery is so called because of the white straw stalactites that glitter in the light.

☎ 066 714 1244

🏛 Craggaunowen `72 A1`

Quin, Co. Clare. Created in the 1960s in the grounds of Craggaunowen Castle, the centre is a recreation of a prehistoric site where traditional crafts and trades are carried out by people in the costume of the period. A Crannog, an artificial island containing clay huts, has been created in the lake and an original iron age timber road is also included.

☎ 061 360788   www.castlesireland.com

⌂ Cratloe Woods House `72 A1`

Cratloe, Co. Clare. Dating from the 17th century, this is the only example of an inhabited longhouse in Ireland. Of interest are numerous works of art, displays of horse drawn farm machinery and a pets' corner. Garranon Oak Wood, which provided the timbers for Westminster Hall in London, is part of the estate.

☎ 061 327028

❊ Creagh Gardens `75 C3`

Skibbereen, Co. Cork. 8ha (20 acres) of informal gardens amongst woodland leading down to the river estuary. There are woodland walks with tree ferns and rhododendrons, a large Regency walled garden, a number of woodland glades, a mill pond and ruined octagonal mill house.

☎ 028 22413   www.gardensireland.com

✹ Croom Mills Waterwheel & Heritage Centre `72 A2`

Croom, Co. Limerick. The history of grain milling in the Croom area and the impact it had on the local community is illustrated in the restored 19th century corn mill beside the River Maquire, where wheat is milled once more. Working conditions for 19th century millers are portrayed in the restored granary and visitors can try out grinding corn on an old quern stone with model milling equipment.

☎ 061 397130

🐾 Curraghchase Forest Park `72 A2`

Askeaton, Co. Limerick. A 240ha (593 acre) plantation which features a lake, arboretum and garden surrounding the ruins of the 18th century home of the de Vere family which included the poet, Aubrey de Vere.

☎ 061 337322

🏛 De Valera Museum & Heritage Centre `72 A2`

Bruree, Co. Limerick. Dedicated to the memory of Eamon De Valera (1882 – 1975), freedom fighter, statesman and President of Ireland, the museum is housed in his former school and contains a collection of his personal belongings. The history and heritage of the local area is also illustrated with artefacts relating to rural life in Bruree in the early 20th century.

☎ 063 91300/90530

❊ Derreen Garden `74 B2`

Lauragh, Kenmare, Co. Kerry. Located on the north coast of the Beara Peninsula, these woodland gardens were created by the 5th Marquess of Lansdowne in the 1870s at a time when exotic plants imported by travellers were in fashion. Sixty feet high Arborerum Rhododendrons, planted in the original garden, are amongst the plants which thrive in the moist climate warmed by the Gulf Stream.

☎ 064 83588   www.gardensireland.com

🏛 Derrynane House `74 A2`

Caherdaniel, Co. Kerry. The former home of Daniel O'Connell 'The Liberator' (1775 – 1847) who fought for civil rights for Catholics and was later elected MP for County Clare. The simply constructed house contains much of his furniture and possessions as a memorial to the great statesman. The grounds of 120ha (300 acres) give access to attractive coastal scenery.
☎ 066 9475113   www.heritageireland.ie

⚔ Desmond Castle `76 A2`

Cork Street, Kinsale, Co. Cork. Also known as the 'The French Prison' due to a tragedy in 1747 when 54 French prisoners died in a fire. Built in the 16th century by the Earl of Desmond for use as a custom house, the castle was subject to occupation by the Spanish in 1601 and was also used to imprison captured American sailors during the American War of Independence. Also houses the International Museum of Wine.
☎ 021 477 4855   www.heritageireland.ie

🏛 Desmond Hall `71 D2`

The Square, Newcastle West, Co. Limerick. An imposing medieval hall used by the Earls of Desmond which includes a restored oak musician's gallery and a limestone hooded fireplace. The 15th century building consists of the hall, vaulted lower chamber and adjoining tower built on the site of a 13th century structure.
☎ 069 77408   www.heritageireland.ie

❊ Doneraile Park `72 A3`

Doneraile, Co. Cork. 160ha (400 acres) of landscaped parkland in a natural 'Capability Brown' style. A number of red deer herds can be seen amongst the mature deciduous trees. The building of a dam, originally in the mid 1750s, created a number of islands in the River Awbeg and also a weir which includes a fish pass allowing trout and salmon to gain access to spawning grounds upriver.
☎ 022 24244   www.heritageireland.ie

⚔ Dromoland Castle `72 A1`

Newmarket-on-Fergus, Co. Clare. Constructed in the 16th century by the Earls of Thomond and converted to a five-star luxury hotel in the 1960s. In the castle grounds is Moghane Fort, the largest hill fort site in the country from which there are fine views of the Shannon Estuary.
☎ 061 368144   www.dromoland.ie

🦅 Dromore Wood `67 C2`

Ruan, Ennis, Co. Clare. Covering an area of 400ha (990 acres) Dromore Wood includes a variety of habitats – wetlands, limestone pavement, woodland and peatland – that enables the diverse flora and fauna to thrive. The 17th century O'Brien Castle stands on the lake side and there are also sites of a castle, church, ring forts and lime kiln.
☎ 065 683 7166   www.heritageireland.ie

❊ Dundrum Plantarum `78 B1`

Dundrum, Co. Tipperary. A Celtic theme runs through this 3.2ha (8 acres) woodland with walks, water features, dolmens and crannogs.
☎ 062 71303

⚔ Dungarvan Castle `79 C3`

Castle Street, Dungarvan, Co. Waterford. Due to reopen in Spring 2002; access will be by guided tour only. Built by Prince John of England in 1185 but considerably altered at various later periods, the castle consists of a 12th century shell keep with an enclosing curtain wall, gate tower and corner tower. Within the curtain wall stands an early 18th century two storey military barracks which has been restored and now houses an exhibition and visitor facilities.
☎ 058 48144   www.heritageireland.ie

🏛 Dunkathel `76 B1`

Glanmire, Co. Cork. The house, which overlooks the River Lee, dates from around 1790 and was built by the wealthy local merchant Abraham Morris. The fine interior includes Adam fireplaces, a magnificent bifurcated stone staircase and a collection of watercolours by Beatrice Gubbins, one of five sisters who previously owned the house. A rare 1880 barrel organ can still be played on request.
☎ 021 482 1014   www.castlesireland.com

★ Dysert O'Dea Archaeology Centre `67 C2`

Corofin, Co. Clare. Built in 1480 the castle now houses the Clare Archaeological Centre which contains a museum and exhibitions about the twenty five archaeological monuments that fall within a 6km (3.7 mile) radius of the castle. These include two stone forts, a 12th century High Cross, a 'fulacht fiadh' (an ancient cooking site), Romanesque Churches and Holy Wells.
☎ 065 683 7401

⚔ Elizabeth Fort `77 B2`

Barrack Street, Cork, Co. Cork. Built in the 16th century it has been used as a prison, barracks and now houses the Garda. The outer walls are 5 – 9m (16 – 30ft) high and the view from them is impressive showing the strategic importance of the location. The Gateway Bar, the oldest pub in Cork, is next to the fort
☎ 021 427 3251

✝ Ennis Friary `67 C3`

Abbey Street, Ennis, Co. Clare. Founded in 1242 by the O'Briens, though most of the building dates from the 14th century. In the 15th century over 300 monks and 600 pupils resided here as it was one of the finest seats of learning in Ireland. The decorated tombs and carvings are of most interest especially the St Francis carving and the 15th century MacMahon tomb.
☎ 065 682 9100   www.heritageireland.ie

⚔ Farney Castle `69 C3`

Holycross, Co. Tipperary. Built in 1495 this Round Tower is currently occupied by the designer Cyril Cullen. The naturally coloured wool from the rare Jacob Sheep that graze in the surrounding fields is used to make the world-famous Jacob sweaters which, along with the home produced Parian Porcelain, are retailed from the shop on the premises.
☎ 0504 43281

★ Fenit Seaworld `70 B3`

The Pier, Fenit, Co. Kerry. Local species together with hundreds from the Atlantic are brought together by use of realistic recreations of the deep ocean floor.
☎ 066 7136544   www.kerrygems.ie/fenitseaworld

🏛 Fethard Folk Farm & Transport Museum `78 B1`

Cashel Road, Fethard, Co. Tipperary. Housed in the former 19th century railway station near the town walls, there are over 1200 exhibits many of which sit in re-creations of authentic surroundings.
☎ 052 31516

❊ Fota Arboretum & Gardens `76 B1`

Carrigtwohill, Co. Cork. Covering an area of 13ha (32 acres) and originally designed by James Hugh Smith-Barry 150 years ago, the excellent soil and mild climate allows a wide range of exotic trees and shrubs from every continent to thrive. There are an orangery, a range of terraces and four walled gardens which include stone ornamental gateways and a summer house in the Italian Garden.
☎ 021 481 2728   www.heritageireland.ie

⛳ Fota Island Golf Club `76 B1`

Carrigtwohill, Co. Cork. Championship course on the 350ha (780 acre) island in Cork Harbour. The Irish Open, Irish PGA and Irish Amateur Open Championships have been held here in recent years.
☎ 021 883700

🦌 Fota Wildlife Park `76 B1`

Carrigtwohill, Co. Cork. The park holds over 90 species of animal including giraffes, bison and cheetahs and is important in the conservation and breeding of endangered species. Wherever possible the animals are encouraged to thrive in unrestricted areas and some, such as lemurs, kangaroos and wallabies, are allowed to roam free through the park.
☎ 021 481 2678   www.fotawildlife.ie

🏛 Foynes Flying Boat Museum `71 D2`

Foynes, Co. Limerick. During the 1930s and 1940s Foynes was the base for flying boats operating between the United States and Europe. The museum commemorates the operational staff and many of the passengers on the transatlantic flights and an audiovisual show brings to life Foynes during the war time era. Features of interest include the original terminal building, weather and radio room with original transmitters, receivers and morse code equipment, a 1940s style cinema and wartime radio.
☎ 069 65416

✝ Gallarus Oratory `70 A3`

Near Ballyferriter, Dingle, Co. Kerry. On the beautiful Dingle peninsula, at Lateevmore is Gallarus oratory, a corbel-roofed dry-stone structure of remarkable perfection and completely waterproof. A thousand year old Christian chapel lacks only the crosses that once decorated the roof.
☎ 066 9155333

★ Gap of Dunloe `75 C1`

Killarney, Co. Kerry. Dramatic mountain scenery formed during the last ice age which is popular with walkers, cyclists and pony trekkers.
☎ 064 31633

⚜ Gleninsheen & Poulnabrone Megalithic Tombs `67 C2`

Gleninsheen, Ballyvaughan, Co. Clare. Gleninsheen is a wedge tomb dating from the late Stone Age period. The distinctive Poulnabrone dolmen is known the world over and is a single chambered tomb dating from 2500BC that would originally have been earth covered.
☎ 065 6828366

❊ Glenleigh Gardens `78 B2`

Clogheen, Co. Tipperary. Set in the northern foothills of the Knockmealdown Mountains, the 5ha (12 acre) natural gardens contain woodland interspersed with lawns and mountain streams.
☎ 052 65251

⚔ Glin Castle `71 D2`

Glin, Co. Limerick. The Fitzgeralds, Knights of Glin, have lived here for over 700 years, first in a castle in the village itself, of which little remains, and then in Glin Castle, a Georgian house which dates from the 1780s. Set in formal gardens, Glin also has a beautiful kitchen garden and many specimen trees and shrubs amongst the woodland. The house interior is decorated with fine plasterwork and is hung with interesting Irish paintings and family portraits. There is also a collection of 18th century furniture by Irish craftsmen.
☎ 068 34173   www.glincastle.com

🦌 Gougane Barra Forest Park `75 C2`

Ballingeary, Co. Cork. The lake on the edge of this 142ha (350 acre) park is the source of the River Lee. Holy Island sits in the lake and is linked to the shore by a causeway and it is here that the patron saint of Cork, St Finbarr, founded a monastery. Unusually, the ring road allows the motorist to drive around the park.
☎ 026 43280

🏛 GPA-Bolton Library `78 B1`

John Street, Cashel, Co. Tipperary. Founded in 1744 by Theophilus Bolton, Archbishop of Cashel. Houses a collection of 12th century books, maps and manuscripts including extracts from Chaucers 'Book of Fame'.
☎ 062 61944

✝ Holy Cross Abbey `69 C3`

Holycross, Co. Tipperary. Founded in the 12th century by Donal Mor O'Brien. Picturesque and in a lovely setting, the abbey is named after the true cross believed to have been presented to the grandson of Brian Ború in 1100AD.
☎ 0504 43241

🏛 **Hunt Museum** `73 B1`
The Custom House, Rutland Street, Limerick, Co. Limerick. Works of Irish and European art and antiquities collected by John and Gertrude Hunt housed in the elegant 18th century custom house. There are paintings by Renoir, Picasso, O'Connor and Yeats, the personal seal of Charles I of England, the cross worn by Mary, Queen of Scots on the day of her execution, a coin revered since the Middle ages as being one of the '30 pieces of silver' and a bronze horse by Leonardo da Vinci.
☎ 061 312833

✷ **Ilnacullin (Garinish Island)** `75 C2`
Glengarriff, Bantry, Co. Cork. The gardens were created in 1910 by the owner Annan Bryce and the garden designer Harold Peto. A particularly mild climate allows plants from all around the world to flourish. Included is an Italian Garden with ornamental lily pool, a New Zealand fernery, a Japanese rockery and a number of follies including a clock tower and a Grecian temple. Access to the island is by boat for which there is a separate charge.
☎ 027 63040   www.heritageireland.ie

★ **Jameson Heritage Centre** `76 B1`
Midleton, Co. Cork. Contains the world's largest pot still with a capacity of 32,000 gallons and a working waterwheel dating from 1825. Guided tours start with an audiovisual presentation, continue through the production process of Irish Whiskey and culminates with a tasting session in the Jameson Bar.
☎ 021 461 3594   www.whiskeytours.ie

★ **Kenmare Heritage Centre** `75 C1`
The Square, Kenmare, Co. Kerry. Opened in 1994 and covering much of local interest including the history of the traditional lace making industry for which Kenmare is famous. The Kenmare Lace and Design Centre above the Heritage Centre gives an opportunity to see the lace being made.
☎ 064 41233

✟ **Kenmare Holy Well** `75 C1`
Kenmare, Co. Kerry. One of a number of historic sites in Kenmare including a large Stone Circle and St Finians Church.
☎ 064 41233

🏛 **Kerry Bog Village Museum** `74 B1`
Glenbeigh, Ring of Kerry, Co. Kerry. A recreation of a 19th century village and turf cutting which is still used as domestic fuel. Thatched cottages, a blacksmith's forge with authentic tools, a hen house and vegetable garden are amonst the buildings on display. There are also rare Bog Ponies.
☎ 066 976 9184   www.kerrybogvillage.com

🏛 **Kerry the Kingdom** `71 C3`
Ashe Memorial Hall, Denny Street, Tralee, Co. Kerry. Comprises three attractions; 'Kerry in Colour' – an audiovisual tour of the Kerry landscape stretching back 7000 years; 'Kerry County Museum' – includes displays, slides, models and audiovisuals showing the lifestyle of settlers through the ages; 'Geraldine Tralee' – a reconstruction of Tralee in the 1450s when the Geraldine family ruled Kerry.
☎ 066 712777

★ **Kerry Woollen Mills** `75 C1`
Beaufort, Killarney, Co. Kerry. Situated on the Ring of Kerry and producing wool for over 300 years. A steel water wheel replaced the original wooden one in 1928 and is still in use. Guided tours and an on-site shop.
☎ 064 44122

✟ **Kilcooley Abbey** `69 D3`
Urlingford, Co. Tipperary. Kilcooley was founded by Donal O'Brien in the 12th century. It has a fine east window and many decorative carvings.
☎ 062 61333

★ **Killaloe Heritage Centre** `68 B3`
Killaloe, Co. Clare. Sited on a bridge on the Shannon, water plays an important part in the Centre's displays as does Brian Ború, High King of Ireland, who was born here in 940AD.
☎ 061 376866

★ **Killarney Model Railway** `75 C1`
Beech Road, Killarney, Co. Kerry. Situated next to the Tourist Information Office, over 50 trains run on a mile of track set amongst recreations of a variety of European locations. A Scalextric race track is also on site.
☎ 064 6434000

🏞 **Killarney National Park** `75 C1`
Muckross House, Muckross, Killarney, Co. Kerry. The National Park covers an area of over 10,000ha (24,700 acres) most of which is given over to the beautiful three lakes of Killarney. The Visitor Centre at Muckross House gives information on the flora and wildlife in the Park, including Killarney Fern, Strawberry Tree, Northern Emerald Dragonfly and a flock of Greenland Whitefronted Geese which reside in the bogs over the winter months. There is also an information point at the 18m (60ft) high Torc Waterfall. Ladies View is a viewpoint on the N71 near Upper Lake so named because of the pleasure it gave to Queen Victoria's ladies-in-waiting in 1861.
☎ 064 31440   homepage.tinet.ie/~knp

🏇 **Killarney Racecourse** `75 C1`
The Racecourse, Killarney, Co. Kerry. National Hunt and Flat racing course with seven race days a year.
☎ 064 31125

🏛 **Kilmallock Museum & History Trail** `72 A2`
Kilmallock, Co. Limerick. A small museum collection reflecting life in the area in the 19th century and 20th century, including aspects of industry and farming. There are also scale models of prehistoric houses excavated in the area and a large model of medieval Kilmallock. The self guiding history trail comprises thirteen points of interest in Kilmallock which are marked by information plaques. The town has retained many of its historic buildings including the early 13th century Collegiate Church and Dominican Friary, and one of the remaining 16th century town gates.
☎ 063 91300

★ **Kilrush Heritage Centre** `71 C1`
Market House, Kilrush, Co. Clare. The effects of the Great Famine and the evictions of 1888 are examined along with the history of the area. A heritage trail through Kilrush starts at the centre.
☎ 065 905 1577

♜ **King John's Castle** `73 B1`
King's Island, Limerick, Co. Limerick. In the old town of Limerick on an island formed by the River Shannon and the River Abbey, the 13th century castle is a fine example of Norman fortified architecture. An exhibition tells of the origin and development of the city and the castle's role in Limerick's dramatic history; life sized wooden sculptures represent the people who inhabited the castle at various times in its history. Costumed animators illustrate the life and trades of 13th century Limerick and there is a display of battering rams and catapults.
☎ 061 411201/360788

🏛 **Kinsale Museum** `76 A2`
Market Square, Kinsale, Co. Cork. Housed in the original market house, the museum tells the story of Kinsale through the ages. Maritime displays based on the shipbuilding heritage include the controversial sinking of the Lusitania in 1915 off the Old Head of Kinsale. There are also displays on the Battle of Kinsale and the Kinsale Giant, Patrick Cotter O'Brien.
☎ 021 477 7930

♜ **Knappogue Castle** `72 A1`
Quin, Co. Clare. The central tower was originally built by the MacNamaras in 1467 and has been added to over the years, mainly in a neo-Gothic style. The grounds are in the process of being restored.
☎ 061 360788   www.castlesireland.com

★ **Lahinch Seaworld** `67 C2`
The Promenade, Lahinch, Co. Clare. The aquarium uncovers the diversity of life at the Clare coastline and of the Atlantic Ocean. Features a 'blow hole' as found in Doolin, a magnificent section of the rugged Clare coastline.
☎ 065 708 1900   www.iol.ie/~seaworld

🏛 **Limerick City Gallery of Art** `73 B3`
Pery Square, Limerick, Co. Limerick. Features a permanent collection of works of art by acclaimed Irish artists from the 18th, 19th and 20th centuries and an extensive programme of temporary exhibitions.
☎ 061 310633

🏛 **Limerick Museum** `73 B1`
Castle Lane, Nicholas Street, Limerick, Co. Limerick. Adjacent to King John's Castle, the award winning museum presents Limerick's long and varied history. The collection includes artefacts from prehistoric and medieval times including currency circulating at the time of the Vikings. Among the museum's treasures are the city charters of Charles I and the Civic Sword and City Maces. There are displays of local crafts, notably Limerick lace, and exhibits relating to trades history.
☎ 061 417826

🏇 **Limerick Racecourse** `72 A2`
Greenmount, Patrickswell, Co. Limerick. National Hunt and Flat racing course with 15 race days a year on a track opened in 2001, 9kms (6 miles) SW of Limerick City.
☎ 061 355055   www.limerick-racecourse.com

✷ **Lismore Castle Gardens** `78 B2`
Lismore, Co. Waterford. Situated above the River Blackwater, the castle was built in the 19th century by Joseph Paxton, architect of the Crystal Palace in London, for the 6th Duke of Devonshire, incorporating the remains of the medieval castle erected by Prince John of England in 1185. The castle is partially surrounded by delightful walled gardens, with areas of woodland, shrubberies, and a yew walk. In early spring the gardens are at their best when the camellias and magnolias are in flower. The Elizabethan poet Edmund Spencer is said to have composed part of the Faerie Queene in the grounds. Lismore is still the Irish home of the Duke of Devonshire and the castle itself is not open to the public.
☎ 058 54424   www.lismorecastle.com

★ **Lismore Heritage Centre** `78 B2`
Lismore, Co. Waterford. Housed in the former courthouse, the heritage centre traces the history of Lismore from its foundation in 636. An multimedia presentation takes up the themes of monastic Lismore, the Vikings, the Normans, Walter Raleigh, and Lismore Castle, Cathedral and Church.
☎ 058 54975   www.lismoreheritage.com

✷ **Lisselan Estate** `76 A2`
Clonakilty, Co. Cork. Laid out in the valley of the Argideen River in the 1850s, the 12ha (30 acre) gardens include an azalea garden, water and rock gardens, shrubbery and orchard and woodland walks. Gum Trees, Handkerchief Trees and Japanese Maples are amongst the wide variety of species from all over the world.
☎ 023 33249   www.lisselanestate.com

🏇 **Listowel Racecourse** `71 C2`
Listowel, Co. Kerry. A rectangular National Hunt and Flat racing course with nine race days a year.
☎ 068 21172

🏛 Lough Gur Stone Age Centre   `72 A2`
Ballyneety, Co. Limerick. Archaeological excavation and survey has shown this to be the most important Stone age site in Ireland, with evidence of Neolithic farming, dwellings and ritual and burial sites dating back 5000 years. The lough side visitor centre in a re-constructed Neolithic house has an audiovisual show illustrating the site's history and there are many artefacts on display. Walking tours cover many of the archaeological features of the site.
☎ 061 360788

🐾 Millstreet Country Park   `75 D1`
Millstreet, Co. Cork. A 200ha (500 acre) park which includes a visitor centre, themed gardens containing rare shrubs, flowers, bogland and an ornamental lake. Wildlife includes red deer, stoats, otters and brown trout. Of archaeological interest are a 4 – 5000 year old stone circle and a Fullacht Fiadh – a bronze age cooking site.
☎ 029 70810   mlcp.foundmark.com

✱ Mitchelstown Cave   `78 B2`
Burncourt, Cahir, Co. Tipperary. A 1km tour through the cave system takes the visitor past spectacular stalagtites, stalagmites and calcite columns. The Earl of Desmond hid from the English in 1601 in the old cave, which is not open to the public, and it was not until 1833 that the current caves were discovered.
☎ 052 67246

✱ Mizen Vision!   `74 B3`
Mizen Head, Co. Cork. Mizen Head not only has the spectacular Atlantic coastline but also the Signal Station Visitor Centre and the 99 steps leading to the famous suspension bridge, the link to the offshore island on which the lighthouse is situated. The lighthouse keeper's house has been converted to contain an audiovisual display, maps and archives, the Fastnet Lighthouse room, an underwater room and a viewing room from where whales and dolphins can be seen.
☎ 028 35591/35253   www.mizenvision.com

✝ Muckross Friary   `75 C1`
Killarney National Park, Co. Kerry. This well preserved friary was built in 1448 though the tower dates from the 17th century and is the only example of a Franciscan tower in Ireland that is as wide as the friary itself. The superbly preserved cloisters surround an old yew tree, probably as old as the friary. In the graveyard are the graves of ancient chieftains and the last King of Desmond.
☎ 064 31440   www.heritageireland.ie

❋ Muckross House   `75 C1`
Muckross, Killarney, Co. Kerry. A Victorian mansion built in 1843 in the Elizabethan style. The interior shows not only the lifestyle of the gentry of the period but also that of the servants. Grounds have water gardens, colourful displays of azaleas and rhododendrons in the spring and a limestone rock garden. There are also craft workers demonstrating weaving, bookbinding and pottery, the Museum of Kerry Life and the Killarney National Park Visitor Centre. Three working farms in the grounds use the traditional farming methods of the early 20th century.
☎ 064 31440   www.heritageireland.ie

🏛 Museum of Irish Transport   `75 C1`
Scotts Gardens, Killarney, Co. Kerry. An impressive display of vintage cars, motorcycles and bicycles including the history of the bicycle from 1825 to the present day. Among the exhibits are an 1898 Benz, a 1907 Silver Stream, the 1914 Wolsey and 1925 Vulcan used in the films The Blue Max and Michael Collins respectively and a 1981 DeLorean.
☎ 064 34677

🏰 Nenagh Castle   `68 B3`
Nenagh, Co. Tipperary. Built in 1200 though the castellations were not added until 1858. The walls are 6m (20ft) thick and it is five storeys and 30m (100ft) high. It was originally one of five towers that linked the curtain wall of the original castle.
☎ 067 31610

✱ Nenagh Heritage Centre   `68 B3`
Nenagh, Co. Tipperary. Housed in the Governor's House of the former gaol, the history of which is a feature of the Centre. There are also details of the seventeen men who were hanged here in the mid 19th century.
☎ 067 33850

✱ Oceanworld   `70 A3`
Mara Beo, Slea Head Road, Dingle, Co. Kerry. The shark tank is the first of its kind in Ireland, the 9m (30ft) long Ocean Tunnel allows fish to swim overhead and the Touch Pool allows interaction with the fish. There are also displays relating to the wrecks in Blasket Sound and the voyages of Brendan the Navigator.
☎ 066 9152111   www.dingle-oceanworld.ie

🏰 Ormond Castle   `79 C2`
Carrick-on-Suir, Co. Tipperary. A combination of the original 15th century fortress and the Elizabethan Mansion House built by Thomas Butler, the 10th Earl of Ormond, a century later. It is Ireland's most impressive example of an unfortified manor house of the period. The Long Gallery is a most impressive room having a decorative plasterwork ceiling and two ornate fireplaces.
☎ 051 640787   www.heritageireland.ie

🏛 Queenstown Story, The   `76 B2`
The Railway Station, Cobh, Co. Cork. The maritime history of Cobh is told covering Irish emigration, transportation of convicts and the loss of the Lusitania. The town reverted to its original name, Cobh, in 1921 after being renamed Queenstown in 1849 after a visit by Queen Victoria.
☎ 021 481 3591   www.cobhheritage.com

✝ Quin Abbey   `72 A1`
Quin, Co. Clare. The village of Quin is noted for a Franciscan friary founded in the early 15th century, the first Observantine house in Ireland. The ruins, incorporating an earlier castle, are sufficiently well preserved to clearly demonstrate the layout of a medieval friary.
☎ 091 844084

🏰 Reginald's Tower   `79 D2`
The Quay, Waterford, Co. Waterford. For more than 1000 years a defensive tower has stood on this site to protect the quays of Waterford. The present circular structure dates back to the early part of the 13th century but has 15th century additions and, besides its defensive role, has also been used as a mint, prison and military store. Recently restored to its medieval appearance, there is now a collection of civic regalia and decorated civil charters in the tower and an exhibition of Viking and medieval artefacts.
☎ 051 304220/873501   www.heritageireland.ie

✱ Ring of Kerry   `74 B1`
Co. Kerry. The Ring of Kerry is a famous circular scenic route of about 185kms (115 miles) around the Iveragh Peninsula. Killarney is generally considered the gateway to the peninsula, though the best section lies between Kenmare and Killorglin. The principal route follows the coast and encircles Irelands highest mountains, Macgillykuddy's Reeks, though some of the finest scenery is to be found along the unmarked roads running through the interior of the peninsula.
☎ 064 31633

🏛 Riverstown House   `76 B1`
Glanmire, Co. Cork. To the east of Cork city is Riverstown House, originally dating from 1602 though it was extensively remodelled and extended in 1745 by Jemmett Browne, later to become Bishop of Cork. There is marvellous ceiling and wall stuccowork by the Lafrancini brothers, a carved wooden fireplace in the Green Drawing Room, original Barry engravings and a marble carving.
☎ 021 482 1205   www.castlesireland.com

✞ Rock of Cashel   `78 B1`
Cashel, Co. Tipperary. One of the most spectacular sights in Ireland, the Rock of Cashel is a steep limestone outcrop surmounted by the ruins of the ancient capital of the Kings of Munster. According to legend, St Patrick baptised Corc the Third here; and Brian Boru, High King of Ireland, was crowned here in 977. In 1101 King Murtagh O'Brien donated the rock to the church after which it became the See of the Archbishopric of Munster. The ruins are extensive and fascinating. Cormac's Chapel, built in the 1130s contains a magnificent carved 11th century sarcophagus; whilst the carved Cross of St Patrick is set into the coronation stone of the Kings of Munster. The main cathedral is essentially 13th century and although it has suffered pillage and neglect, it remains a fine example of Irish Gothic architecture.
☎ 062 61437   www.heritageireland.ie

✱ Roscrea Castle & Damer House   `69 C2`
Castle Street, Roscrea, Co. Tipperary. The Castle includes a gatehouse, curtain walls and twin corner towers dating from the 1280s. In the courtyard stands Damer House which was on the verge of being demolished in the 1970s but was saved by the Irish Georgian Society. Restoration since then has included the magnificent carved wooden staircase and an elegant carved stone doorway.
☎ 0505 21850   www.heritageireland.ie

✝ Roscrea Priory   `69 C2`
Abbey Street, Roscrea, Co. Tipperary. Of this 12th century priory only the west gable survives with its arched doorway. Nearby there are also remains of a round tower and a 15th century Franciscan Friary.
☎ 067 31610

🏰 Ross Castle   `75 C1`
Killarney, Co. Kerry. Recently restored 14th or 15th century castle which stands at the entrance to a peninsula extending into Lough Leane in the Killarney National Park. It was the last stronghold in Munster to fall to Cromwell's army in 1652. Two of the four corner towers were removed in 1688 to allow room for expansion though the remaining two still survive.
☎ 061 35851/2   www.heritageireland.ie

✝ St Fin Barre's Cathedral   `77 B2`
Bishop Street, Cork, Co. Cork. Cork's triple spired Church of Ireland Cathedral was founded in 1870 on the site of St Fin Barre's 7th century monastic school and replaced the medieval cathedral which was badly damaged during the siege of Cork in 1690. Built in the Gothic style by William Burges the cathedral is relatively small though the design gives a spacious feel. There are more than 1200 sculptures built into the structure and several relics from the old cathedral have been preserved including two doorways which have been built into the south wall of the grounds.
☎ 021 496 3387   cathedral.cork.anglican.org

✱ St John's Theatre & Arts Centre   `71 C2`
The Square, Listowel, Co. Kerry. The transformation of the old Church of Ireland into the St John's Theatre & Arts Centre started in 1988 and took two years. It is now host to numerous local and national theatrical productions and arts, dance and musical events. It is also the site of the Tourist Information office.
☎ 068 22566

✝ St Mary's Cathedral   `73 B1`
Bridge Street, Limerick, Co. Limerick. Founded in 1168 by Donal Mor O'Brien, King of Munster, the cathedral has many notable architectural features and furnishings: a pre-Reformation stone altar, the Reardos of the High Altar carved by the father of Patrick Pearse, and the renowned Misericords, a collection of 23 carved oak seats used by the clergy which date back 450 years. The cathedral was built on the site of O'Brien's home and the door is reputed to be the original door of his house.
☎ 061 310293

✝ **St Mary's Church** `78 B2`

Irishtown, Clonmel, Co. Tipperary. The medieval town walls bound the grounds of this church which has an unusual octagonal tower and was built on the site of an earlier 14th century church.
☎ 052 22960

✱ **Scattery Island Centre** `71 C1`

Merchants Quay, Kilrush, Co. Clare. Scattery Island (Inis Cathaig in Irish) in the Shannon Estuary is named after the mythical monster, 'Cathach', which St Senan drove out in the 6th century before founding one of the earliest Christian settlements. Amongst these remains is a 10th century round tower which unusually has its entrance at ground level. Though last inhabited in 1979, the island is easily accessible from Kilrush where the Scattery Island Centre can be found which tells the story of the island.
☎ 065 9052139 www.heritageireland.ie

✱ **Schull Planetarium** `75 C3`

The Community College, Schull, Co. Cork. Situated in the grounds of the community college, this is the only planetarium in the Republic of Ireland. It includes recreations of the night sky – there are three different star shows each week which are unsuitable for young children.
☎ 028 28552

▥ **1796 French Armada Exhibition Centre** `75 C2`

East Stables Bantry House, Bantry, Co. Cork. An exhibition housed in the outbuildings of Bantry House telling the story of the attempted invasion by the French fleet and the United Irishmen led by Theobald Wolfe Tone in 1796. A storm, however, forced them to turn back with the loss of 10 ships, including 'la Surveillante' which was scuttled after being badly damaged. The wreck was declared a Irish National Monument in 1985.
☎ 027 50047 www.bantryhouse.ie

✱ **Skellig Experience, The** `74 A1`

Skellig Heritage Centre, Valentia Island, Co. Kerry. Skellig Michael has a remarkable series of 1000 year old steps cut into the cliff face rising to the remains of a 6th century monastery. The monks abandoned the island in the 12th century. The Skellig Experience offers information about the island's history and the abundant bird and marine life.
☎ 066 9476306

✱ **Springfield Castle & Deer Farm** `72 A3`

Springfield, Dromcollogher, Co. Limerick. The wooded Springfield Castle estate has a breeding herd of deer, one of the finest in Ireland, and the breeding programme involves the cross breeding of red deer with elf hybrids. Tractor and trailer rides take visitors through the grazing deer and there are woodland walks, a nature trail and children's playground. A restored cottage illustrates the evolution of deer and the history of deer farming in Ireland.
☎ 063 83162

⛫ **Staigue Stone Fort** `74 B2`

Castlecove, Co. Kerry. Amid the beautiful scenery overlooking Kenmare Bay, Staigue is a stone 2500 year old ringfort made up of a 4m (13ft) thick rampart divided into terraces and linked by a system of stairways.
☎ 064 31633

✱ **Swiss Cottage** `78 B2`

Kilcommon, Cahir, Co. Tipperary. Designed by Regency architect, John Nash, and built in the early part of the 19th century for the 1st Earl of Glengall, the Swiss Cottage is a large ornate cottage style building which was fashionable amongst the wealthy of Europe. The elegant interior has a graceful staircase and the salon is decorated with one of the first commercially produced Parisian wallpapers.
☎ 052 41144 www.heritageireland.ie

✱ **Tarbert Bridewell** `71 C2`

Tarbert, Co. Kerry. Originally a courthouse and gaol built in 1831, now restored to include cells, exercise yard, courthouse and gaoler's quarters to show how 19th century justice was handed out. There is also a Famine Exhibition showing the effects of the famine both locally and nationally.
☎ 068 36500

▤ **Tarbert House** `71 C2`

Tarbert, Co. Kerry. A fine collection of Georgian furniture including a Chippendale mirror. The original trestles and gunracks still exist in the walls of the entrance hall. The Leslie ancestral home since 1690 and host to such visitors as Benjamin Franklin, Winston Churchill, Charlotte Brontë and Lord Kitchener.
☎ 068 36198

✝ **Thurles Cathedral** `69 C3`

Cathedral Street, Thurles, Co. Tipperary. Building of the cathedral was completed in 1872 and consecration took place in 1879 after completion of the interior. Major renovation work was carried out for the centenary celebrations. One of the features of the interior is a tabernacle that was created by Giacoma dello Porta who was a pupil of Michelangelo. It is ironic that the cathedral was designed to face a link road which has still not been built to alleviate the through traffic. This is why the first view is of the rear of the building.
☎ 062 51457

🏇 **Thurles Racecourse** `69 C3`

The Racecourse, Thurles, Co. Tipperary. National Hunt and Flat racing course with ten race days a year.
☎ 0504 22253

✝ **Timoleague Abbey** `76 A2`

Timoleague, Co. Cork. The origins of the abbey are unknown but probably date back to the 13th century. The remains are significant and include the church, infirmary, refectory, wine cellar and a walled courtyard. The abbey was sacked by the English in 1612 and remained in use until 1629.
☎ 023 33226

✱ **Tipperary Crystal** `79 C2`

Ballynoran, Carrick-on-Suir, Co. Tipperary. Only established in 1988 but, with the acquisition of Tyrone Crystal in 2000, are now firmly established as a major player in Irish crystal. This is the original site, which is now housed in two thatched cottages, where production started although there is another visitor centre at Birdhill, near Limerick. Mouthblowing and handcutting by master craftsmen is carried out as it has been for over 200 years.
☎ 051 641188 www.tipperarycrystal.com

🏇 **Tipperary Racecourse** `78 A1`

Limerick Junction, Tipperary, Co. Tipperary. A left handed oval National Hunt and Flat racing course with nine race days a year.
☎ 062 51357

▥ **Tipperary South Riding County Museum** `78 B2`

Emmet Street, Clonmel, Co. Tipperary. The history of South Tipperary from prehistoric times to the present day is exhibited in this custom built museum.
☎ 052 34550

✱ **Tralee & Dingle Steam Railway** `71 C3`

Ballyard Station, Dingle Road, Co. Kerry. Europe's most westerly line and part of the Tralee-Dingle Light Railway which ran from 1891 to 1951. Trains run every hour during the summer on the 3km (1.9 mile) section between Tralee and Blennerville which takes about 20 minutes.
☎ 066 7121064

✱ **Tralee Aqua Dome** `71 C3`

Tralee, Co. Kerry. Leisure centre including a 75m (250ft) flume, gushers, waves, a castle with water cannon and also a sauna, steam room and cool pool.
☎ 066 71228899 www.discoverkerry.com/aquadome/

🏇 **Tralee Racecourse** `71 C3`

Ballybeggan Park, Tralee, Co. Kerry. A round, left handed, National Hunt and Flat racing course with seven race days a year.
☎ 066 26188/36148

❀ **Tramore House Gardens** `79 D2`

Tramore, Co. Waterford. A steep, sloping garden surrounding an elegant Victorian Town House dating from the late 1880s. The garden is undergoing restoration with both formal and informal planting. Box edged old rose beds front the house, there is a long herbaceous border, woodland and shrubbery. A stream cascades down the garden into a canal and thence to a pool. Other features include a rock garden, stone grotto and timber pavilion.
☎ 051 386303 www.gardensireland.com

🏇 **Tramore Racecourse** `79 D2`

Tramore, Co. Waterford. National Hunt and Flat racing course with nine race days a year including the four day summer festival meeting in August.
☎ 051 381425 www.tramore-racecourse.com

❀ **Vandeleur Walled Garden** `71 C1`

Vandeleur Demesne, Kilrush, Co. Clare. Opened in 2000, this was once the walled garden of Kilrush House and has been restored using the original network of paths. A horizontal maze, arboretum and water features have been added and the old farmyard buildings have been developed into the Vandeleur Centre which includes meeting and conference rooms.
☎ 065 905 1760

✱ **Waterford Crystal Visitor Centre** `79 D2`

Cork Road, Waterford, Co. Waterford. Visitors are guided through the production areas to see the glass blowers, master cutters and engravers at work creating what is regarded by many as the world's finest crystal. The manufacture of crystal in Waterford has a history going back to 1783 and an audiovisual presentation traces the history of glassmaking.
☎ 051 373311 www.waterfordvisitorcentre.com

✱ **West Cork Heritage Centre** `76 A2`

North Main Street, Bandon, Co. Cork. Housed in Christchurch which was deconsecrated in 1973 and is reputedly the first building in Ireland to be built for the Church of Ireland. The exhibition includes a trip back in time with recreations of an old shop, schoolhouse and wheelwright and harness makers' workshops. There are also displays of archaeological interest, in fact some of the old town walls are incorporated into the fabric of the building.
☎ 023 41677

✱ **West Cork Model Railway Village** `76 A2`

The Station, Inchdoney Road, Clonakilty, Co. Cork. Including an exhibition of the pre-war cultural and industrial life of West Cork housed in a replica of the original station house at McCurtain Hill. Though not yet complete, there are new additions every year, the model village will comprise 1:24 scale reconstructions of all of the towns on the route of the West Cork Railway, which closed in 1961 – Bandon, Bantry, Clonakilty, Dunmanway, Kinsale and Skibbereen.
☎ 023 33224 www.clon.ie/mvillage.html

▥ **West Cork Regional Museum** `76 A2`

Western Road, Clonakilty, Co. Cork. Amongst the historical exhibits are displays about Clonakilty's own Michael Collins (1890 – 1922) and his role in the 1916 rebellion and the War of Independence.
☎ 023 33115

✱ **Youghal Heritage Centre** `78 B3`

Market Square, Youghal, Co. Cork. The development of Youghal from the 6th century is outlined in the Heritage Centre which is located in the same building as the Tourist Information Centre.
☎ 024 92447

Index to place names & places of interest

The following is a comprehensive listing of all named places and places of tourist interest which appear in this atlas. The places of tourist interest are in purple type and they are also listed and described in the separate Places of Interest section for each province. The letters and numbers around the page edges form the referencing system used in this atlas. The place name is followed by a page number and a grid reference specific for that page. The place can be found by searching that grid square. Where more than one place has the same name, each can be distinguished by the county name shown after the place name, for example Ardglass *Co Down* can be found on page 17 in grid square D2.

L